The Rise of Historical Sociology

The Rise of
Historical
Sociology

DENNIS SMITH

Temple University Press
Philadelphia

HM 104
S 65
1991

Temple University Press, Philadelphia 19122
Copyright © Dennis Smith 1991

ISBN 0–87722–919–8 (cloth)
ISBN 0–87722–920–1 (paper)

CIP data available from the Library of Congress

Printed in Great Britain

This book is printed on acid-free paper.

Contents

Preface

I hope this book is relatively easy to read. It is intended to be, since one of its objects is to widen the audience for historical sociology. This is presented as a discipline which tries to make sense of the past (and present) by investigating how societies work and change. The chapters which follow provide many ways into this literature, and some readers might want to start by dipping into sections on particular writers or themes (e.g. Braudel on the Mediterranean world).

I have traced a number of themes running through historical sociology over the past few decades, especially in the United States and Britain. Readers with particular interests will be able to compare the approaches taken by various historians and sociologists to topics like feudalism, the growth of cities, the rise and decline of agro-bureaucratic states, class formation, nation-building and nationalism, citizenship, revolution and war. The long-running debate between evolutionists and discontinuity theorists also is discussed. This survey culminates in an analysis of the present state of historical sociology as an intellectual field (in the first part of chapter five).

In this book I develop a historical sociology of historical sociology itself. I argue that the post-war resurgence of this discipline, and successive phases of its growth, are related to changes in the broader political and ideological context. The text presents three successive phases, each characterized by a distinctive approach to democracy, capitalism, power and values within historical sociology. This argument is drawn to a conclusion in the second part of chapter five.

The present book is part of a larger project. A decade ago I published a historical comparison of class formation processes in two English cities, entitled *Conflict and Compromise* (Smith, 1982a). I set out to follow it up with a transatlantic comparison on the same lines, focusing on Birmingham and Chicago. I soon discovered that this meant coming to terms with the fact that approaches to (for example) the city, the state, capitalism, democracy, human nature and power differed greatly between the two societies. As a result I have spent some time trying to make sense for myself of intellectual tendencies within the western liberal tradition, especially the American and British variants.

This has resulted in studies of Barrington Moore (Smith, 1983) and the Chicago school of sociology (Smith, 1984a) and, of particular relevance here, a book entitled *Capitalist Democracy on Trial: The Transatlantic Debate from Tocqueville to the Present* (Smith, 1990). Like the present work, it tries to identify the unfolding logic and recurrent lines of convergence and divergence within a debate central to the western liberal tradition and to locate this debate within its historical and political contexts.

I am grateful to all those people who have helped or tolerated me in these various activities. This includes colleagues, past and present, in the sociology department at Leicester University and at the Aston Business School – as well as many others.

Val and Ian Riddell have helped the process along, aided by Harriet and Bilbo. Val commented on the manuscript at various stages. Tanya, Pen, Sue, Ed, Freda and Cleo Smith have all been prepared to let me get on with it, for which much thanks.

Figures

1   Like a Phoenix Rising

The post-war resurgence of historical sociology

Fifty years ago historical sociology was on the verge of extinction. Fascism and Stalinism were deeply hostile to its critical perspective. It remained weak throughout the 1940s and early 1950s. However, since then it has emerged from the ashes like a phoenix. By the 1970s and 1980s it was soaring high. Works by Immanuel Wallerstein, Michael Mann, Perry Anderson, Anthony Giddens and others display enormous ambition. Authors like Simon Schama and Paul Kennedy have found a massive audience. This mix of intellectual dynamism and popular attention gives historical sociology a great opportunity to make its mark on civic culture. Through their work, historical sociologists have the chance to give their fellow citizens knowledge and skills which may help them to assess competing views about what is 'possible' or 'impossible'. In brief, historical sociology can be a positive force for democratic citizenship.

At its best, historical sociology is rational, critical and imaginative. It looks for the mechanisms through which societies change or reproduce themselves. It seeks the hidden structures which frustrate some human aspirations while making others realizable, whether we appreciate it or not. This knowledge is well worth searching for. After all, it is useful to know, in any particular case, whether you are pushing against an open door or beating your head against a brick wall. One of historical sociology's objectives should be to distinguish between open doors and brick walls and discover whether, how, and with what consequences, walls may be removed.

The search for mechanism of social reproduction and transformation is closely related to a second concern. This is to explore the social preconditions and consequences of attempts to implement or impede such values as freedom, equality and justice. In the post-war period this line of enquiry has involved leading practitioners such as T. H. Marshall, E. P. Thompson, Reinhard Bendix and Barrington Moore. Historical sociology is used to dealing with power and values.

We are now on the crest of the second long wave of historical sociology. The first wave began in the mid-eighteenth century, in Britain and France especially. Like the second, it was driven by the need to make sense of contemporary political events. These presented a formidable intellectual challenge. For example, the British crown was humiliated twice by its own subjects – during the Glorious Revolution and the American Revolution – yet it defeated absolutist France in India and Canada. An Ernest Gellner put it: 'A strong civil society, conjoined with a relatively weak or at least non-dominant central state, constituted a unit more powerful than more thoroughly centralized polities. The Enlightenment pondered the lesson' (1988, p. 115). The French Revolution, British industrialization, the American democratic experiment, and German nation-building all posed equally difficult problems in subsequent decades.

This first long wave – from Montesquieu and Hume, Tocqueville and Marx to Durkheim and Weber – finally crashed against the wall of totalitarianism, right and left, in the late 1920s. Regimes which 'knew' the future and invented the past rejected historical sociology. Most disastrously, German intellectual life was devastated. Its most creative people were driven underground or overseas. American society at that time was a harsh place of sanctuary for historical sociology. Big business and big science were the main repositories of values and knowledge in the leading capitalist democracy. They did not like foreign intellectuals offering competition. Anti-Semitism played its part, too.[1]

Historical sociology survived. The questions it had wrestled with did not go away. They were the central moral dilemmas of western liberalism. For example, Max Weber had worried about the nature of rationality and the relationship between justice and order. Such moral concerns were preserved through the 1930s and 1940s in the writings of European exiles like Theodor Adorno and Max Horkheimer, the studies of Chicago sociologists like Robert Park, and the thoughts of evolutionist sociologists such as Morris Ginsberg working in the tradition of L. T. Hobhouse. During the 1950s, these issues became prominent once more, in the work of T. H. Marshall and Reinhard Bendix. By that time the second long wave was under way.[2]

Between 1958 and 1978, American doctoral dissertations in social history quadrupled. In two successive three-year periods during the 1970s, the number of articles with significant historical content in the *British Journal of Sociology* rose from nine (1973–5) to twenty-four

(1976–8). *History Workshop*, *Social History*, and the Social History Society were all founded in 1976.[3] By the early 1980s, nearly a quarter of the articles in the main sociological journals had a historical dimension. Comparative Historical Sociology was one of the largest sections in the American Sociological Association. This was, it was said, 'the golden age of historical sociology' (Collins, 1985, p. 107).

What is historical sociology?

To oversimplify, historical sociology is the study of the past to find out how societies work and change. Some sociologists are 'non-historical': empirically, they neglect the past; conceptually, they consider neither the time dimension of social life, nor the historicity of social structure. Similarly, some historians are 'non-sociological': empirically, they neglect the way processes and structures vary between societies; conceptually, they consider neither the general properties of processes and structures, nor their relationships to acts and events. By contrast, historical sociology is carried out by historians and sociologists who investigate the mutual interpenetration of past and present, events and processes, acting and structuration. They try to marry conceptual clarification, comparative generalization and empirical exploration.

There is considerable internal specialization within this intellectual field. However: 'The important lines of difference all cross disciplines [and] . . . are substantive: they lie in the arguments put forward, which are inescapably, if not always systematically, theoretical' (Calhoun, 1987, p. 625). In fact, 'there simply are no logical or even methodological distinctions between the social sciences and history – appropriately conceived' (Giddens, 1979, p. 230). History and sociology are 'one single intellectual adventure' (Braudel, 1980, p. 69). The two disciplines may be integrated 'as a single unified programme of analysis' (Abrams, 1982, p. xviii).

There is a danger that these assertions might simply become empty ideological slogans for a new academic vested interest. According to Charles Tilly, the institutionalization of historical sociology – 'fixing of a labeled speciality in sections of learned societies, journals, courses, a share of the job market' – could have a stultifying effect: 'first, because the "field" lacks intellectual unity and, by its very nature, will forever lack it; second, because institutionalization may well impede the spread of historical thinking to other parts of sociology. The other parts need that thinking badly' (1988, p. 709).

In fact, the danger identified by Tilly is far less serious than domination by a rigid orthodoxy, as occurred in the 1950s when historical sociology was held in check by the strait-jacket of structural functionalism. It broke free during the 1960s. By the 1970s and 1980s it was presenting ambitious world-views intended to fill the void left by the collapse of cold-war certainties. This book analyses that process through the work of scholars centrally involved. In the final chapter it also asks what kind of an intellectual field historical sociology has become, and how it might develop in the future.

The focus is on Britain and the United States. However, the *Annales* school of French historians is very relevant. Their work has become familiar and influential in the English-speaking world in the last few decades. Between the wars, the *Annalistes*, under the leadership of Lucien Febvre and Marc Bloch, were 'marginal men and *heretics*' (Stoianovich, 1976, p. 14; emphasis in original).[4] Things improved after World War II. Following the student troubles of 1968, and the French university reforms of the early 1970s, the academic heirs of Bloch and Febvre acquired a solid base in the École des Hautes Etudes en Sciences Sociales. They became increasingly well-known across the English Channel and across the Atlantic.[5] Many of their works have since been translated into English, including Marc Bloch's *Feudal Society*, Braudel's work on the Mediterranean, and his three-volume series on civilization and capitalism between the fifteenth and eighteenth centuries. In view of their influence in the English-speaking world, all three works will be examined in later chapters.[6]

Three phases of post-war historical sociology

The current revival of historical sociology has so far passed through three phases, to be discussed in successive chapters. Each phase has been marked by a specific political 'conjuncture' and a characteristic mood among historical sociologists. The first phase, before the mid-1960s, was shaped by the battle with totalitarianism. Liberal orthodoxy insisted that capitalist democracy could solve any major human problems without fundamental institutional changes. The 'American way' ruled. In Britain the liberal establishment retained great self-confidence. Key figures in this first phase were Talcott Parsons and T. H. Marshall, although the argument will also bring in Neil J. Smelser, S. N. Eisenstadt, Seymour Martin Lipset, and Reinhard Bendix.

Marc Bloch and Norbert Elias became more widely known in the

English-speaking world during the early 1960s. Their ideas contributed to the second phase, although its tone was mainly set by contemporary politics: especially, protest movements for student rights, Black power, and an end to the Vietnam war. Marxian approaches became fashionable, almost respectable. Historical sociology rediscovered domination, inequality and resistance movements. Key figures in this second phase were Barrington Moore and E. P. Thompson, although, once again, others will also be discussed, especially Charles Tilly and Theda Skocpol. Major publications by these writers appeared throughout the 1970s and 1980s.

The current of protest flowed on into the 1970s and 1980s, energized by the women's movement. This movement was quite slow to develop. A paper composed in the early 1960s recorded that 'the organized feminist movements, if they continue at all today, can only be counted alongside vegetarianism and nudism as bordering on the cult' (Banks and Banks, 1964a, p. 548).[7] By the late 1960s consciousness-raising classes had become common, especially in colleges and universities. The impact on historical sociology was felt during the 1970s and 1980s.[8] The link between feminism and historical sociology was dramatized in the early 1980s by the well-publicized protest against gender discrimination over tenure filed at Harvard by Theda Skocpol. Skocpol, 'a woman from the sixties', later wrote: 'the general esteem in which protest against perceived injustice is held by my generation gave me the courage to sustain what turned out to be a many-year game of "chicken" with the leaders of the most arrogant university in the Western world" (1988, p. 638). She won her case.

The third phase overlaps the second. It began in the mid-1970s, under the impact of the fragmentation of the stable bi-polar world of the Cold War. In 1974 key works were published by Perry Anderson and Immanuel Wallerstein. Their wide-ranging surveys of historical development, especially in Europe, marked a new level of ambition and self-assurance among historical sociologists. This third phase saw American retreat from Vietnam, Soviet withdrawal from Afghanistan, growing anxiety about Japanese economic power, and revolutionary uprisings in Eastern Europe. As old political boundaries became more permeable, new imaginative resources were brought into play. Anderson explored the East/West division in Europe from a fresh angle. Wallerstein produced a novel interpretation of relations between the First, Second and Third Worlds. Braudel brought back into focus the old trading networks linking Europe, the Americas and Asia. Mann worked on a canvas stretching from Mesopotamia to the Atlantic.

Skocpol – whose work, like Tilly's, overlaps the two phases – brought three revolutions, clearly separated by history, geography and ideology, into one interpretative framework.[9]

Randall Collins set out to codify 'a powerful science in the making' (1975, p. ix), beginning with over four hundred theoretical propositions in his *Conflict Sociology* (1975). The following year, Anthony Giddens published his *New Rules of Sociological Method* (1976). Both authors surveyed existing contributions, juxtaposed them in a new way, and laid down the foundations for large-scale projects of their own. Collins's approach was explicitly historical from the beginning, Giddens's implicitly so: three years later, he criticized the division of labour whereby 'sociologists have been content to leave the succession of events in time to the historians, some of whom as their part of the bargain have been prepared to relinquish the structural properties of social systems to the sociologists' (Giddens, 1979, p. 8).

Between the mid-1970s and the mid-1980s a stream of books and articles expressed the heightened self-consciousness of historical sociology (e.g. Genovese and Genovese, 1976; Zeldin, 1976; Tilly and Tilly, 1980). Meanwhile, interest in methodology increased. For example, in 1978 there were books by E. P. Thompson, Arthur Stinchcombe, G. A. Cohen and Norbert Elias. These were followed by many others.[10]

This third phase had a paradoxical aspect. On the one hand, historical sociology achieved increasing institutional success within academe, especially in the United States. On the other hand, political tendencies moved against the critical spirit of historical sociology – especially the Marxian approaches adopted by Wallerstein and Anderson. Public affairs in the 1980s were dominated by the right-wing rhetoric of Ronald Reagan and Margaret Thatcher. The dominant intellectual emphasis among historical sociologists gradually changed. Debates within Marxism (of the Thompson vs. Anderson vs. Wallerstein variety) were displaced from centre stage by arguments which marginalized Marxian approaches. The same pattern was found in attempts to build grand theory (e.g. Randall Collins, W. G. Runciman, Anthony Giddens, Ernest Gellner). The wholesale collapse of communist regimes in Eastern Europe late in 1989 undermined still further the residual prestige of Marxian approaches.

Ironically, this has brought a new ideological crisis in the West. Current forms of capitalist democracy can no longer be legitimized simply by pointing to tyranny in the East. Until some new devil is found (Islam? Japan?), critics of our own political, economic and cultural institutions will not be so easily dismissed as 'disloyal'. Meanwhile, there is intense interest in how to make power 'moral', how to make capitalist democracy 'work'. Before tackling those questions, we will look at the three phases through which historical sociology has passed so far.

Chapter two looks at the first phase, when historical sociology was emerging 'out of the ashes' during the 1950s and early 1960s. Chapter three traces the process of 'taking flight' in the mid and late-1960s and during the 1970s. Chapter four deals with the most recent period, when historical sociology has been 'soaring high'. The final chapter considers historical sociology in the 1990s. It asks: what are the characteristics of historical sociology as an intellectual field? How are its past, present and future development related to the challenges posed by successive phases of capitalist democracy? Who are the audience for historical sociology? And what can it give them?

2   Out of the Ashes

War and peace

War and its aftermath have shaped the preoccupations and careers of historical sociologists. Marc Bloch's personal experience as an army officer in World War I must have helped him, years later, to recreate imaginatively the Europe of one thousand years before when, confronted with alien invasions, the assembled bishops of the province of Rheims lamented:

> you see before you the wrath of the Lord breaking forth . . . there is naught but towns emptied of their folk, monasteries razed to the ground or given to the flames, fields desolated . . . Everywhere the strong oppresseth the weak and men are like fish of the sea that blindly devour each other. (Bloch, 1961, p. 3).[1]

That quotation is from the first volume of *Feudal Society* (Bloch, 1961) which appeared in 1939. The second volume was published in 1940, with German troops advancing into France and Bloch in uniform once more as an army captain. Four years later, he was shot by the Germans in his home town of Lyons where he had been active in the French resistance.

Bloch's career is an extreme example of war's impact. There are other examples. In the year France fell, T. H. Marshall was writing a discussion paper for the Foreign Office on how a defeated Germany would be dealt with. Marshall had spent four years as a civilian prisoner of war on a race course in Germany during World War I. This experience was mirrored by Norbert Elias's internment in Liverpool and on the Isle of Man during World War II. Elias's incarceration, though painful to bear, was relatively brief. Fernand Braudel's much longer confinement in

Germany between 1940 and 1945 helped shape his approach to the analysis of historical time.[2] According to Edward Shils, World War II 'enhanced the confidence of the sociologists' (Shils, 1980, p. 119). In the United States, many of them joined the Information and Education Branch of the Office of the Adjutant General. Other historians and sociologists, including recent immigrants from Europe, joined the Research and Analysis Branch of the Office of Strategic Services.[3]

World War I destroyed imperial regimes in Russia, Turkey, Austria–Hungary, and Germany. It helped create conditions for successful revolution in Russia, attempted revolution in Germany and, for a short while, fear of revolution in Britain. Established authorities collapsed in the midst of widespread death and destruction. These events intensified debate on two unresolved issues within Western liberalism. One was the relationship between justice and order within modern societies. More specifically, between, on the one hand, unmet claims for the legal, political and social rights of citizenship and, on the other hand, the need for a stable political framework guaranteeing life, property and peaceful economic exchange. The other unresolved issue was the relationship between the rational and the non-rational in thought, experience and behaviour.[4]

Max Weber met both issues head on. As is well known, he was interested in the nature of rationality and the part played by intuitive understanding and interpretation. He also analysed in depth the conflict between democracy and bureaucracy, especially after the fall of Bismarck. Democratic government needed a powerful bureaucratic organization to assert its will against aristocratic institutions. However, bureaucracy itself had to be held in check by inspired and intelligent political leaders within a strong parliamentary system: 'a merely *passive democratization* would be a wholly pure form of *uncontrolled bureaucratic domination*' (Weber, 1978, p. 1453; emphasis in original).[5]

If the nation were to be strong, justice and order had to be reconciled by active bourgeois reformers such as Weber himself. Unfortunately, between the two world wars in Europe the rise of mass movements promising 'justice' was followed by social breakdown, political oppression, or both. This situation was transformed by Allied victory in World War II. The 'American way' was advertised as the 'best' form of democracy. It was supposedly free from the tensions troubling Weber and his contemporaries. Consensus was based upon emotional commitment and rational assent to a just social order offering equality of opportunity. Patriotic commitment and calculated self-interest were in harmony. Rational and non-rational aspects of human nature were both positively engaged within a moral and stable polity.

In this atmosphere Talcott Parsons developed his structural-functionalist approach. It exercised a major influence on historical sociology before the mid-1960s. The rest of this chapter looks at two aspects of this phenomenon. Its first theme is the impact on American intellectuals of the two world wars and European politics during the interwar years. Second, the contribution of structural-functionalism to historical sociology is studied in the work of Talcott Parsons, Neil J. Smelser, S. N. Eisenstadt and Seymour Martin Lipset. The argument then turns to T. H. Marshall and Reinhard Bendix. Parsons, Marshall and Bendix were alike in two respects. First, they were broadly satisfied that capitalist democratic ideology as it stood in the aftermath of the Second World War accurately described the dominant tendencies within American and British society. Second, they believed values made a systematic contribution to regulating societies. However, Marshall and Bendix took more interest than Parsons in the evidence ideologies provided about social tensions and conflict.

The end of ideology?

When Daniel Bell proclaimed the 'end of ideology' (Bell, 1962), he was reflecting a mood widespread on both sides of the Atlantic. By the 1950s, it seemed, fascism had been defeated and communism outfaced. Social planners had learned a sense of proportion (cf. Hayek, 1976). There was a broad consensus in favour of political pluralism, the mixed economy, the welfare state, and power-sharing between central government and more decentralized authorities.

Not all contemporaries responded in the same way to the defeats and victories of the 1930s and 1940s. One pattern is exemplified by Seymour Martin Lipset. During his youth in the late 1930s, while at the preparatory school for the City College of New York, Lipset belonged to the Young People's Socialist League (YPSL), the youth section of the Socialist Party, and to the American Student Union, an organization dominated by communists. Later in his undergraduate career, he was national chairman of the YPSL. However, by 1961 he was attacking C. Wright Mills for the latter's Marxist bias.[6]

A quite different example of the intertwining of personal experience and intellectual development is provided by Reinhard Bendix. He was born in Weimar Germany, grew up under Hitler's regime, and for a short time joined the Socialist Labour Youth. He came to Chicago in 1938 as 'a twenty-two year-old German-Jewish refugee' (Bendix, 1984, p. 1).[7] He had a 'European' concern with moral and political dilemmas which, according to official American ideology, had been solved. Lipset and Bendix have collaboratored on several projects;[8] but the message of their individual work is that, while Lipset thinks 'the American way' is 'the best possible,' Bendix merely regards it as 'one of the best available'.

The American way: Parsons and Smelser

Talcott Parsons's intellectual and moral development reflected his Calvinistic, Midwestern background and his experiences in Europe between the wars. Parsons had visited Germany on an exchange fellowship during the 1920s:

> The state of Western society which might be designated as either capitalism or free enterprise – and on the political side as democracy – was clearly in some kind of state of crisis. The Russian Revolution and the emergence of the first socialist state as controlled by the Communist party had been crucial to my thinking since undergraduate days. The Fascist movements affected friendships in Germany. Less than two years after the publication of [*The Structure of Social Action*] . . . the Second World War was to begin, and, finally, came the Great Depression with its ramifications throughout the world. (1970, p. 831)

During World War II, Parsons worried about the effects of Nazi propaganda upon immigrants poorly integrated into American society. This helps account for his later insistence on the importance of integrating values within social systems.

Parsons told Americans how their society worked – or at least how it should work.[9] In principle at least, Parsons's main concerns – with socialization and social control, the maintenance of integration within social systems, and the part played by consensus with respect to values – could have been pursued through comparative and historical analysis. This approach was implied by, for example, his early piece entitled 'Some sociological aspects of the fascist movements' (Parsons, 1942) which concluded that 'one of the most important reasons for the different degrees of success of the fascist movement in different countries has lain in the different degrees in which national traditions and with them pride and honour, have been integrated with the symbols of the rationalized patterns of Western culture.' (p. 145)

In *The Social System* (1951), Parsons provided insights into specific historical situations and processes: for example, the rise to power of technologists and professional managers in the United States. This had 'a great deal to do with the fact that the "business elite" of the great era of capitalist expansion during the period following the Civil War failed to become consolidated as anything closely approaching a "ruling class" in America' (p. 509). Parsons also analysed the rise of national socialism in Germany, and the implications for Russian communism of its success in capturing the state. All these examples were relevant to his concern with the development of responsible leadership in American society.

There is little doubt that Parsons 'was greatly intrigued by empirical variety and extremely well-informed about historical and comparative issues on many fronts' (Robertson and Turner, 1990, p. 550). However, comparative and historical explorations came second in Parsons's work to the challenge of clarifying the responsibilities of the intelligentsia in modern society. In his view, it was the job of professional men and women, especially sociologists, to help maintain a rational, moral and integrated social order (see, for example, Buxton, 1985).

Interpreting social dynamism

In Parsons's view, it was necessary to distinguish between three aspects of social dynamism: dynamism which maintained particular social systems (e.g. through socialization and social control); dynamism which carried forward 'particular sub-processes of change *within* such systems' (e.g. within the institution of the family); and dynamism which contributed to 'the over-all processes of change *of* the systems as systems' (e.g. the rise of a 'charismatic revolutionary movement' such as National Socialism in Germany) (1951, pp. 486, 520–1).

It was possible to go 'beyond description' and produce explanations with respect to change *within* social systems – under certain conditions. For example, 'explanatory generalization' was possible if you understood the relevant 'structural imperatives' within such systems. The 'paradigm of motivational process' was also a useful explanatory device. By this, Parsons meant his assumption that 'value-orientations' became internalized in 'role-expectations' and 'the personalities of individual actors' (pp. 484–5).

In 1951 Parsons believed that '*a general theory of the processes of change of social systems is not possible in the present state of knowledge*' (p. 586; emphasis in original). Instead of a theory, Parsons offered: first, a set of interrelated concepts for describing some aspects of change; second, the Weberian assumption that 'the process of rationalization' was 'a general directional factor in the change of social systems' (p. 499); and, third, the observation that change was often accompanied by 'strains' (p. 513) due to the resistance of vested interests and the disruption of established expectations.

During the late 1950s Parsons began to incorporate societal change more fully into his thinking, mainly through his association with Neil Smelser, to be discussed shortly. In fact, by the mid-1960s Parsons had developed a neo-evolutionist analysis. According to this view, societal change took the form of increasing differentiation leading to problems of integration handled by 'adaptive upgrading' of differentiated systems, improving their capacity to survive (Parsons, 1966, p. 22).[10] Ironically, in some respects, these ideas took Parsons towards Herbert Spencer, whose work he had criticized three decades before in *The Structure of Social Action*.[11]

By taking historical change seriously, in the mid-1960s Parsons was following the example of academic colleagues who had been trying to apply structural-functional approaches in that sphere for a decade or so. Parsons's best-known student, Robert K. Merton, falls into a special category. He carried out important historical work in the middle and late-1930s, leading to his *Science, Technology and Society in Seventeenth Century England* (1970), originally published in 1938. Unlike Parsons, Merton concentrated on developing middle-range theories which could be operationalized in empirical research. Merton's approach interested English sociologists such as W. G. Runciman who were, by contrast, rather dismissive of Parsons. Merton managed to combine a rich vein of irony and human feeling in his work which is largely absent from Parsons. However, despite his early work Merton was not, in the main, a historical sociologist.[12]

Another American sociologist working on historical themes was George Homans, whose *English Villagers of the Thirteenth Century* was published in 1942. This fascinating work could almost have been produced by an early member of the *Annales* school, opening as it did with over a hundred pages on medieval field systems and agricultural methods, followed by long sections on family structures, the social organization of the manor, and the annual pattern of work and ritual. However, this was very much an individual effort from a scholar whose interests also encompassed social theory, poetry and the study of small groups. Like Parsons, Homans was a Harvard sociologist. However, Homans found Parsons 'guilty of both fuzzy thought and sloppy writing' (Tilly, 1990a, p. 263).[13]

Unlike Merton and Homans, the three sociologists now to be discussed all developed approaches to historical analysis which drew upon Parsonian structural functionalism to a significant degree in their work of the late 1950s and early 1960s. The most thoroughly committed was

Neil J. Smelser, who insisted on the close relationship between the validity of his historical analysis and the validity of the theory itself. S. N. Eisenstadt and Seymour Martin Lipset were less heavily committed, but drew upon the structural-functional approach to a significant extent.

Handling and channelling social change

When Talcott Parsons came to deliver the Marshall lectures at Cambridge University in the autumn of 1953, he met Neil Smelser who was a Rhodes Scholar studying Philosophy, Politics and Economics at Oxford. Smelser, previously a sociology student at Harvard, collaborated closely with Talcott Parsons from the early 1950s. The problems of 'growth and institutional change' were tackled in their *Economy and Society* (Parsons and Smelser, 1956).

In their view, institutional change affected the 'boundary-maintaining' conditions of a social system: for example, it disrupted the processes of integration carried out through the family. Change typically meant a period of instability followed, eventually, by a restoration of equilibrium. This was an advance beyond Parsons's position of the early 1950s. Smelser and he were now discussing changes of the system itself, rather than changes within the system. The key was structural differentiation, meaning an increase in the number of sub-systems and a shift to a higher degree of complexity in the relationships between them. Structural differentiation passed through a cycle containing a number of 'logical steps' (p. 270).

This cycle, to be discussed shortly, was the basis of Smelser's argument in *Social Change and the Industrial Revolution* (1959). In this book, Smelser's overt purpose was to demonstrate the utility in historical analysis of the structural-functional approach. As his subtitle made clear, it was 'an application of theory'. The book's subject was the Lancashire cotton industry between 1770 and 1840. This was not an innocent choice of theme. Since Marx and Engels, the mechanization of English textile production has been the *locus classicus* of debates on the early development of industrial capitalism, including its implications for the rise of the bourgeoisie and the working class. Smelser focussed on two closely-related spheres: the cotton industry, and 'the family economy of its working classes' (p. 4). He did not discuss the family economy of the factory owners. This curious omission had the consequence, intended or not, that he was able to ignore the broader issue of the interplay between kinship and property relations. 'Class' disappeared into the interstices between 'industry' and 'family'.

Smelser argued that structural differentiation typically happened as a consequence of two conditions: dissatisfaction with 'the goal-achievements' of a social system, perhaps caused by an inhibiting 'external pressure'; and the 'prospect of facilities . . . to correct this imbalance' (p. 15). Subsequently, social control mechanisms ensured that disturbances were handled and channelled in such a way that resources were mobilized, producing innovations which would then be routinized. These processes were broken down into seven steps: (i) feelings of dissatisfaction and frustrated opportunity; (ii) symptoms of disturbance, including unreasonable hostility and unrealistic aspirations; (iii) covert handling of these tensions, along with attempts to restore commitment to existing values; (iv) official tolerance of experimentation, but without acceptance of responsibility for implementation or consequences; (v) positive attempts to specify the new ideas and encourage entrepreneurial commitment to them; (vi) the implementation of new ideas with the innovators being either rewarded with success or punished by failure; and (vii) the consolidation of gains from innovation through the institutionalization of new ways of doing things.

Having established his 'empty theoretical boxes' (p. 7), Smelser filled them up three times. First, he produced empirical evidence for cycles of structural differentiation in spinning and, more briefly, weaving. For example, he argued that the spread of Methodism in the manufacturing districts strengthened values legitimizing manufacturers' complaints about bottlenecks in the existing industrial structure (steps i and ii). The law courts handled and channelled disturbances (step iii); the Patent Office showed tolerance of new ideas (step iv); and so on (pp. 69–85). Steps v to vii were illustrated through innovations such as the spinning jenny, the water-frame, carding machinery, mule spinning, the self-acting mule, steam power, and the factory system (pp. 85–128).

The other two box-filling exercises involved the family economy. Smelser examined, in turn, changes in the family division of labour and its consumption functions. He traced the emergence of new specialized roles by examining labour market patterns, protest activity (e.g. machine breaking), factory reform agitation, the cooperative and trade-union movements, and institutions such as the poor laws, friendly societies, and savings banks. Confronted with the need 'to offer industrial labour on new terms [e.g. to become a factory hand instead of a domestic worker] *and at the same time* maintain its functions of socialization and tension-management . . . the family rose to this challenge by a process formally identical with that of the industrial change itself – the process of structural differentiation' (p. 180; emphasis in original).

Smelser's achievement was to order a great deal of historical material, more or less plausibly, in terms of his seven-step model of structural differentiation. As he put it: 'the nature of our "explanation" was to relate a multitude of complex social phenomena to a single set of analytical propositions without varying the logic of the propositions themselves' (p. 384). However, this achievement was more limited than Smelser implied.

Smelser argued that a number of competing theoretical explanations – referring variously to economic motivations, resistance to capitalist exploitation, responses to misery and the working of the free market – were all less discriminating than his own. Each relied too heavily upon a single causal factor, and ignored or glossed over cases which contradicted that approach. Smelser made these points in a chapter only eighteen pages long in a text of over four hundred pages. Apart from a brief passage in the introduction (p. 5), this is the only place where competing theories were mentioned. A serious attempt to consider such theories would surely have involved, first, a more detailed comparison of their assumptions and logic, and second, consideration of the alternative explanations offered by these theories at several points in the various empirical applications by Smelser of his seven-step sequence.

Although Smelser's overt project was to use his analysis of historical data to validate structural-functionalist theory, in practice the reverse occurred: the prestige of the theory was used as a means of validating his historical analysis. The key lies in chapters two and three (pp. 7–49). These contain the general theory of action, the seven-step sequence, eight diagrams, two technical appendices and a lot of algebraic notation. In effect, these chapters issue a challenge: who will quarrel with a theory worked out in such detail and with such sophistication?

Smelser's work can be compared, very briefly, with a book which had appeared five years earlier: J.A. Banks's *Prosperity and Parenthood* (1954). Banks was concerned with the relationship between the fall in middle-class fertility in England from the 1870s and changes in middle-class standards of living. Although the period is slightly later than Smelser's, Banks's book directs attention to a highly relevant theme which was, as has been noticed, neglected by Smelser; the strategies and social constraints associated with family life among the educated and property-holding part of the population.

Like Smelser, Banks was interested in the part played by economic and normative factors in bringing about changes in the family. However, the latter's approach was very different. Instead of invoking the transcendent logic of structural differentiation, he explored the situational logic implicit in middle-class responses to increasing social competition. Briefly, Banks found evidence supporting the hypothesis that deliberate limitation of family size in the English middle-class was a response to a perceived threat to their social superiority. For example, in the late nineteenth century the wealth of their immediate inferiors, the lower middle-class, increased disproportionately. So did the costs of bringing up children and preparing them for middle-class careers.

With a little ingenuity, it would not be difficult to 'translate' Banks's analysis into Smelserian terms, describing how middle-class dissatisfaction and frustration associated with 'unrealistic' aspirations (the wish to maintain both relative social superiority *and* large families) produced 'tensions' which were 'handled and channelled' by the institutionalization of new ways of doing things (the adoption of birth control techniques). However, carrying out such a translation does not represent an advance in knowledge.

Confronted with a historical phenomenon (the decline in fertility from the 1870s) and a large list of possible causes ranging from the growing prestige of science to the emancipation of women, Banks isolated a strategic aspect of the phenomenon – the decline of *middle-class* fertility – and focused upon one possible cause: changes in the middle-class standard of living considered with reference both to established aspirations and actual consumption. Empirical investigation was then carried out to identify how the middle class expected to live – what kind of housing? how many servants? what forms of personal transport? and so on – and the changing level of expenditure required. The strategy adopted by Banks of carefully investigating the interrelationship between specific variables allowed a chain or web of causal connections to be built up gradually. From the perspective adopted by Banks, a fact has significance if its causal connection with another fact can be demonstrated through careful empirical work, not because it can be located within a 'theoretical box'.

Old empires, new nations: Eisenstadt and Lipset

At the end of *Social Change and the Industrial Revolution*, Neil Smelser called for further studies of structural differentiation: for example 'the segregation of political parties from the system of aristocratic family cliques . . . [and] the segregation of the military and civil service from the earlier system of political and class patronage' (1959, p. 408). In 1963 two works appeared dealing with these issues, especially the development of specialized political institutions and movements resisting 'traditional' ways of doing things. They were S. N. Eisenstadt's *The Political Systems of Empires* (1963), and Seymour Martin Lipset's *The*

First New Nation (1963). The latter book was an application to a specific case, the United States, of a theoretical approach developed a few years earlier in *Political Man* (1981; originally published in 1960).

Eisenstadt and Lipset both operated within a structural-functionalist framework at the time these books were written. They dealt, respectively, with pre-industrial societies (Eisenstadt) and societies which have undergone or are undergoing industrialization (Lipset). The works were written in very different styles. Lipset made no secret of his admiration for American democracy and his contempt for extremism of the left and right. He conveyed a strong sense of political commitment to the American way. Eisenstadt had a much drier and more abstract style. His book was completely free from evaluations (or, indeed, any evidence of feeling).

A laboratory report

The Political Systems of Empires resembled a laboratory report on a crucial scientific experiment. The subjects of the experiment were the political systems within the historical bureaucratic empires: e.g. Egypt, China, Rome, Byzantium, and the major European states between feudalism and the end of absolutism. Eisenstadt set out to identify, firstly, the conditions for the development of specialized political systems within such societies, and, secondly, the conditions which allowed such systems to be perpetuated.

As a type, historical bureaucratic empires stood between 'traditional' and 'modern' political regimes. As in traditional societies, the masses were politically passive. However, the 'historical' regimes had certain modern characteristics: a relatively unified and centralized polity, bureaucratic administration and, not least, institutionalized political conflict between elites for the support of social groups.

Almost a third of the book consisted of bibliographical citations indicating the sources of the 'data', and a large collection of tables containing Eisenstadt's manipulation of variables. Some of these tables compared five pre-bureaucratic societies (e.g. the Mongol and Carolingian empires) with twenty-seven historical bureaucratic societies. Others compared particular societies within the latter category. One, for example, displayed relationships between 'autonomy of ruler's goals, differentiation of institutional spheres, and extent of development of centralized polity' (p. 449). Within the tables, specific societies were given scores for different variables, or located in various categories.

Eisenstadt's book is frustrating. The empirical evidence on which he

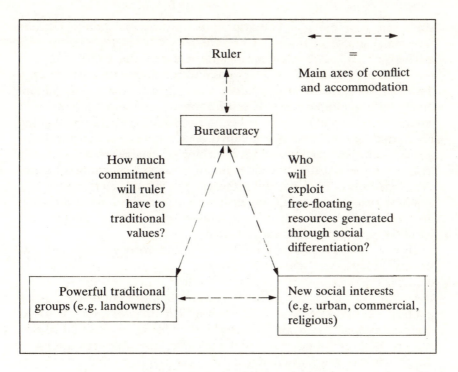

Figure 2.1 Eisenstadt on historical bureaucratic empires

based his generalizations is largely kept under wraps. It is also tendentious, because the criteria according to which his data were manipulated in the tables remain covert. There is the suspicion of inspired guesswork here and there. However, the book remains very interesting because of Eisenstadt's clever analysis of structural conflicts within historical bureaucratic empires (see Figure 2.1). Eisenstadt argued that political systems became institutionalized within historical bureaucratic empires when two conditions were fulfilled: first, when rulers began to pursue their own objectives rather than simply accepting the traditional values and goals of the society; and, second, when social differentiation through urbanization, the spread of the market, new religious movements and so on, brought into being 'free-floating resources' (p. 27) which were not trapped by traditional institutions and attitudes. This 'created a reservoir of generalized power' which could be used by the ruler, the governmental bureaucracy and new social groups such as merchants and other town-dwelling groups.

The ruler and the bureaucracy had to regulate interchanges between the political system and other groups and activities within the society. This task involved them in conflict. For example, the ruler's 'auton- omous' goals differed from those of powerful traditional groups, with whom he or she had to compromise. A cross-cutting factor was that the ruler typically shared many traditional values. Relations with new social groups were also complex. Not surprisingly, they resisted the ruler's attempts to restrict their independence and rake off a sizeable share of the new surplus they created. At the same time, bureaucrats were torn between their responsibility to maintain an orderly flow of resources within the society, and their inclination to line their own pockets and build themselves up as an independent power.

These conflicts created constant pressure for change. Eisenstadt dis- tinguished between three kinds of change: total, marginal and 'accom- modable'. Total changes occurred when, following uprisings or usurpa- tions, 'dislocated groups' could not be accommodated in the existing political system without a fundamental alteration of its framework. Marginal changes were much less serious, involving negative attacks on aspects of the existing order. Finally, 'accommodable' change intro- duced innovations which did not affect '*basic* norms, symbols, and levels of activity of the central political institutions' (pp. 313–4; emphasis in original).

One possible outcome of total change was a more differentiated political system; in other words, the modern state. In such a polity, state and society interpenetrated in a more complex way. Distinctions between the aspirations of the rulers and those of the ruled became blurred. Within modern polities, the 'latent despotic and totalitarian power' of the state might become fully realized. On the other hand, there might be 'fuller freer participation of different groups in the political process' (p. 371).

As will be recalled, Smelser argued that structural differentiation occurred in a repeated pattern: an initial disruption of the harmony of means, ends and values, and subsequent restoration of this harmony. S. N. Eisenstadt discerned a similar pattern, but with two differences of emphasis. First, Eisenstadt stressed the potential for disruption to recur, rather than the tendency for harmony to be re-established. Second, while Smelser assumed that 'handling and channelling' of discontent and maladjustment occurred within each specialized institutional order – e.g. the family, the economy – Eisenstadt saw that conflicts between groups cut across different institutional orders. Specifically, the differentiation of goals and institutions within historical bureaucratic empires led to conflicts among traditional groups (especially landowners), the beneficiaries of 'free-floating resources' (e.g. bureaucrats, merchants), and those with investments in both camps (e.g. rulers). They were not contained within sub-systems, but were society-wide.

To recap: in Eisenstadt's view, historical bureaucratic empires were 'in-between'. The appearance of a differentiated political system disrupted a more harmonious traditional order. The re-establishment of a more integrated order would occur with the establishment of the modern state, in the form either of dictatorship or democracy. The rhythm of change – harmony/disruption/harmony – was the same as in Smelser's model but the scale was different. Smelser worked with specialized institutions and decades, Eisenstadt with whole societies and centuries.

Eisenstadt concluded his book by suggesting that historical bureaucratic empires contained the seeds of modern dictatorship and modern democracy. This provides a natural bridge to Lipset, who was very interested in the distinction between these two political forms.

The sociologist as patriot

The first part of *Political Man* (first published in 1960) was concerned with 'the conditions of the democratic order'. In exploring these conditions, Lipset applied a methodology similar in some respects to that used by Eisenstadt. For example, he classified a number of modern societies according to whether they were 'stable democracies' or 'unstable democracies and dictatorships'. By tabulating various indices of wealth, industrialization, education, and urbanization, he was able to show that in all cases the 'stable democracies' had the higher score (1981, pp. 31–8).

A second similarity is that Lipset and Eisenstadt were both interested in the conditions under which conflicts arising from competing goals and values could be accommodated within the political system. Lipset's view was that a certain amount of institutionalized conflict was helpful in maintaining a democratic consensus. He had drawn this conclusion from his earlier study of the internal politics of the International Typographical Union (Lipset, Trow and Coleman, 1956).

Third, Eisenstadt and Lipset, like many other American social scientists in the early 1960s, were both interested in the development of ex-colonial states in Africa and Asia. Eisenstadt pointed out that the interaction of 'traditional' and 'differentiated' elements within the political systems of historical bureaucratic empires generated problems which 'may be akin, to some degree, to those of various "new states" now undergoing processes of modernization' (1963, p. 4).[14]

In *The First New Nation*, Lipset was more direct:

> The United States may properly claim the title of the first new nation. It was the first major colony successfully to break away from colonial rule through revolution. . . So perhaps the first new nation can contribute more than money to the latter-day ones; perhaps its development can give us some clues as to how revolutionary equalitarian and populist values may eventually become incorporated into a stable nonauthoritarian polity. (1963, p. 15).

This book was written against the background of American fears that post-colonial societies might become communist. One of the difficulties confronting attempts to establish stable democracies was, in his view, the 'world-wide totalitarian conspiracy seeking to upset political and economic development from within, and holding up an alternative model of seemingly successful economic growth through the use of authoritarian methods' (p. 91).

Lipset sought to undermine 'the appeal of a vulgar Marxism which would have democracy wait solely upon economic development' (p. 313). His own analysis gave a larger place to elite strategies, political institutions and, above all, values and national character. In his view, 'Basic alterations of social character or values are rarely produced by changes in the means of production, distribution and exchange.' Instead, as societies became more complex their institutions adjusted to new conditions 'within the the framework of a dominant value system' (p. 103).

New nations required a strong national authority and a stable national identity. The social and constitutional arrangements of the United States had acquired legitimacy by 'being *effective*' (p. 59; emphasis in original); in other words, by 'taking off' economically and giving symbolic rewards to American citizens. These rewards included a sense of nationhood deriving, in particular, from the American Revolution and the Puritan religious heritage. Since the population was homogeneous and law-abiding, political stability was not threatened by tension between the equalitarian values of the Revolution and the Puritan stress on achievement. This tension has persisted in American life. Although Lipset did not make the point, this tension has a strong family resemblance to the contradiction between the social rights of citizenship and the inequalities of the market, as explored by T. H. Marshall in his essay on 'citizenship and social class' (1963d).

However, Lipset's main point was that through its particular history, the United States had 'produced a particular set of "structured predispositions", which is one way of defining values, for handling strains generated by social change' (p. 207). The predispositions were favourable to stable democracy, aided by institutional factors such as a two-party system. This type of party system also prevailed in Britain, another stable democracy. A bi-polar system promoted generalized leadership and support, rather than the fragmentation occurring after World War II in France with its multi-party arrangements.

Newly developing nations might not possess a stable two-party system. They might not enjoy the relatively equitable land ownership and vigorous spirit of enterprise that made achievement values so strong in the early American Republic. However, they might still derive benefits from having stable traditional regimes promoting diffuse and ascriptive values. What mattered was how a traditional upper class reponded to the rise of new groups with industrialization, and how traditional values such as elitism, diffuseness, ascription and particularism became embedded in the modernizing society. Lipset developed this argument through a comparison between the United States, Britain, France, Germany and Sweden.

Lipset took a modified Schumpeterian view of democracy. In other words, complex societies were best served by a political elite competing for the votes of a mainly passive electorate. The struggle could only be 'meaningful' (p. 208) if individuals were motivated to pursue their interests actively within a political system with well-defined rules. The United States, Britain and Sweden were stable democracies in this sense. Germany and France did not qualify for that label. The cases will be briefly described in turn (see Figure 2.2).

The United States emphasized the mutually-supportive values of achievement, equalitarianism, universalism and specificity (with the major exceptions of ethnic and racial issues and, more generally, the South – here dealt with in a single short paragraph and a footnote). It was favoured with non-revolutionary lower-class groups, and upper classes able to accept improvements for the lower strata *without feeling morally offended*' (p. 214; emphasis in original).

In Britain, the economy and polity were a mix of achievement and universalism on the one hand, and elitism and diffuseness on the other. By contrast, the social class system retained a great deal of ascription, elitism, particularism and diffuseness. Instead of the open competition

	Economy	*Polity*	*Upper strata*	*Lower strata*
Stable cases				
United States	Ach, U Sp	Eq, U Sp	open	moderate
Britain	Ach, U; Asc, El, Part, Diff	Ach, U; Asc, El, Part, Diff	incorporating	moderate
Sweden	El, Part, Diff; becoming Eq, Ach, U	Asc, El, Part, Diff; becoming Eq	insulative; becoming incorporating	moderate
Unstable cases				
France	Ach, U; Asc, El, Diff Sp	Eq, U Sp	insulative	immoderate
Germany	Ach, U; Asc, El, Diff	Asc, El, Diff	insulative	immoderate; becoming moderate

Key   Ach = achieved
      Asc = ascriptive
      Diff = diffuse
      El   = elitist
      Eq = equalitarian
      Part = particularistic
      Sp = specificity
      U   = universalist

Figure 2.2   Lipset on conditions for stable democracy

of '*contest mobility*' found in American education, British schoolchildren were selected from above through a system of '*sponsored mobility*' (p. 222; emphasis in original). However, the British upper strata were flexible and open, willing to receive successful people from business and elsewhere. The deference accorded to members of this open and 'incorporating' (p. 239) upper class reinforced political stability.

France, like the United States, emphasized achievement, equalitarianism, universalism and specificity in its value system. Unfortunately, the French Revolution had left fundamental ambiguities and social cleavages. White-collar culture was divided between the deferential Catholicism of the private sector and the assertive egalitarianism of the public sector. Workers shared the latter spirit, but were confronted by an unyielding bourgeoisie which retained substantial quasi-aristocratic pretensions.

French workers achieved full participation in politics, but were denied this in industry. The German working-class experience was the reverse. Its members enjoyed substantial rights and protection in the industrial sphere, but had only limited political access. The main source of opposition was a traditional middle-class which feared for its privileges and was prepared to support Nazism. As in France, the German upper strata were not 'incorporating', but 'insulative' (p. 239), a response leading in both cases to political polarization. Although this spirit had weakened in the political sphere since World War II, German management remained authoritarian.

Sweden demonstrated how Germany might have developed into a stable democracy:

> In many ways, pre-World War I Swedish social structure resembled that of Germany. The Swedish privileged classes strongly resisted universal suffrage, and adult suffrage was adopted only in 1909 for the lower house and in 1921 for the upper one. Swedish social life contained many of the new authoritarian patterns that characterized Germany's and Sweden instinctively looked to Germany for intellectual and cultural leadership. But Sweden was both small and geographically isolated from European wars; it escaped the tensions resulting from the overthrow of a monarchy after military defeat. Its radical Socialist party became moderate and its extreme conservatives and upper class came to accept the right of the workers to participate in, and ultimately to dominate, the polity. (pp. 235–6)

In other words, a society with a culture and social structure almost diametrically opposed to the American pattern could still develop in a very favourable direction.

Three ways to persuade

On the face of it, Lipset was more tentative than either Smelser or Eisenstadt. Smelser insisted on the ubiquity of his seven-stage sequence of structural differentiation. Eisenstadt presented his conclusions about historical bureaucratic empires with all the confidence of a biologist drawing on a well-stocked sample cupboard full of labelled specimens. By contrast, Lipset contented himself with an apparently modest objective: 'merely to demonstrate that values are one important source of variation among social systems' (1963, p. 4). He provided much more evidence than Eisenstadt about particular cases, especially the United States, and his conclusions were less dogmatically expressed than Smelser's. Lipset

> tried to think in terms of a dynamic (that is, moving or unstable) equilibrium model, which posits that a complex society is under constant pressure to adjust its institutions to its central value system, in order to alleviate strains created by changes in social relations; and which asserts that the failure to do so results in political disturbance. (pp. 7–8)

The model was explicitly offered as a guide to thinking, rather than a product of empirical enquiry.

Lipset claimed not to have 'proved' anything, but to have 'attempted . . . to use a certain conceptual framework to point out possible relationships' (pp. 343–4) between values and the internal differentiation of social systems. He concluded by stressing the importance of 'looking at the same problem from different theoretical perspectives' so that we may 'increase knowledge about social processes' (p. 347).

However, Lipset's text carried a concealed weapon. The tentatively presented hypothesis about the central importance of values such as equality and achievement in American society was four-square with a vital tenet of American ideology. This is that America remains strong as long as its citizens continue to believe in the principles of the Declaration of Independence. This background assumption gave Lipset's hypothesis considerable latent power. There was a strong 'structured predisposition' on the part of his American readers to accept it as the truth without serious question. Belief in its central proposition was a major aspect of national identity, of being American. Furthermore, Lipset's support for the American way was evident. Indeed, he was offering American experience as an exemplar to Third World nations, in the context of intense international competition for their support.

The three structural-functionalist approaches to historical analysis drew on different sources of legitimacy. Smelser evoked the reader's respect for complex theory. Eisenstadt exploited the reader's deference to the model of the natural sciences. Finally, Lipset tapped the power of political ideology. All three approaches marginalized the liberal dilemmas associated with the limitations of rationality and the conflict between political order and social justice. Eisenstadt swept aside these issues by presenting his analysis as a scientific study of systems whose pressures and counter-pressures could, in principle at least, be objectively measured. Smelser and Lipset both acknowledged that social protest was typically fed by moral outrage as well as collective fear and anger. However, both assumed that within advanced industrial societies a mutual adjustment tended to occur between, on the one hand, integrating values, and, on the other, the needs and demands arising within differentiated institutions and groups. In other words, social systems usually solved the problems that were set for them. Increasingly, it was assumed, these problems were limited to technical matters requiring pragmatic adjustments.

At this point in the argument it is necessary to cross the Atlantic.

Ideology and social conflict: Marshall and Bendix

> I was born on 19 December 1893 in London, the fourth child, and second son, of a successful architect. Two younger sisters raised the total to six – enough to constitute a very self-contained social unit. Our home was, I suppose, typical of the higher professional classes of the period – intellectually and artistically cultured and financially well endowed. Although we lived, officially, in London, we spent our holidays in the country, either in our house in Hindhead or, in the summer, at the seaside or in the Lake District, and it was in the country that we felt we really belonged . . . I knew nothing of working-class life, and the great industrial north was a nightmare land of smoke and grime through which one had to travel to get from London to the Lake District. My feelings on this point were unaffected by the fact that I was enjoying a share – only a modest one by that time – of the fortune my great-grandfather had made in industry a hundred years before. (Marshall, 1973, p. 88)

T. H. Marshall's solid upper middle class origins, capped by a public school education and a Cambridge fellowship, helped sociology become respectable in Britain after the last war. They gave Marshall, 'one of the deans of British sociology' (Lipset, 1963, p. 9), a secure position within the professional and social establishment.

There are similarities between the post-war national contexts which nurtured Marshall, on one side of the Atlantic, and Parsons on the other. The British, like the Americans, felt insulated from the troubles of the Continent. They generally shared the American assumption that the existing social order was good rather than bad. Intellectuals in both countries were more aware of society's capacity to solve human problems, than its capacity to create misery. A pervasive liberal ethos had

become part of English identity in the late nineteenth and early twentieth centuries.[15] As in the United States, universal laws of historical
development had gone out of fashion by the 1940s. However, the
evolutionist legacy of L.T. Hobhouse continued to shape the British
intellectual agenda.[16] Moral issues were not marginalized. In his
inaugural lecture at the London School of Economics, Marshall insisted
that:

> Sociology can find a better patron saint than Autolycus, that 'snapper-up
> of unconsidered trifles', and some of us may still prefer to spend time over
> such gross and obvious things as law, justice, authority and citizenship,
> instead of joining the merry hunt after the laws that determine whether
> men lean their right or left side against the bar when drinking, and what
> social conditions determine the rate at which they empty their glasses.
> (Marshall, 1963b, pp. 14–15)

Citizenship and social class

After World War II, Marshall held university appointments in history,
social work and sociology. All three perspectives were combined in his
long essay on 'Citizenship and social class' (Marshall, 1963d; originally
published in 1950). As with Parsons's *The Structure of Social Action*, the
economist Alfred Marshall provided the point of departure. T. H.
Marshall seized upon Alfred Marshall's speculation that, despite persisting inequalities, at some future date every human being might live like a
gentleman or 'achieve the standard of civilized life' (Marshall, 1963d, p.
72). This would imply full membership of the community, being as much
a citizen and having the same rights and duties as everyone else, rich or
poor.

Societies in which the idea of citizenship was developing

> . . . create an image of an ideal citizenship against which achievement can
> be measured and towards which aspiration can be directed. The urge
> forward along the path thus plotted is an urge towards a fuller measure of
> equality, an enrichment of the stuff of which the status is made and an
> increase in the number of those on whom the status is bestowed. (p. 87).

In England this equalizing process had coincided with the growth of
capitalism, a system producing inequality: 'in the twentieth century,
citizenship and the capitalist class system have been at war' (p. 87).

Marshall's analysis concentrated upon, firstly, the inner logic of the evolution of citizenship and, secondly, its implications for social inequality, social justice and economic dynamism.

In the medieval period, all rights depended on a person's status in the local community. As these local communities gradually disintegrated, distinctions emerged between civil, political and social rights, each administered by specialized national institutions such as the royal law courts, parliament, and the poor law (managed locally within a national framework). The three kinds of rights evolved in different ways and at different speeds. Civil rights advanced strongly during the eighteenth century, political rights during the nineteenth, social rights during the twentieth.

The courts successfully upheld the rule of law against royal or parliamentary attempts to weaken the principle of individual liberty embodied within it. In fact, this latter principle was extended. Restrictive practices enforced by Tudor legislation like the Statute of Artificers were eroded, freeing people to work in any trade if they were technically qualified. The extension of civil liberties meant giving more substance to a universal right, one already enjoyed by all. By contrast, the extension of political citizenship meant giving the right to vote, whose substance was already fully developed, to a greater proportion of the population. Political rights were 'defective . . . not in content, but in distribution' (p. 80). The property and income qualifications attached to the franchise after 1832 made political rights dependent upon successful use of civil rights in the economic arena. In principle at least, the franchise could be obtained by any one. This economic hurdle was gradually lowered until political rights were given to all, irrespective of their economic means, as a direct attribute of citizenship (see figure 2.3).

Political and civil rights developed in counterpoint. The first began as a collective attribute and became an individual attribute; the other moved in the opposite direction. In the earliest days, Members of Parliament represented whole communities. By 1918 they represented individual voters. The civil dimension of citizenship developed originally in defence of individual liberty. By the late nineteenth century, however, it was providing protection for collective bargaining by trade unions. The unions were using this power to demand a decent standard of living. Furthermore, this demand was put forward as a legitimate expectation, due to citizens irrespective of market conditions. Originally, civil rights had enabled economically-successful individuals to acquire political rights. Now they were enabling economically-powerful industrial groups to bargain for social rights.

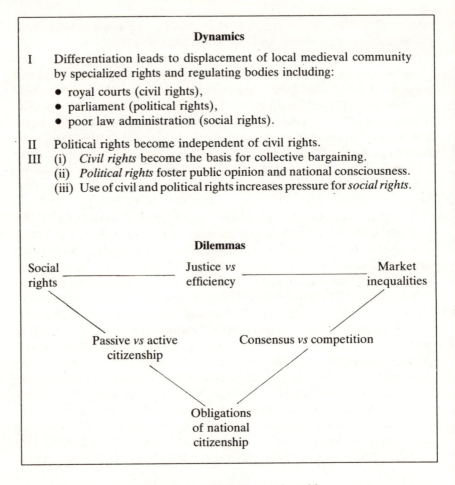

Dynamics

I   Differentiation leads to displacement of local medieval community by specialized rights and regulating bodies including:

- royal courts (civil rights),
- parliament (political rights),
- poor law administration (social rights).

II   Political rights become independent of civil rights.

III   (i)   *Civil rights* become the basis for collective bargaining.
(ii)   *Political rights* foster public opinion and national consciousness.
(iii)   Use of civil and political rights increases pressure for *social rights*.

Dilemmas

Social rights ——————— Justice *vs* efficiency ——————— Market inequalities

Passive *vs* active citizenship   Consensus *vs* competition

Obligations of national citizenship

Figure 2.3   Marshall on citizenship

In fact, bargaining for rights was a contradiction in terms. The problem was the absence of signals within the competitive market indicating what degree of inequality or poverty was morally acceptable. Indeed, under the Victorian poor law, if you sought shelter from the cold blast of the market by going 'on the parish', you forfeited your civil or political rights. During the nineteenth century, social rights guaranteeing minimum living standards had been whittled away, along with occupational restrictive practices. However, the situation changed during the latter part of the century with the development of public opinion and national consciousness, encouraged by the spread of political rights. This stimulated a new determination to make national citizenship mean equality of social worth. In practical terms, this meant a right to welfare, a health service, education, an old-age pension, and so on.

Unfortunately, this added a new set of dilemmas. First, social rights were being expanded to limit inequalities deriving from social class and the market economy. But what limits were there on the drive towards equality of status implicit in citizenship? Second, how were social duties, deriving from national needs, to be reconciled with individual rights satisfying the dictates of social justice? And, finally, how would the equalizing effect of citizenship impinge upon the working of the market economy? To summarize the central problem: the rights and obligations created by contracts in the market place were simultaneously dependent upon and challenged by the rights and obligations bestowed through citizenship.

Governments attempted to meet conflicting expectations by a pragmatic mix of strategies in spheres such as legal aid, health and housing. Education was the key area, because of its strategic significance for both individual opportunity and the success of the national economy. Educational channels fed directly into different points within the job market. As pupils passed through their schools, they were placed into a few broad categories. The hierarchical categorization of students which resulted located them in a system of social stratification which would affect them throughout their lives. In this way, citizenship had invaded the realm of social class. People accepted these new inequalities because of 'the compression, at both ends, of the scale of income distribution [and] . . . the great extension of the area of common culture and common experience' (p. 121) in modern society. However, they complained loudly if they did not get the jobs their education entitled them to. This caused Marshall some nagging doubts, expressed at the end of his argument.

Educational selection should, ideally, be both socially just and economically efficient. Competitive selection was bound to create inequality. However, the egalitarian spirit of democratic citizenship with full civil, political and social rights would only tolerate 'undynamic' inequalities: in other words, inequalities which did not create deep dissatisfaction or make people want to bring about change. This was unfortunate, because such inequalities were 'economically functionless' (p. 125). They were much less useful to society than inequalities generated within the market.

In Marshall's view, inequality could be

> . . . justified only if it *is* dynamic, and if it *does* provide an incentive to change and betterment. It may prove, therefore, that the inequalities permitted, and even moulded by citizenship will not function in an

economic sense as forces influencing the free distribution of manpower.
Or that social stratification persists, but social ambition ceases to be a
normal phenomenon, and becomes a deviant behaviour pattern – to use
some of the jargon of sociology. (p. 121; emphasis in original)

These conflicts and ambiguities were endemic. In his later work, Marshall suggested that modern Western societies were 'hyphenated' (1981b, p. 110). They embodied an uneasy compromise between democratic, welfare and capitalist principles. Marshall had very little sympathy with Daniel Bell's argument that the democratic-welfare-capitalist society had led to consensus over basic values, an end of ideology. In 1972 he commented: 'Even the most cursory glance at the history of western Europe during the last ten or fifeen years shows that it did not' (p. 120). Disagreements about how to handle social inequality were a 'deeply-rooted threat . . . The trouble is that no way has been found of equating a man's value in the market (capitalist value), his value as a citizen (democratic value) and his value for himself (welfare value)' (p. 119).

Marshall focused upon persisting structural conflicts, avoiding grand theory and irrelevant detail. Models of 'social systems' were valid if it were accepted that alongside 'pro-system' phenomena there were also 'anti-system' and 'non-system' phenomena (1963c, p. 27–8). Max Weber and Emile Durkheim were useful but he would not 'swallow either of them whole' (1973, p. 95). Concepts and explanations should be 'stepping stones in the middle distance', an idea similar to Robert K. Merton's 'theories of the middle range' (1963b, p. 13; 1973, p. 98).

With these intellectual tools he was able not only to carry out historical analyses, such as his study of social policy in Britain since the Victorian era (Marshall, 1965), but also to range across other national cases, including India, the Soviet Union and the United States (Marshall, 1981a). On the question of Black protest, for example, he argued in 1969 that while political and social rights could not be used effectively against an unjust regime, civil rights were in general much more difficult to neutralize or ignore. They were 'a hydra-headed monster' (1981d, p. 142) built into the personality and encouraging group formation. The Blacks faced a serious difficulty, however. They were not 'heirs to the full complement of the civic culture' (p. 148). Their collective status in American society imposed a heavy load, which civil rights could not easily overcome. Means had to be found to lift this burden and give Blacks the will and courage to defend their interests. In fact, Marshall was quite sympathetic to the Black Power movement insofar as its aim was to 'replace the anomic weakness of the Negroes by a new internal power generated by self-realization' (p. 150).

This last comment goes to the heart of Marshall's approach. Whether he was serving in the post-war Control Commission in Germany, standing as a Labour candidate, working for UNESCO, or writing and lecturing on sociological themes, T. H. Marshall remained at heart a liberal Englishman. What really mattered to him was the moral vigour of the individual and the community. Human energy had to be stimulated, and legitimate aspirations satisfied. This did not

> ... necessarily imply actual equality of treatment for all persons, any more than it implies equality of powers. It does, I think, imply that whatever inequality of actual treatment, of income, rank, office, consideration, there [is] ... in a good social system, it would rest, not on the interest of the favoured individual as such, but on the common good.

Other questions were raised, for example:

> How far is it possible to organize industry in the interests of the common welfare without either overriding the freedom of individual choice or drying up the springs of initiative and energy? How far is it possible to abolish poverty, or to institute economic equality without arresting industrial progress? ... What is the real meaning of 'equality' in economics? ... What is the province of justice in economics?

These are Marshall's sentiments and Marshall's preoccupations, but they are not his words. In fact, the extracts come from *Liberalism*, by L. T. Hobhouse (1911, pp. 131, 173–4).

Order and justice

Both T. H. Marshall and Reinhard Bendix put conflicts within and between principles of social regulation at the centre of their work. They specialized in tracing contradictions in the justifying creeds developed by vested interests in competition with each other. Marshall focused upon institutions such as the political, welfare and educational orders, Bendix upon social groups such as industrial entrepreneurs and managers. Reinhard Bendix made use of Marshall's work in his own *Nation-Building and Citizenship* (1964), also citing Marc Bloch and Norbert Elias in the same volume (pp. 234, 261). As the most 'European' of the American writers considered so far, Bendix accepted that sociology was not 'useful' in the short run. It could not provide 'secular answers to the ultimate questions of human existence, such as the meaning of life or of history' (1984, p. 127). He was very aware of the dynamic, historical character of the cultural tradition which supplied his intellectual tools. This approach put him at odds with his contemporaries.

For example, in *Political Man* Lipset declared, notoriously, that 'the fundamental political problems of the industrial revolution have been solved' (1981, p. 442).[17] He broadly accepted Daniel Bell's argument that the age of grand political ideologies was over. Like Marshall, Reinhard Bendix had a different view. The 'age of ideology' (1970b), begun in the seventeenth century, would continue as long as there were disputes over goals, and doubts about the rationality of human beings.

Bendix has been preoccupied with 'the circumstantial, institutional, and . . . irrational foundations of knowledge' (1974, p. xviii). Producing reliable sociological knowledge was a difficult task within a culture plagued by ideological mystifications, misleading theories and unwise reliance on the model of the natural sciences. Such knowledge had to be pursued with dogged faith in 'embattled reason', and in full awareness of its implications for moral issues (1970a).

In the year that *Social Change in the Industrial Revolution* came out, Bendix was busy undermining its basic approach. For example, he pointed out that a concept like 'successful adaptation' could be seriously misleading, especially if it failed to balance the short-run and long-run consequences of conflict. A 'dysfunctional' strike might bring increased efficiency and stability in the long run. It was tempting 'to advance judgements with an air of assurance: e.g. strikes jeopardise the consensus required for social integration.' However, 'From a scholarly standpoint such judgements are ideological shortcuts of doubtful value' (1966, pp. 134–5; originally published in 1959). Social structure was 'not . . . a natural system with defined limits and invariant laws governing an equilibrating process, but rather . . . a system of historical dimensions which we examine in terms of the piecemeal solutions men have found for the characteristic problems of that structure' (1963, p. 537).

Like his adopted mentor, Max Weber, Bendix saw national cultures as complex mosaics of beliefs and tendencies produced by past conflicts and the domination of successive elites.[18] Integration and consensus were always incomplete. The intellectual matrix within which modern sociologists formed their theories and concepts was a kaleidoscope of ideologies thrown up in the course of historical development – a fact which escaped many modern students of society. For example, 'given the decreasing interest in the history of ideas among sociologists, a number of them may no longer be aware of the evolutionary theory implicit in their use of "pattern variables" ' (1963, p. 533). However, a sensitive and self-aware historical sociologist could exploit these complexities. Ideologies and associated social structures provided clues to the way specific problems were coped with in the past. Changes in the ideologies of closely-related groups (e.g. industrialists and their employees) could give important evidence of shifts in power relationships and socio-political strategies.

Comparing different societies increased the visibility of distinctive national patterns. In contrast to the reifying tendencies of structural-functionalism, 'Comparative sociological studies are likely to impart a salutary degree of nominalism to the terms we use' (p. 538). The openness of historical change and the coexistence of conflicting tendencies could be captured by using 'paired concepts' (1966, p. 127) as 'benchmarks that can facilitate detailed analysis' (p. 129): for example, bureaucracy and social class could be paired as rival tendencies of action, in Bendix's view. This approach and other aspects of his methodology may be illustrated by looking at two of his works: *Work and Authority in Industry* (1974; originally published in 1956), and *Nation-Building and Citizenship* (1964).

Unlike many of his fellow sociologists, Bendix did not marginalize the dilemmas of Western liberalism. They were central to his work. As has been seen, he paid great attention to the problem of human rationality. He also examined the ways in which developing societies, including the western democracies and their totalitarian rivals, had confronted the dilemma of reconciling order and justice.

In *Work and Authority in Industry*, the emphasis was upon the problem of order generated by industrialization. In *Nation-Building and Citizenship* the area of interest widened. It included the forms of authority implemented within political communities and in the employment relationship. It also encompassed the origins, character and consequences of lower-class demands for fuller rights within the nation-state.

Work and Authority in Industry was mainly concerned with two things: the impact of the factory system upon the employment relationship; and the implications of industrialization for the wider set of relations between workers, industrialists, the state, and the landed class. Industrialization posed the problem of how the new labour force would be disciplined within and outside the factory. It also raised the issue of how industrialists and the working class would fit in to the existing society. Bendix argued that in societies faced with these problems, employers tended to unite together in thought and action, either on the basis of the shard interests of social class, or on the basis of authoritative directives within bureaucracies. Bendix analysed these tendencies and the ideologies developed to justify them in four contexts: eighteenth-

and nineteenth-century England; eighteenth- and nineteenth-century Russia; the United States during the twentieth century; and East Germany after World War II. In all four settings the analysis focused upon the emergence of entrepreneurs and, later, managers as distinct groups with ideologies justifying their demands upon society.

In the English case, early industrial entrepreneurs faced hostility from both the aristocracy and the working population. Industrialists fought for social recognition by competing with the former for the support of the latter. Entrepreneurial ideologies emphasized the power and excitement of new technology. However, the interests and attitudes of factory masters were in conflict with the traditionalism of their workforces. Parents were willing to send their children to work in the factories, but adults fought a rearguard action against the discipline imposed by new forms of production. At the same time, the new entrepreneurs refused to accept the traditional obligation to care for the interests of their employees. Instead, they applied Malthusian principles and punished the poor for their poverty.

Industrialization brought degradation and social isolation to working people. Aroused by the denial of their 'rightful' place in society, they turned to Methodism and Chartist radicalism. Both 'enlisted the active participation of the common people and thereby satisfied their inarticulate quest for social recognition' (Bendix 1974, p. 46). On the other side, the entrepreneurs' harsh rejection of social responsibility was modified in a number of ways. Evangelical preaching insisted on the moral worth of every individual. Employers led popular political campaigns, for example against the corn laws. The task of improving the condition of the people came on to the political agenda. In sum, the class relationship between employers and employees was brought inside a single moral community encompassing both.

The three other cases will be discussed more briefly. Industrialization in eighteenth- and nineteenth-century Russia was initially promoted by central government and subsequently controlled by the aristocracy on their rural estates. As mercantile and industrial groups struggled for greater independence they received encouragement from central government. In the event, entrepreneurs failed to develop a cohesive sense of group identity. In Bendix's terms, they were coordinated in terms of bureaucracy, rather than social class. During the late nineteenth century, government regulation of industry increased, legitimized by the ideology of Tsarist paternalism.

However, urbanization and the freeing of the serfs caused considerable social disruption. The lower orders were detached from their traditional place within an authoritarian rural order. Paternalistic regulation was quite unable to meet the challenge of satisfying the demands of the workers. Unlike England, the workforce could not be satisfactorily reintegrated into the moral and political community. The eventual consequence was revolution and the overthrow of the Tsarist regime.

In the twentieth century, the managerial task has become more complex in both East and West. In the case of the United States, Bendix saw a long-run shift. Late nineteenth-century managerial ideology had stressed the need to reward individual effort and character. This justified executive authority over an obedient workforce in which, paradoxically, initiative was discouraged. Later, this ideology was succeeded by others emphasizing technical competence and intelligent cooperation between management and workers. Psychological manipulation of the shopfloor was attempted and more attention given to the social relationships in which workers were embedded.

In post-war East Germany, the Communist Party and the state tried to regulate all key economic and political relationships. Party bureaucrats and state officials formed a dual hierarchy, each monitoring the other. Industrial production was surrounded by an all-pervasive atmosphere of insecurity. Within both hierarchies there was the constant threat of being overruled, purged or forced to engage in self-criticism. Continuing pressure upon industrial managers to fulfil impossible demands created repeated crises. These drew in party officials hunting for evidence of slackness or sabotage. Failures of executive planning at the highest level were often disguised by blaming middle-level management for supposedly failing to keep in touch with the masses (see figure 4).

Like Smelser, Bendix argued that in the English case complex social struggles passed through phases of disruption and reintegration. Throughout, there was a great deal of institutional continuity. However, compared to Smelser, Bendix had a greater feel for the opposing forces at work, a livelier sense that in other circumstances things might have turned out differently. This grasp of alternative possibilities is displayed through his comparison with the eastern cases, where the strains of industrialization were not successfully 'handled or channelled' (Smelser, 1959, p. 39). On the contrary, they undermined the Tsarist regime and prepared the way for violent revolution. Surprisingly, Smelser made no reference to Bendix's book in his *Social Change in the Industrial Revolution*.

In *Nation-Building and Citizenship*, Bendix presented an argument which encompassed not only the 'historical bureaucratic empires' analysed by Eisenstadt, but also Lipset's concern with the development of 'new nations'. Bendix incorporated a moral dimension absent from

Eisenstadt's former work. He rooted this dimension in his detailed analyses of the dilemmas and choices confronting key social groups in the course of nation-building. As for Lipset, Bendix criticized his *The First New Nation* for assuming that 'the achievement of political independence in the middle of the eighteenth century is comparable with a similar achievement in the middle of the twentieth century', an assumption apparently made on the grounds that 'all achievements of independence by former colonies are comparable – irrespective of time and place'. Bendix commented: 'I do not consider the utility of that assumption very great' (1970e, p. 224).

Lipset and Bendix agreed that two criteria of a national political community were that the state must possess legitimate authority, and the inhabitants must share a national cultural identity. As far as Lipset was concerned, stable democracy required an appropriate set of 'structured predispositions' – e.g. orientation towards achievement and equality – and political institutions inhibiting excessive fragmentation or monopolization of power. His comparative-historical analyses in *The First New Nation* ran the relevant data through a kind of sieve, designed to distinguish between favourable and unfavourable conditions and outcomes. By contrast, Bendix paid much more attention than Lipset to the shape and dynamics of historical processes, especially the development of the central relationship between state and citizen in the course of nation-building. This process, he argued, was just as significant as industrialization. In *Nation-Building and Citizenship* he examined both processes, focusing upon Western Europe, Russia, Japan and India (see figure 2.4).

His analyses of western Europe, partly influenced by T. H. Marshall's work, identified four phases of development, beginning with the medieval age. In this first phase, most people were locked into dependency relations and had no direct political involvement – although they sometimes engaged in unlawful violent protest in defence of established customs. Political rights and obligations were not individual, but collective. They derived from membership within corporate bodies (e.g. manorial estates, guilds, municipalities), each with its distinctive law. These separate jurisdictions, overlapping and conflicting, enjoyed considerable autonomy in relationship to each other. Feudal tendencies of this kind were in conflict with royal patrimonialism. The king, who claimed a general responsibility for all subjects, exploited conflicts between corporations, built up the administrative capacity of the royal household, and tried to extend the effective power of kingship beyond the immediate royal domain.

During the second phase, patrimonialism triumphed and developed

Industrialization

West	East
Class competition/conflict mediated by the market	Centralized bureaucratic regulation
18th/19th century Britain: Crisis of paternalism, leading to civic reincorporation.	*19th/early 20th century Russia*: Crisis of paternalism, leading to revolution.
19th/20th century United States Shift from individualistic Social Darwinism to effective psychological and social manipulation of workforce by managers as a social group.	*20th century East Germany* Conflicting demands upon atomized middle management by centralized dual hierarchy of state and party officials.

Nation-building

I	II	III	IV
Royal patrimonialism *vs*. localized feudal jurisdictions.	Absolutism; estates; masses excluded from participation in political life.	Royal patrimonialism replaced by public bureaucracy; eradication of estates; masses demand entry to political sphere.	Increase in power and scope of state apparatus; civic incorporation of masses; class inequalities limit effective power of the people.

Figure 2.4 Bendix on modernization

into absolutist monarchy, backed by an apparatus of royal justice and taxation. The feudal corporations were transformed into estates. These assemblies represented groups with particular rights within a rigid status hierarchy. They retained control over many legal and administrative functions. Most of the population remained outside the political community, protected only by the obligation of a master to care for his subordinates within the sphere of private authority.

In the third phase, public and private authority relations were transformed. In the wake of the French Revolution the estates were swept away, increasing the power and functions of the state. Commercialization eroded the traditional obligations of employers in the private sphere, although not their power. Meanwhile, new ideas of liberty and equality stimulated a rejection of dependency from below. Outraged and alienated, the people demanded entry in their own right to the political community, the sphere of public authority. This was the point of maximum danger in nation-building.

However, in the fourth phase the crisis was overcome as a result of three factors: the increased willingness of industrialists to assume political leadership on behalf of the people; the civic reincorporation of the masses through the extension of citizenship rights to the urban workforce; and an increase in the strength and scope of the state apparatus. There were major limitations on the power of citizens. In Western Europe and elsewhere, the relationship between state and citizen was embedded in differentiated and unequal social orders. Formal political and legal equality was quite consistent with economic inequality. Also, traditional interests retained significant influence within some nation-states.

By contrast, in Russia a plebiscitarian franchise legitimized a dominant state which suppressed independent pressure groups. In Japan and Germany, industrialization and nation-building were shaped by the continuing political influence of aristocracies. In India, the power of local interests organized through the caste system meant that the state had considerable difficulty in establishing its authority within an integrated polity. Bendix used distinctions developed in his analysis of Western Europe – such as state/society, authority/association, public authority/private authority – to explore these cases at length. The case studies in *Nation-Building and Citizenship*, with the exception of India, were explored in even more historical detail in *Kings or People* (1978).

Bendix's approach evoked a sense of direction and coherence by focusing on major structural dilemmas common to all cases and exploring the principles exhibited in attempts to cope with these dilemmas. In the works mentioned, Bendix did not develop an overall explanation of historical change. Nor, however, did he assert the supposed certainties of grand theory, science or ideology. His agnosticism carried an authority of its own. The influence of structural-functionalism in historical sociology was undermined by Bendix's reasoned attacks on its central postulates. Along with Marshall, he exploded the assumption that normative consensus was either normal or necessary. This helped prepare the way for the second phase.

3   Taking Flight

Injustice and domination

Historical sociology was transformed during the 1960s. By mid-decade its agenda was dominated by power, privilege, and social justice. These issues were tackled, for example, by W. G. Runciman and Gerhard E. Lenski.[1] In the second phase, historical sociologists remembered that social 'actors' were human beings of flesh and blood. This lesson was made easier by the brilliant examples of Marc Bloch and Norbert Elias. Although their key texts were produced in 1939 and 1940, their ideas did not begin to attract much attention in the English-speaking world until the 1960s.

Human interdependence: Bloch and Elias

Bloch and Elias belonged to the continental European tradition of historical sociology forced underground or overseas during the 1930s and 1940s. Both had served in the front line. In fact, somewhere in northern France during World War I Marc Bloch and Norbert Elias, both in military uniform, may conceivably have come within a few dozen miles of each other. Elias joined the German army in 1915 at the age of eighteen and, after a brief spell in Poland, served on the Western front in the Signals Corps. He was a reluctant soldier: 'I have never been a patriot – I was strongly anti' (quoted in Mennell, 1989, p. 6). By contrast, Bloch was eager to serve his country. He was following the example of his great-grandfather, who had fought against the Prussians in 1793 (Fink, 1989, p. 17). There is a strong connection between Bloch the patriot and Bloch the historian.

Eleven years Elias's senior, Bloch had trained as a historian in Paris before the war. There was intense academic rivalry with the Germans. Leopold von Ranke and his disciples had pioneered professional scholarship. This was dedicated to careful interpretation of primary sources as a means of accurately reconstructing the past. By contrast, French historians around the turn of the century developed a methodology emphasizing the professional utility and republican worth of geographical knowledge.[2]

Bloch's early research on landholding patterns reflected the influence of the geographer Pierre Vidal de la Blache. The latter's guiding ideas – such a *milieu, mentalités, genres de vie* and *civilisation* – were taken up by Bloch and his colleagues, including Lucien Febvre. Bloch became an expert in the scientific assessment and imaginative interpretation of a wide range of evidence: textual, topographical, archaeological, architectural, and so on. He used this evidence to build up a coherent understanding of the underlying structures at work within society. Narrative frequently took second place.[3]

The close interweaving of Bloch's professional identity with his patriotism recalls Max Weber in Germany. Like Weber, Marc Bloch despaired of his nation's lack of effective social and political leadership (Bloch, 1949). Each man tried very hard to achieve encyclopaedic knowledge in the quest for maximum understanding, making use of varying mixtures of comparison, causal explanation and trained intuition. The parallels could be explored further in view of their shared interest in agricultural history and the interplay of the material substratum and religious ideas.

However, Bloch was more influenced by Emile Durkheim, a fellow son of Alsace. As a liberal republican, Durkheim saw a need for a national moral and social order in which the ideals of the French Revolution could be achieved. The complex industrial order had to be integrated through a form of democratic government based on active citizenship and strong occupational solidarities.[4] Similarly, while Bloch despaired of the invertebrate French upper class, he did not look for a great charismatic leader. Instead, he accepted a responsibility to serve France as a member of the solid professional middle class.

Durkheim's influence appears in early works by Bloch such as *The Royal Touch* (1973) and the paper entitled 'Reflexions d'un historien sur les fausses nouvelles de la guerre' (Bloch, 1963b). The first, originally published in 1923, explained beliefs about the healing power of monarchy in England and France, with reference to the Durkheimian concept of 'collective conscience'.[5] In the latter, which first appeared in 1922,

Bloch examined the way false shared perceptions spread in wartime, an example of social currents at work.[6]

However, Bloch was no more the disciple of Durkheim than was Fernand Braudel, a generation later, the disciple of Georges Gurvitch. In both cases, there was careful but measured admiration. Bloch was influenced as much by the historians Henri Pirenne and Lucien Febvre.[7] Durkheim was put in his place by Febvre's friend, Henri Berr, in the founding issue of his *Revue de synthèse historique* in 1900:

> We believe that sociology, to establish itself as a discipline, must be primarily a study of what is social in history; we believe that its point of departure must be the concrete data of history. It seems to us, that among French sociologists, the great merit of M. Durkheim and his group . . . is to have applied a precise, experimental, comparative method to historical facts . . . [But] For all the importance and legitimacy of sociology, is it the whole of history? We do not think so . . .

Henri Berr spoke for both Febvre and Bloch when he added:

> It is doing a real service to the sociologist – and to the anthropologist and the ethnographer as well – to invite him to be more specific . . . instead of allowing him . . . to solve all problems, both great and small, from his own point of view . . . And it seems . . . that these various undertakings, amalgamated through historical synthesis, must lead ultimately to psychology. The comparative study of societies must lead to social psychology and to a knowledge of the basic needs to which institutions and their changing manifestations are the response. (Quoted in Stern, 1956, pp. 252–3)

In other words, before pronouncing on human beings and social facts, particular instances should be studied in detail. True to this ambition, in 1920 Berr established a multi-volume series on society, history and culture, entitled *L'évolution de l'humanité*. Sixty-five works had been published in this series by the time Berr died in 1954. One of them was Marc Bloch's *Feudal Society* (1961).

Feudal society

This work appeared in two parts. The first, subtitled 'The growth of ties of dependence', examined a new development beginning in Europe during the ninth century. Hierarchical bonds were formed between powerful military leaders and armed followers (vassals). The latter were supported by conditional grants of land (fiefs). The vassal (as lord of the manor) was responsible for administering justice on his estate; the local population were obliged to provide economic services for their lord.

These feudal bonds grew up because kinship ties were unable to provide sufficient protection for people in a highly turbulent human environment. Men and women suffered the penalties of institutional breakdown (with the Roman legal system in disarray), military vulnerability (shown by repeated invasions by Moslems, Hungarians and Scandinavians), economic weakness (due to worsening communications, declining trade, emptying towns, falling population) and psychological insecurity (fear of hell, the Apocalpyse, the supernatural).

The second volume of *Feudal Society*, 'Social classes and political organization', was mainly concerned with the 'second feudal age' beginning in the mid-eleventh century. This was a more expansive period, with forest clearances, rising agricultural production, and a vigorous revival of urban trade. An intellectual renaissance occurred. Roman law revived. Universities were founded. Self-consciousness developed: 'Human affairs were newly emerging as subjects for reflection' (1961, p. 107). Feudal institutions were transformed. For example, the fief became property to be sold or bequeathed by the vassal – a fundamental change. The military obligations of vassalage were commuted to financial payments. Manorial labour services were likewise replaced by cash transactions, or evaded altogether by migration to towns. The lines of feudal loyalty and obligation became obscured.

Medieval Europe became increasingly structured in terms of estates and classes, rather than of networks of hierarchical interdependence among individuals. The feudal nobility developed a shared code, mixing chivalry, courtliness and Christianity. The urban institutions of wealthy burgesses were less martial and more egalitarian than the old feudal pyramid. Commercial revival helped royal government build up its bureaucracy and so strengthen its capacity to tax subjects. In this way kings could assert their independence from feudal lords. Finally, the church built up its own bureaucracy, centred on Rome. Church, crown, nobility and urban burgesses were bound together in a complex structure of shifting conflicts and alliances.

In *Feudal Society* Bloch explored the structural logic of a particular civilization. A 'civilization' typically lasted several 'generations' (another key term for Bloch). The historian had to recognize that within a civilization, 'everything is mutually controlled and connected: the political and social structure, the economy, the beliefs, the most rudimentary as well as the subtlest manifestations of the mind' (1954, p. 188). Bloch took a kind of X-ray of feudal society, or rather a series of

X-rays, showing how it was held together and the dynamic tensions transforming it. The implicit underlying principle, as Daniel Chirot has pointed out, was the pursuit of human survival (Chirot, 1984, p. 39).

Bloch's model of feudal society was richly impregnated with empirical detail, and specific to medieval Europe. It was built up by interrogating a wide range of evidence, from legal documents to epic poems. Bloch was obviously interested in generalizations about human society, but he was very cautious. He did not create or draw upon any Grand Theory. And he was most comfortable when applying the comparative method to societies close to each other in space and time.[8] *Feudal Society* is rife with comparative analyses within medieval Europe, but has only a brief reference to Japanese feudalism.

Bloch did not assign causal priority to any specific order of facts. *Feudal Society* would probably have paid more attention to the material aspects of medieval life had he not dealt with these some years earlier in his *French Rural History. An Essay on Its Basic Characteristics* (1966). However, he did assert that 'in the last analysis it is human consciousness which is the subject-matter of history'. By this he meant that 'the only real being' was the 'man of flesh and bone', who synthesized '*homo religiosus*, *homo oeconomicus*, *homo politicus* and all that rigmarole of Latinized men' created as 'convenient . . . phantoms' by scholars (1954, p. 151). Bloch's work was a long quest to get in close touch with this 'being . . . of flesh and blood', to discover how his 'mental climate' had changed over time, and to learn about the 'more or less unconscious drives behind individual or collective attitudes' (pp. 42–3). As will be seen, there are certain parallels with Norbert Elias in this respect.

Bloch's point of departure was not a particular theory, but a specific national identity. The 'geography' of this identity was complex. Bloch was evidently most comfortable as a Parisian. His doctoral thesis dealt with the eradication of serfdom in the Paris region; the Île de France was used as a recurrent example in his work thereafter. His 'forward position' was Strasburg, a university town in Alsace regained from the Germans in World War I; he helped reconstruct the University of Strasburg as a French institution in the 1920s. Bloch's 'defensive position' was in the south-west, at Lyons, his birthplace and the centre of the French resistance during World War II. From this secure psychological base, Bloch was able to concentrate on his mission of making human history intelligible. In this particular respect there is a marked contrast with Norbert Elias, to whom the analysis now turns.

The civilizing process

Elias was much more distrustful of patriotism. His career included decades of relative obscurity and lengthy periods of residence in four European countries. It both required and reinforced a strong and independent personality, whose defences were pitched much closer in than any national frontiers. Bloch engaged on a quest for historical truth fired by curiosity and a sense of republican duty. By contrast, Elias was intent upon pinning down, elaborating and transmitting to others a creative personal vision that for several years encountered neglect or hostility from academic establishments.

Norbert Elias's career included the posts of Reader in Sociology at Leicester University, Professor of Sociology at the University of Ghana, and Professor Emeritus at the University of Frankfurt. As a young man he did his postgraduate studies with Alfred Weber and served as academic assistant to Karl Mannheim. The start of Elias's academic career was delayed until the return of peace after World War I. Following an initial period of study in his home town of Breslau, Elias arrived at Heidelberg in 1925 with a doctorate in philosophy and psychology.

Intellectual debate in Heidelberg still echoed with Max Weber's ideas. Weber had died there a mere five years earlier; his widow still conducted a prestigious salon. Talcott Parsons arrived in Heidelberg the same year as Elias. It is unlikely that the two met, although not impossible, since Parsons attended the seminars of Karl Jaspers, with whom Elias was acquainted.[9] If they had met, they probably would have disagreed. Nearly half a century later, when they encountered each other during a round table discussion on 'grand theories of evolution' at the Seventh World Congress of Sociology, Elias praised Parsons's power of synthesis but added:

> I cannot persuade myself that this gift has been used in the right cause. Even for analytical purposes, the assumption that 'actions' form a kind of atoms of human societies appears to me one of those barren formal generalizations too remote from research tasks to be either confirmed or refuted by reference to observable data. Why put 'actions' in the center of a theory of society and not the people who act? If anything, societies are networks of human beings in the round, not a medley of disembodied actions. (Elias, 1970, p. 277)

Elias could not see how this atomism could be combined with 'a decidely not atomistic theory' of society as 'well oiled machinery where all parts are harmoniously geared to each other'; nor how the latter related to 'the rough and tumble of men's social life, as one can actually observe it' (p. 277).

Elias's own approach had begun to take shape in his Breslau days when, straight out of the army, he enrolled to study philosophy and medicine. Stephen Mennell reports that his medical studies made a lasting impression. The complicated interconnections of bones, muscles, nerves and so on were suggestive of 'the idea of complex interweaving of social interconnections' (1989, p. 7) which Elias used prominently later. Furthermore, the way biological endowments were implicated in human communication did not, in Elias's view, fit easily with current neo-Kantian assumptions that the external world and the internal world of the mind were sharply differentiated.

These positive and negative reactions helped push Elias towards studies of long-term processes of social development. He pursued these studies at Heidelberg and Frankfurt before going into exile, first in France and subsequently in Britain. At the same time that Bloch's work was becoming better known in the English-speaking world, following the translation of *Feudal Society* in 1961, Elias's influence and reputation were also spreading gradually. Between the mid-1950s and mid-1970s he was based at Leicester University. Under Ilya Neustadt the Department of Sociology at Leicester became large and influential, replacing LSE during the 1970s as the main provider of sociology teachers in British higher education. Elias and a number of colleagues infused his distinctive approach into undergraduate teaching at Leicester.

J. A. Banks, a graduate of LSE who later held a chair in sociology at Leicester, has recalled that 'What was taught by [Elias, Neustadt] . . . and their assistants at Leicester was an amalgam of the Eliasian and Ginsbergian conceptions of sociology as the comparative study of different societies at different levels in their development.' A large number of historians were recruited to the department. Banks adds: 'Such people were familiar already with . . . the scientific technique elaborated by modern historians and they learned their sociology usually after they had been appointed to the department, mainly from their colleagues' (Banks 1989, p. 533). As a member of the Leicester department during the 1970s, the present writer can record that even though, with a few exceptions such as Eric Dunning, colleagues referred to Elias's work relatively rarely in their publications, Eliasian issues dominated the departmental culture. This was despite the fact that, apart from *The Established and the Outsiders* (Elias and Scotson, 1965) and a few articles, the key texts remained unavailable in English until the late 1970s and early 1980s. The Eliasian approach was largely carried by word of mouth before then.

Since the early 1970s, Elias has become more widely recognized, especially in continental Europe. He continued to refine his approach until his death in 1990. However, his key work was first published half a century earlier. It is the two-volume *The Civilizing Process*, which originally appeared in 1939, the same year as the first volume of *Feudal Society*. In fact, Elias's subsequent work only makes sense by referring back to *The Civilizing Process*. Broadly speaking, this subsequent work covered three areas. First, it elaborated further the strategies of sociological analysis practised in that major work.[10] Second, it examined specific aspects of the civilizing process, in a wide range of fields from psychiatry to the naval profession.[11] Third, it defined Elias's approach to the development of knowledge, including science.[12]

All of this, and more, stemmed from the decision of a young German Jew in the early 1930s, a member of the archetypal European 'outsider' group in its hour of greatest danger, to prepare his *habilitationsschrift* on the subject of that archetypal European establishment, French court society in the age of Louis XIV. The structured processes of social development, including the modes of perception and feeling, which produced and resulted from that dynamic human figuration are a major concern of Eliasian sociology.

In *The History of Manners* (1978a), the first volume of *The Civilizing Process*, Elias began by linking his project to an issue high on the German intellectual agenda after World War I: the differences between German *kultur* and French *civilisation*. Elias skillfully showed how this debate was relevant to the relations between aristocratic and bourgeois society. In France, the bourgeoisie was drawn into courtly society early on. The court played a central role in shaping national culture – and much more. By contrast, the fragmentation of German territory and the distance between classes were major obstacles to this outcome. They stood in the way of 'the formation [in Germany] of a unified, model-setting central society, which in other countries attained decisive importance at least as a stage on the way to nationhood, setting its stamp in certain phases on language, on the arts, on the manners and on the structure of emotions' (p. 22).

In Elias's view, understanding between members of different European nations would be improved if these processes were better understood. Court society was, however, only one phase in the civilizing process. In this first volume, Elias examined *courtoisie*, *civilité*, and *civilisation* as three successive phases in the expression of the human psyche in social relationships. To oversimplify, they appeared in medieval, absolutist and bourgeois societies, respectively. These phases were explored through manuals of etiquette dealing with, for example, the use of knives and forks, how to eat meat, nose blowing, sexual conduct and aggressive behaviour. In the second volume, *State Formation and Civilization* (1982a), there were long chapters on the dynamics of feudalism (including an excursus on troubadour culture), the sociogenesis of the state, and the civilizing process as a whole.

Elias argued that the social and psychological aspects of human life were intimately related. Changes in social 'figurations' (or human interdependencies) and in the human psyche had a clear pattern and structure. Particularly important was a shift away from relatively simple and rather violent human figurations (e.g. in early feudal society) towards more centralized, densely interdependent and increasingly pacified figurations. At the same time, power relations between interdependent functional interests tended to become equalized.

More specifically, power struggles between competing territorial lords were subject to a monopoly mechanism (1982a, p. 104) which led to pacification under a central ruler. People learned to exercise self-control in order to survive. Pacification brought functional differentiation, aided by monetization. Conflict between competing functional interests could, to an increasing extent, be consciously manipulated from above.

Violence was marginalized as competing interests grew to depend on the peace preserved by the central state, as well as upon each other. Two other changes occurred. The activities of the state establishment and related functional interests (e.g. the leading property owners) became 'public business' for the 'public sphere'. And 'civilized behaviour', a complex expression of the invisible wall of effects regulating pacified social relations, became available as a resource which could be used by establishments to put aspiring outsiders in their place.

Elias made three more general points. First, whenever conflict between 'haves' and 'have nots' led to the formation of a new establishment, it was always greatly influenced by its predecessor. For example, the bourgeoisie adopted many aspects of courtly civilized behaviour, although mainly as a preferred (rather than obligatory) style in the private (rather than the public) domain. Second, the civilizing process described in Elias's two volumes was not engineered deliberately. It was 'set in motion blindly, and kept in motion by the autonomous dynamics of a web of relationships, by specific changes in the way people are bound together' (1982a, p. 232).

Third, through exposure to differentiation and competition within figurations, people acquired 'an increasingly differentiated regulation of impulses'. One consequence, as has been noted, was an increase in 'conscious self-control'. This was a means of adjusting to a complex reality and maintaining socially acceptable behaviour. Unfortunately, another consequence was the creation of a 'wall of deep-rooted fears' which reinforced inhibitions. However, since this self-protective psychological response 'operates blindly and by habit, it frequently indirectly produces . . . collisions with social reality' (p. 233). In a later work entitled *What is Sociology?* (1978b), Elias argued that a major task for sociology was to overcome these blind fears, since they were a breeding ground for dangerous myths. Sociology could free the human mind of fantasy-ridden perceptions.

There is no space to explore in greater detail Elias's later work.[13] A fuller assessment would obviously have to take account of the further half-century of creative work enjoyed by Elias, a benefit obviously denied to Bloch.

Some years ago, Johan Goudsblom, a notable advocate of Elias's approach to sociology, suggested that: 'It would be most interesting to compare *Uber den Prozess der Zivilisation* with Marc Bloch's standard work on feudalism, *La societé féodale*, which appeared at approximately the same time' (Goudsblom, 1977, p. 86). *The Civilizing Process* and *Feudal Society* do indeed have some remarkable similarities, which go beyond the fact that Elias drew on some of Bloch's earlier work (e.g. Elias, 1978b, pp. 338, 342, 345, 353).

Although their emphases differed, both works were concerned with the development of networks of human interdependence: the subtitle of Bloch's first volume is 'The growth of ties of dependence'. Both were sensitive to the dynamic interplay of processes of integration and disintegration.[14] Both focused upon the shift within medieval Europe from a violent society dominated by local warrior chiefs to a more centralized, commercialized and pacified society (see figure 3.1).

Each scholar paid particular attention to the connection between what Bloch called 'the reconcentration of authority' and the 'Corresponding changes [which] took place in the mentality of men' (Bloch, 1961, pp. 421–2). While Elias emphasized the increase in self-control required by the courtier, Bloch stressed 'the growth of self consciousness' (p. 106). By the twelfth century, 'Human affairs were newly emerging as subjects for reflection . . . every man had to be something of a lawyer'. Legal education flourished, inculcating 'the habit of reasoned argument' (pp. 107–8). Finally, both were interested in 'human beings in the round' (Elias 1978a, p. 277), 'men of flesh and blood' (Bloch 1954, p. 151), not latinized abstractions.

Each work had its particular strengths. Elias was at his most powerful

Bloch	Elias
First Feudal Age: Breakdown of public bureaucracy, cash nexus, extended kinship. Leads to vulnerability, insecurity and spread of localized feudal hierarchies	The history of manners passes through the phases of: • *courtoisie* – in the medieval castle; • *civilité* – in the absolutist court; • *civilisation* – in bourgeois society.
Second Feudal Age: Commericalization, pacification, urbanization. Leads to demilitarization of vassalage, market in fiefs and conflicts/alliances between crown, Church, aristocracy and urban burgesses.	Passage through these phases is accompanied by increases in: pacification, monetization, functional differentiation, interdependence, centralization, self-restraint, and inhibition.

Similar strategic issues

(a) The development of networks of human interdependence.
(b) The interplay between processes of integration and disintegration.
(c) The shift from violent localized society to more centralized and pacified society.
(d) The relationship between military/political centralization and transformations in the human psyche (e.g. growth of self-awareness).
(e) The unconscious drives expressed in human values and social relationships.
(f) The human struggle for survival under conditions of vulnerability and uncertainty.

Figure 3.1   Convergences between Bloch and Elias

when exploring the moulding and expression of human perceptions and feelings within social bonds. When confronted with dense and potentially alien data, he was able to lead the reader right into the middle of the action, while also allowing him or her to step back from it. He brilliantly explored the transmutation of violence into etiquette and art – although he perhaps did this even more successfully in *The Court Society* (1983). Elias's strength in this respect compensates for a hiatus in Bloch's analysis: for while the latter recognized that the 'second feudal age' saw more refined rules of courtly conduct, he could not quite pin down why French aristocratic culture should have dominated European society. He concluded that it 'seems to be beyond our understanding – the ethos of a civilization and its power of attraction' (1961, p. 307). Elias, of course, had a detailed and highly persuasive answer, as has been seen.

However, the answer invites qualifications.[15] Elias focused his argument upon the secular 'upper class' and explored the formation of the royal court, a crucial institution of socialization and social control – or rather 'a unified, model-setting central society' (Elias, 1978a, p. 22). He argued that the psychic balances and figurational constraints engendered and expressed there subsequently became generalized (and transformed) within bourgeois society. Elias's argument is both narrow (relative to feudal society as a whole) and challengeable.

An alternative approach has been offered by, for example, Clifford Geertz, whose *Negara* (1980) related courtly etiquette in Bali to the shared task of constructing meaning within a highly localized society, rather than implementing political survival strategies within a centralized polity. In *The Fall of Public Man* (1977) Richard Sennett emphasized the function of elaborate codes of etiquette in providing meaningful order for urbanized strangers (as opposed to intimate courtly enemies) in the *ancien régime*. Finally, Michel Foucault found not sexual inhibition, but deliberate incitement to discourse on sexuality, in Europe from the sixteenth century onward (Foucault, 1981).

These alternative approaches do not diminish the powerful beam of light that Elias throws forward on to nineteenth- and twentieth-century Europe. The cost of Elias's insight, however, is a relatively narrow view of feudal society.

In particular, Bloch was able to pay more attention to the part played by Christianity and the Church, factors quite consciously set aside by Elias (1982a, p. 7) in favour of the secular court. Elias's references to the Church (e.g. 1982a, pp. 20, 21, 94, 97, 103, 121–3, 181–3, 187) generally concern its capacity to manipulate political and economic resources, rather than the psychic and social effects of its ritual enactment of a complex supernatural order.

There are, of course, connections between these two aspects of religion. After all, according to Randall Collins, 'The first bureaucratic state in modern times was not a secular state, but the Papacy' (Collins, 1986d, p. 48) – although he went on to point out that Buddhist monasteries, equally centres of strict personal discipline, were not managed through centralized legal bureaucracies, such as existed in the medieval Church. Buddhist monasteries notwithstanding, there obviously *are* important connections between the centralization of administrative capacity and the development of psychic balances and controls as described by Elias. And at the royal court the connection is close and obvious.

However, what went on at court has to be seen in the same context as, say, the long-term effects of literacy throughout society. This innovation is generally, and quite plausibly, assumed to be closely tied up with the development of the state. But the capacities created by literacy may not only survive the breakdown of the state in particular instances, but also extend beyond the grasp of the state, as in early medieval Europe in the wake of the Roman Empire. Religions of 'the Book', including Christianity, were a major expression of these capacities (cf. Mann, 1986).

The age of the knight was also the age of the monk. Monasteries were complex institutions built upon self-restraint, deliberately-created arenas of social experience reflecting and shaping a complicated inner life. Marc Bloch, like Elias, noted the 'emotional instability' of a feudal order 'in which moral or social convention did not yet require well-bred people to repress their tears and their raptures' (1961, p. 73). However, this society produced institutions orientated to the not-here and not-now, where 'the influence of mortifications of the flesh and the repression of natural instincts was joined to a mental attitude centred on the problems of the unseen' (p. 73). Self-examination, self-control and mutual surveillance; the pursuit of holiness through voluntary submission to the divine will: these practices were not the reflex of a presiding secular state. This religious culture eventually produced Erasmus of Rotterdam, author of a book of manners much cited by Elias. Was it entirely coincidence that the concept of *civilité* wes popularized by a man who had trained as a monk?

An uppity generation?

The work of Bloch and Elias did not attract the kind of following achieved by Barrington Moore and E. P. Thompson in the late 1960s. In part, this reflects the way the first pair handled values in their writings. Bloch's own passionate commitment to freedom and justice was expressed in his life [and in his contemporary document, *Strange Defeat*], rather than directly through his historical publications (Bloch, 1949). The emphasis in his academic work was upon sweeping aside ignorance and prejudice, in order to look clear-sightedly upon the past.

Detachment was a virtue also practised by Elias, whose central interest was the challenge of replacing misleading myths with 'object-adequate' knowledge which enhances the possibilities of human control.

Until late in his life, his published work focused less upon the human search for meaning, than the struggle for survival.[16] In sum, both Bloch and Elias kept the question of values in a compartment separate from their concerns as historical sociologists. By contrast, Moore and Thompson brought the discussion of values fully into the practice of historical sociology. They were duly acclaimed by the 'sixties generation'.

Some members of this generation eventually became historical sociologists themselves. They were infused with a pioneer spirit:

'How did someone from your background come to write such a book?'
The questioner was Perry Anderson, and the question was directed at me, Theda Skocpol, as the two of us sat together on a wintry day in 1978, eating lunch at Grendel's Den, down Boylston Street from Harvard Square. I had just finished the manuscript for *States and Social Revolutions: A Comparative Analysis of France, Russia and China . . .*
As I tried, a bit lamely, to explain to Perry Anderson that day, the answer lies partly in the impact on my thinking – and on the thinking of many others who were then becoming young adults and students of society – of the indelible domestic and international events of the 1960s. The 1960s created an 'uppity generation', which has not only caused trouble for its elders in all of America's major institutions but has also revitalized the macroscopic and critical sides of our discipline. (Skocpol, 1988a, pp. 627–8)

In her 'reflections at mid-career by a woman from the sixties', Theda Skocpol argued that her generation was at odds with its predecessor. The latter accepted the Cold War opposition between capitalist-democratic 'freedom' and communist 'tyranny'. By contrast, most of the 1960s generation developed 'an acute sense that existing relations of power in state, economy and society could be very unjust' (p. 630). They did not trust authority:

It is not incidental that sixties-generation sociologists, along with a few older ones whose work resonated well with the experiences of the 1960s, have led the way in reorienting much of sociological theorizing and research from the study of prestige and mobility to the study of class relations, from the study of political attitudes to the study of the state, and from the study of irrational deviance to the study of resourceful collective action. (p. 631)

In this piece, Theda Skocpol effectively conveyed the mood of the 1960s as recalled two decades later: a heady mixture of political enthusiasm and ebullient self-confidence. It is an intriguing self-portrait of a generation.

In fact, the part played by the 'few older ones' was crucial. As historical sociology 'took off' during the 1960s, it implemented and developed the programme outlined in *The Sociological Imagination* (1959). Its author, C. Wright Mills, was a product of the student generation of the 1930s. E. P. Thompson and Barrington Moore were also from earlier generations. Thompson, educated at an English public school and Oxford University, was a student in the 1940s. Moore, 'perhaps the most radical American sociologist' (Lipset, 1971, p. 210) belonged to the generation of the 1930s. He was the product of a comfortably-off patrician background. Apparently, George Homans once remarked: 'Barry's got some funny ideas but he must be all right, since his grandfather was commodore of the New York Yacht Club' (Tilly, 1990a, p. 265). Neither Moore nor Thompson pursued a conventional academic career. They did not found 'schools'. But anyone who claimed to be interested in historical sociology had to be familiar with their work. Eugene D. Genovese, 'probably the leading Marxist historian in the United States', who 'lost his position at Rutgers University . . . because of his open advocacy of a victory for the Viet Cong' (Lipset, 1971, p. 211), was born in 1930.

After 1974, equal prominence was achieved by Immanuel Wallerstein and Perry Anderson. Wallerstein had been a student in the 1950s, Anderson's student career ran into the early 1960s. There will be disagreement about specific individuals and relative rankings, but any list of the 'foundation scholars' of post-war historical sociology in the English-speaking world must include Thompson, Moore, Wallerstein and Anderson. Only one of these four, Perry Anderson, was a member of the (early) 1960s student generation.

However, Theda Skocpol did draw attention to an important truth. During the 1960s there was widespread dissatisfaction among students, women, Blacks and others with the way capitalist democracy was treating them. This created a potential new audience for historical sociology. Members of categories denied proper citizenship or social justice had a vested interest in asserting a strong and confident identity as one means of strengthening morale and increasing their collective power. 'New' histories of these insurgent groups were in demand. This brought dangers. One was that by focusing attention exclusively upon specific groups – such as women, Blacks, the working class – the complex bonds linking these groups into the wider society might be neglected or over-simplified. Another was that the fine line between 'recovering the truth' and creating a useful myth might be overstepped.

Krishan Kumar was correct to suggest recently that although 'The rise of various forms of "segmental history" – "labour history", "black history", and so on – have had readily understandable origins and motivations . . . it is less easy to sympathise with the narrowness of vision, and restricted terms of analysis, imposed by the method of considering events predominantly from the participants' point of view, as "their history" ' (Kumar, 1983, p. 43). As Theda Skocpol has pointed out, the ideological world-views which sustain cohesion and aid mobilization are often at odds with reality (Skocpol, 1979, pp. 168–71).

Fortunately, during the 1960s there were scholars around who were not deeply compromised by career ambitions within the existing academic establishment, or the demands of political activism. In the vanguard of this second wave of historical sociology were writers who did not seek or depend upon conventional success within the academic world. They were active within or strongly sympathetic to radical movements, but certainly not bound to a strict 'party line' of any kind. Like C. Wright Mills, Thompson and Moore were individualists, prepared to accept the risk of asserting independent moral and intellectual positions, and relatively unconcerned with institutional rewards. Members of the sixties generation came into prominence after the advances of the mid-1960s and the mid-1970s. They were able to build upon an established beach-head when their turn came round in the late 1970s and 1980s. Theda Skocpol's work will be examined later, but first more detailed attention will be paid to Barrington Moore and E. P. Thompson.

Two critical rationalists: Moore and Thompson

The work of Barrington Moore and of E. P. Thompson has three striking characteristics: a great sensitivity to the human cost, not least in violence, of the transition to modern capitalist democracy; considerable interest in the potential human benefits that have been denied realization by the suppression of alternative patterns of historical development; and an imaginative capacity enabling them to 'get inside' the cultures of subordinate and dominant classes, explaining them in terms of their structural location and the situational logic confronted by their members.

No one could accuse Moore and Thompson of being hippies. In fact, they both belong to a cultural tradition, shaped by the Enlightenment, which fused the moral and intellectual imperatives of Christianity and classicism.[17] From eighteenth-century Edinburgh and Glasgow and, a little later, the literary and philosophical societies of the English provinces, this tradition crossed to the east coast of America. Moore, whose first degree was in Greek and Latin, belongs to the classical side of the tradition. In the early 1970s he implicitly compared 'critical rationalists' such as himself to 'intelligent pagans in the last phase of classical civilization' (1972, p. 103).

Moore's 'natural' arena is the seminar, or small gathering. It is quite appropriate that he should have published a book entitled *Privacy* (1984). Emotive (as opposed to evaluative) language is kept strictly to a minimum in his writing, making it all the more effective when it is used. The excitement comes from the moral and intellectual quest itself, in which the reader is allowed to play Watson to his Holmes. By contrast, the 'natural' place for Thompson is the pulpit, preferably in debate with the occupant of another pulpit. One such debate, arising from *The Poverty of Theory* (Thompson, 1978a), was held at St Paul's Church, Oxford, a building converted to an arts centre. According to an eye-witness from *New Society*, Thompson's own contribution was 'delivered with maximum theatrical force. The result was that subsequent discussion was almost impossible. The aftermath of the Saturday night's fusillade hung like a pall of smoke over the rest of the conference' (Martin Kettle, quoted in Samuel, 1981, p. 378).

It is worth briefly indicating the background to this occasion. Between 1946 and 1956 Thompson was a member of the Communist Party Historians Group along with, for example, Christopher Hill, Eric Hobsbawm, Rodney Hilton and John Saville (Kaye, 1984). At the base of Thompson's socialism and his work as a historian was a humanistic 'faith in the ultimate capacity of men to manifest themselves as rational and moral agents' (Thompson, 1978c, p. 156), a fundamental optimism about the power of collective will over material circumstances. In 1956–7, following the Soviet invasion of Hungary, Thompson and others actively dissented from the official line of the British Communist Party, not least through their journal the *Reasoner*. Thompson soon left the party and the journal became the *New Reasoner*. In 1960 it amalgamated with *The Universities and Left Review* to emerge as the *New Left Review*. Thompson and a number of his old associates were on the editorial board.

Two decisive events occurred in the early 1960s. First, *The Making of the English Working Class* appeared. Second, control of the *New Left Review* passed to a younger generation led by Perry Anderson. The new people were not preoccupied with 1956, had little taste for the popular traditions of British Labour, and wanted to learn from a study of continental Marxism – Gramsci, Lukacs, Althusser and so on. Thompson left the editorial board. Political disagreements were interwoven with fierce disputes over how history, especially English history, should be understood and written. The so-called 'culturalism' of Thompson's work was roundly criticized, directly and indirectly.[18] *The Poverty of Theory*, a sustained polemic against structuralism, was Thompson's most powerful counterattack.

Thompson stems from the Christian side of the Enlightenment. His father was an educational missionary in India who sent his son to Kingswood, a Methodist public school. According to Thompson's own ironic self-description in the early 1970s, he was inclined to 'minority-minded self-isolation . . . a representative of a residual tradition, like Old Dissent' (1978c, p. 182). His drive is a missionary one: 'I am seeking to rescue the poor stockinger, the Luddite cropper, the 'obsolete' hand-loom weaver, the 'utopian' artisan, and even the deluded follower of Joanna Southcott, from the enormous condescension of posterity' (1968, p. 13). It is not surprising that the earliest of Thompson's major academic writings, published in 1955, was a study of William Morris: a middle-class moralist who became 'our greatest diagnostician of aliena-tion' (Thompson, 1976a, p. 801), a rebel against the depravity of industrial capitalism, who turned to practical socialism.

Since the mid-1950s Thompson has moved in two directions. As a historian of class cultures, he has gone backwards into the early nine-teenth and eighteenth centuries: for example, in *The Making of the English Working Class* (1968), *Whigs and Hunters. The Origin of the Black Act* (1975), and the essays on capitalist work-discipline (1967), the crowd (1971), and popular culture (1975; 1978e). As a political polemi-cist, he has moved forward into the twentieth century: for example, in *Writing By Candlelight* (1980) and *Beyond the Cold War* (1982). These two aspects of Thompson's work were united in *The Poverty of Theory* (1978).

Moore, like Thompson, has been concerned with structures of domi-nation. For example, *Social Origins of Dictatorship and Democracy* (*Social Origins* hereafter) was mainly about the effects on the rural order of modernization in six commercialized agrarian societies (Eng-land, France, the United States, China, Japan and India). Its subtitle was 'Lord and peasant in the making of the modern world'. *Injustice. The Social Bases of Obedience and Revolt* (1978) looked at the develop-ing consciousness of the lower orders, especially the German proletariat in the nineteenth and early twentieth centuries. By contrast, in his earliest books, *Soviet Politics – The Dilemma of Power: The Role of Ideas in Social Change* (1950) and *Terror and Progress USSR: Some Sources of Change and Stability in the Soviet Dictatorship* (1954), Moore looked at the content and consequences of the ways of thinking of the Soviet modernizing elite.

More recently, in *Authority and Equality under Capitalism and Socialism* (1988), Moore has explored the varying ways in which bureaucracies have been implicated in shaping relations of authority and inequality; and also the potential consequences of a variety of possible bureaucratic regimes for maximizing freedom and rationality. As well as the works just mentioned, Moore has published two collections of essays: *Political Power and Social Theory* (1958), which tried to find out which elements of the industrial social order were unique and necessary, and the splendidly-titled *Reflections on the Causes of Human Misery and upon certain Proposals to Eliminate Them* (1972).

Social origins of dictatorship and democracy

At the centre of both *Social Origins* and *The Making of the English Working Class* are two interacting processes: the penetration of the market into local communities within agrarian societies; and the extension of the bureaucratic reach of the central state. Moore's book will be discussed first. Its novel message was that modern political systems were fundamentally shaped by aristocrats and peasants in pre-industrial societies. To oversimplify, a crucial process was the commercialization of agriculture, since this provided food for the towns, while generating cash to pay taxes. Was this process a result of peasant initiative, or aristocratic enterprise in each society? How did the great landowners take their share of the surplus? What was the role of physical coercion?

In Prussia the *junkers* exploited serf labour on large estates producing cash crops. In France the nobility demanded their feudal dues from the profits of peasant entrepreneurship. In England sheep farming prospered as peasants were swept off the common land. Strategies such as these led the aristocracy into closer interdependence with either the central state or the urban bourgeoisie; or both, as in the case of France, where the growth of absolutism was a major consequence. In England, aristocrats and merchants combined to hold the crown in check. In Japan and Germany, the landed interest aided by the state kept the urban bourgeoisie politically weak, though economically strong. In Russia and China, the bourgeoisie's political weakness coincided with a lack of entrepreneurial vigour. As a consequence, the dominant agro-bureaucratic coalitions were unable to inhibit or contain peasant uprisings.

Peasant revolution was possible where reciprocity with landlords was weak, the repressive capacity of government low, and village social structure conducive – three conditions satisfied in France by 1789,

Russia by 1917, and China by the 1940s. It was inhibited in India by the caste system, in Japan by high levels of rural inter-class solidarity, in Germany by repressive labour control, and in England by the destruction of peasant society through the enclosure movement; in the United States there was no peasantry.

To summarize: major transforming events such as revolutions (in France and China) and civil wars (in England and the United States) were explained in terms of specific alliances, inter-group conflicts, and changing patterns of integration and perception; these were stimulated by the challenges of modernization, especially the commercialization of agriculture. Moore distinguished between democratic, fascist and communist outcomes. Democracy assumed shared responsibility for making political rules, and protection for individual freedom. It developed where the only use of violence had been to cut back rural interests hostile to the free market economy; the bourgeoisie had profited from this to establish a dominant, but not monopolistic, position.

Fascism was a direct inversion of democratic principles. It prospered where repression, especially state violence, was used to squeeze the peasantry, protect the great landowners and incorporate the lower orders within an authoritarian polity. Communism asserted a 'higher' freedom beyond bourgeois democracy. Peasant revolution was one condition; another was the use of repressive measures against the peasantry itself by a revolutionary elite intent upon transforming rural conservatism.

It should be emphasized that although Moore's book is largely about the impact of commercialization and bureaucratization on rural society, his cross-national empirical generalizations refer to the end-state reached via these processes, rather than the way these processes unfold. More specifically, he suggests that the outcome of the triangular conflicts and accommodations among aristocracy, bourgeoisie and the state determines whether the 'modern' polity will be democratic, fascist or communist (see figure 3.2). His generalizations are about the political consequences of the outcome of the triangular conflict. His causal explanations – about how the impact of commercialization and bureaucratization on rural society shapes the unfolding struggles – are specific to individual cases. Moore makes brilliant use of cross-national comparisons in demonstrating the individuality of each case.

Since 1966, Moore's propositions in *Social Origins* have been criticized extensively. They have also been tested, elaborated, and revised.[19] It is not possible to review these critiques here, but three weaknesses in Moore's argument cannot be overlooked. They are: his neglect of inter-societal relations, his lack of sustained attention to the

	Modernizing class or coalition	Role of violence
Democracy	Bourgeoisie achieves dominant, not monopolistic, position.	Repression of rural interests opposed to extension of the free market.
Fascism	Landed interest retains privileged position in the state; bourgeoisie remains politically subordinate, though economically vigorous.	Violence used to squeeze peasantry, protect landed interest, and bind urban working class into authoritarian polity.
Communism	Neither bourgeoisie nor landed interest able to effect adequate economic or political modernization; revolutionary elite achieves state power.	Peasant revolution eliminates ruling class and allows revolutionary elite to seize the state; state violence follows against 'reactionary' peasantry.

Figure 3.2 Moore on violence and the origins of democracy, fascism, and communism

role of capitalist-democratic ideology, and his rather Whiggish treatment of English history, especially during the nineteenth century.[20] Moore stated, without apparent irony, that this was 'the age of peaceful transformation when parliamentary democracy established itself firmly and broadened down from precedent to precedent' (1969, p. 29). This highly debatable point provides a natural transition to Thompson's work on the making of the English working class. The strengths and weaknesses of the latter complemented Moore's own.

The making of the English working class

Thompson agreed with Moore that two master processes of modernization were the forceful intrusion of market forces into local communities, and the increase in local and central governmental powers. In fact, the 'truly catastrophic nature of the Industrial Revolution' for the English labouring population was due to their being 'subjected simultaneously to an intensification of two intolerable forms of relationship: those of economic exploitation and of political repression' (Thompson, 1968, p. 217). The beneficiaries were the industrialists and landed aristocracy, driven into alliance by fear of popular radicalism.

Moore acknowledged Thompson's 'excellent and detailed description of what life was like for the lower classes in England' between the 1790s and the early 1820s (Moore, 1969, p. 443). However, in Moore's view this 'reactionary upsurge was no more than a passing phase' (p. 444). The bourgeoisie was mainly interested in guaranteeing an untrammelled free market, not building up the state. From the 1820s onward, manufacturing and agrarian interests competed for popular support, each frustrating the more selfish measures of the other. Thompson did not agree with Moore's view that this repressive period was succeeded by an increasingly encompassing bourgeois democracy. On the contrary, in his view its major outcome was the making of a working class conscious of its collective interests, sharing a common culture and rigidly excluded from the political nation.

The Making of the English Working Class did not present a consecutive narrative; it was 'a group of studies, on related themes' (1968, p. 12). Each of its three parts emphasized one element of a historically specific sequence of class formation. This process operated according to an understandable situational 'logic', specific to particular groups and their experiences, but not in obedience to any universal 'law' (p. 10). This last point was made against two sets of rivals: on the one hand, Marxists who treated culture and experience as mere superstructure and, on the other, Parsonian historians (especially Smelser) who regarded consciousness as an element to be 'handled and channelled' in the interests of social harmony (p. 11).

The central message of 'The Liberty Tree', the first part of Thompson's book, was summed up in the observation that John Bunyan's *Pilgrim's Progress* and Tom Paine's *Rights of Man* were 'the two foundation texts of the English working-class movement' (p. 34). The tradition of Dissent was complex. On the one hand, it embodied a 'slumbering radicalism' (p. 33), reaching back to the Putney debates on property and liberty in Cromwell's army. On the other hand, under the rule of John Wesley and his immediate successors, Methodism, Dissent's great success story of the late eighteenth century, was centralized and authoritarian.

In a similar way, conservatism and insurrectionary potential were mixed in the secular tradition of the labouring population. The 'freeborn Englishman' and his neighbours were ready and able to act collectively – as participants in mobs, crowds, processions, shared rituals and so on – but mainly in defence of unwritten communal codes. Hostility was directed in particular against the corrupt political system and the corrosive free market.

Paine provided 'a new rhetoric of radical egalitarianism' (p. 103), focused on the demand for general citizenship rights. This dug deep into the popular consciousness during the early and mid-1790s. However, it also led to a quarter of a century of counter-revolutionary repression on behalf of aristocratic Old Corruption. The manufacturing class gave its support to this, in return for the repeal of paternalistic industrial legislation.

The rest of the book will be summarized more briefly. In the second part, 'The Curse of Adam', Thompson carried out two tasks. Firstly, he explored the objective and subjective character of exploitation as experienced by outworkers, artisans, weavers and related workers. Secondly, he argued that working-class consciousness was powerfully shaped by Methodism. It inculcated a discipline compatible with bourgeois utilitarianism. However, it also gave an outlet for the anguish and hysteria – the 'chiliasm of despair' (p. 411) – generated by political and economic oppression. The third part, 'The Working-Class Presence', traced the strands which made up the positive response of the working class to the counter-revolution. This response was most coherent and resistant to upper-class penetration when it remained highly localized.

Three distinctions ran through the analysis: between the open electoral politics of the Westminster constituency, and the provincial movement with its radical press, reading circles and Hampden clubs; between the constitutional thrust of public meetings and peaceful mass demonstrations, and the conspiratorial tradition of midnight drills and armed uprising; and between these political initiatives, and the campaigns for industrial justice, whether pursued through union activity or machine-breaking.

Two events were crucial. One was the Peterloo massacre in 1819, when the military attacked a peaceful crowd. The widespread horror this caused undermined the old regime. It also taught the middle class that it needed to restore its influence over the labouring population – especially since alternatives to industrial capitalism were being mooted widely. Ironically, when Old Corruption was undermined in 1832, it was through a parliamentary act with explicitly denied the propertyless the right to vote. This was the second important event. The 1832 Reform Act gave the working class – now imbued with a strong collective self-consciousness – a national definition: they were the *excluded* class.

The Making of the English Working Class remains central to a continuing debate, both within the circles of English Marxism and, equally important, beyond. It is impossible here to summarize this debate, which encompasses, for example, the part played by Methodism, the significance of time and work-discipline, the dynamics of class consciousness, and, more generally, the culture of capitalism.[21]

Moral codes and human choice

Thompson and Moore have both been centrally concerned with the impact on each other of two factors: first, conflicts and accommodations between the peasantry, working class, aristocracy and bourgeoisie; and, second, the organization and *modus operandi* of the state. In this context they have both drawn attention to the interplay between exploitation, violence and injustice. A major indication of injustice was the moral outrage of the victims. Thompson and Moore agreed that although exploitation took a variety of forms, it always entailed infringement of customary norms embodying popular rights. As such, it was objectively identifiable by victims and outside observers alike. Thompson insisted that:

> The exploitative relationship is more than the sum of grievances and mutual antagonisms. It is a relationship which can be seen to take different forms in different historical contexts, forms which are related to corresponding forms of ownership and State power. The classic exploitative relationship of the Industrial Revolution is depersonalized, in the sense that no lingering obligation of mutuality – of paternalism or deference, or of the interests of 'the Trade' – are admitted. There is no whisper of the 'just' price, or of a wage justified in relation to social or moral sanctions, as opposed to the operation of free market forces. (Thompson, 1968, p. 222)

Compare Moore's similar sentiments, applied to rural class relations:

> Within limits broad enough for society to work, the objective character of exploitation seems so dreadfully obvious as to lead to the suspicion that the denial of objectivity is what requires explanation. It is not hard to tell when a peasant community gets real protection from its overlord and when the overlord is either unable to keep enemies out or is in league with them . . . The thesis put forward here merely holds that the contributions of those who fight, rule, and pray must be obvious to the peasant, and the peasants' return payments must not be grossly out of proportion to the services rendered. Folk conceptions of justice, to put the argument in still

another way, do have a real and realistic basis; and arrangements that depart from this basis are likely to need deception and force the more they do depart. (Moore, 1969, p. 471)

Thompson was not prepared to go quite as far as Moore in arguing that folk conceptions of justice have a 'real' basis, i.e. are validated and discoverable by reason, as well as sanctioned by communal tradition. However, both men saw history as involving the imposition of the interests of powerful minorities upon (sometimes resisting) majorities – a process registered in the cultures and ways of life of both predators and victims.

What was the alternative? Both Moore and Thompson saw the basis for a fairer society in the norms of reciprocity and justice according to which participants evaluated the conduct of class relationships.[22] For example, at the end of his *Whigs and Hunters*, Thompson argued that the English legal system as shaped by the seventeenth-century struggle against royal absolutism was not simply 'a mystifying and pompous way in which class power is registered and executed' (1975, p. 267). In fact, it embodied 'a logic of equity (which) . . . must always seek to transcend the inequalities of class power' (p. 268). Obviously, this often conflicted with class interest, never more so than in the period between 1790 and 1832, when England's rulers found it increasingly difficult to maintain their hegemony under the existing constitution. They were faced with a choice: either dispense with the spirit and letter of the law and rule by force, or submit to their own rules and, as a consequence, 'surrender their hegemony' (p. 269). They chose the latter, a demonstration of the power wielded by the 'logic of equity', even against class interest.

However, the routine application of English law normally benefited large property owners and worked against the interests of the common people. These interests were expressed in an unwritten popular code with its own standards of right and wrong – and a capacity to change in response to traumatic learning experiences, as described in *The Making of the English Working Class*. Thompson left unsettled the question of how far the ideals (rather than the self-interested practices) of the ruling legal code and the informal moral economy of the crowd were compatible with each other.

In *Injustice*, Moore took up very similar themes, acknowledging the influence of Thompson (Moore, 1978, pp. 379, 474). In this book Moore had two main objectives. The first was to examine the structure and consciousness of the German working class between the early nineteenth and early twentieth centuries. He studied popular responses to a series of political crises from the 1848 Revolution to the Nazi takeover.

They have both been concerned with:

- the interplay between class structures and forms of state domination;
- the way exploitative relationships shape the cultures and ways of life of both predators and victims;
- the analysis of suppressed historical alternatives;
- identifying immanent norms of reciprocity and justice as potential bases for a fairer society; and
- the responsibility of the historian and sociologist to contribute reasoned moral evaluations of social structures and human choices made in the past.

Figure 3.3   Convergences between Thompson and Moore

The second objective was to demonstrate that in a wide range of human societies there was normative support for a social contract legitimating the exercise of rational political authority; in other words, government which used all available means to minimize human misery and make a decent life available to all (see figure 3.3).

The analysis complemented Thompson's in two ways. It paid more attention than did Thompson to what Perry Anderson called the 'objective coordinates' within which working-class consciousness was moulded (Anderson, 1980, p. 33). It also generalized two issues central to Thompson's work: the part played by moral codes in shaping action; and the existence of suppressed historical alternatives, as witnessed by the frustrated English revolution of 1792–6 and the failed German revolution of 1918–20.

This last point is worth expanding briefly. When analysing crucial historical turning points, Moore was as interested in the outcomes which did not occur, but which might have been feasible given the structural conditions, as those outcomes which did. He believes it is possible, by marshalling available data and imaginatively exploring the situational logic, to assess the practicability, chances of success, probable structural consequences, and likely costs and benefits of various potential human choices; e.g. between tradition, rationality and totalitarianism in a post-Stalinist Russia (Moore, 1954). Human choice is not only historically significant, but can also be morally evaluated; e.g. the strategy of the SPD leadership in the face of a revolutionary uprising in Germany after World War I (Moore, 1978).

There is also some basis for systematic consideration of political choices in the present, and their future implications – even though the possibility of choice may be generally unacknowledged by the human actors involved (Moore, 1972). Thompson's campaigning on behalf of civil liberties and nuclear disarmament stems from the same standpoint.[23] Moore shares Thompson's 'faith in the ultimate capacity of men to manifest themselves as rational and moral agents' by making choices (Thompson, 1978c, pp. 156, 171–2) – although these choices are constrained by 'historically emergent *potentia*' (p. 155) shaped by particular technological levels and social systems.

Moore and Thompson developed their distinctive approaches to historical sociology in response to different theoretical traditions. Thompson has been preoccupied with the Marxian distinction between 'the kingdom of necessity' and 'the kingdom of freedom' (Thompson, 1978c, p. 156). Moore developed his stance through a critical engagement with functionalism and evolutionary theory, and a long-running debate with his friend, Herbert Marcuse (Smith, 1983, p. 53).

While neither founded a school, both men influenced other work. There are, for example, convergences between *The Making of the English Working Class* and Eugene D. Genovese's *Roll, Jordan, Roll* (1974), a study of plantation life in the American South. Each book dealt with a labour force whose members were unwillingly torn away from an established way of life and forced to conform to a harsher mode of production. In both cases, a phase of resistance (the focus of Thompson's argument) was eventually succeeded by the installation of a paternalistic regime (the focus of Genovese's book). Both works began by exploring tensions between dominant and subordinate classes, went on to examine religion, work, domestic life and the community, and concluded by analysing how the victims expressed resistance to the established order. The climax of both accounts was an emancipation which failed to bring the promised rewards: in one case, the English parliamentary reform bill of 1832; in the other, the freeing of the slaves during the 1860s.

In Richard Johnson's view, Thompson and Genovese both produced 'socialist-humanist history' (Johnson, 1978). He believed they over-emphasized culture, at the expense of economic structures. Another critic, more sympathetic, was Ira Katznelson who argued that Thompson failed to distinguish clearly between the shaping of a class-in-itself by external conditions, and the making of a class-for-itself through heightened consciousness and increased organization. Katznelson proposed a distinction between four levels with respect to class: class as shaped by economic structure, class as patterns of life, class as dispositions and, finally, class as collective action.[24]

Reason and revolution: Skocpol and Tilly

The rest of this chapter is devoted to two scholars who came under the powerful influence of Barrington Moore. Charles Tilly carried out his doctoral research at Harvard in the 1950s. He recalled 'leaving graduate school with a fistful of draft chapters and thoughtfully commented bibliographies from Moore's monumental work in progress [*Social Origins*] and then returning years later to discover new versions of chapters and bibliographies in circulation, Moore still arguing with his students, colleagues and himself about the significance of his cases, and the book still in progress' (Tilly, 1984, p. 124). Along with George C. Homans, Moore directed Tilly's dissertation, later published as *The Vendée* (1964). Theda Skocpol's Harvard thesis, which eventually became *States and Social Revolutions* (1979), was completed in the 1970s. In the introduction, Skocpol noted: 'My most fundamental scholarly debt is to Barrington Moore, Jr.' Reading *Social Origins* while an undergraduate had taught her 'that agricultural structures and con-flicts offer important keys to the patterns of modern politics'. Moore's seminars were 'crucibles' for the development of skills in comparative analysis (1979, p. xv).[25]

Just as Marshall and Bendix helped ease the passage of historical sociology from the first phase to the second phase, so Skocpol and Tilly properly belong to both the second and third phases. On the one hand they maintained the emphasis placed by Moore and Thompson on domination and resistance within societies. On the other hand, they each developed a global perspective which gave due recognition to the importance of relations between – not just within – societies and states.

Unlike Genovese and Katznelson, both admirers of Gramsci, Tilly and Skocpol have not tried to anchor their approaches within an explicitly Marxian framework.[26] Actually, it is easier to locate the latter initially through their approaches to methodology. Tilly's contributions include his *As Sociology Meets History* (1981), and *Big Structures, Large Processes, Huge Comparisons* (1984), Skocpol was editor of, and a major contributor to, *Vision and Method in Historical Sociology* (1984).

The logic of comparative analysis has been one of Skocpol's main concerns (e.g. Skocpol and Somers, 1980). Tilly has not regarded this topic as his 'own turf' (Tilly, 1984, p. ix). By contrast, he has devoted considerable attention to the processual aspect of historical analysis; in other words, to the detailed examination of processes such as proletar-ianization, urbanization and state-making. The main works to be consi-dered here are *The Vendée* (1964), *The Rebellious Century 1830–1930*

(Tilly, Tilly and Tilly, 1975) and *Coercion, Capital and European States AD 900–1900* (1990).

Theda Skocpol's intellectual trajectory has been the reverse of Tilly's in one respect, at least. Tilly began with the detailed study of a single case (the counter-revolutionary movement in the Vendée), and gradually worked towards a comparative approach. By contrast, Skocpol's first book, *States and Social Revolutions* (1979), was a full-scale exercise in comparative macro-historical analysis. Since then she has been moving steadily towards an extended and detailed analysis of a single case. Her next major book is to be 'a macroscopic reflection on American history over the last one hundred years, tracing the development of US social policies from Civil War pensions, through the Progressive Era and the New Deal, down to the present-day debates over the future of social security and welfare'.[27]

States and social revolutions

Theda Skocpol has described herself as 'an upwardly-mobile midwesterner' (Skocpol, 1988, p. 633). In her view, the confidence and 'sense of being "special"' she imbibed at Michigan State University and Harvard gave her 'the chutzpah to undertake the virtually impossible'. Under this heading she included her long battle for tenure at Harvard and the composition of *States and Social Revolutions*. Here the focus will be on the latter.

The approach she developed in *States and Social Revolutions* (1979) had three characteristics. Firstly, she adopted a 'nonvoluntarist, structural perspective' (p. 14), discarding the 'purposive image of the process by which revolutions develop' (pp. 15–16). Paying too much attention to the wishes or intentions of revolutionary vanguards was misleading. Far better to examine relations between groups and societies. This showed that revolutionary situations were not 'made' – they emerged. Revolutionary outcomes were the unintended product of multiple conflicts, shaped not by any single presiding group, but by existing socio-economic and international conditions.

Secondly, the inter-societal and world-historical contexts in which social revolutions have occurred count for a great deal. Depending on the point in world-historical time, there may or may not be previous instances of social revolution to emulate. The same factor also determines which technological or organizational breakthroughs the revolutionary regime can benefit from. The international context has two aspects:

transnational economic relations, and the international system of competing states. Neither is reducible to the other.

Modern social revolutions had only occurred in countries located 'in disadvantaged positions within international arenas' (p. 23). International pressures were transmitted to national politics via the political regime, since the state apparatus had a major stake in both spheres. This leads directly to the third characteristic of Skocpol's approach.

Skocpol insisted on 'the potential autonomy of the state' (p. 24). The state was more than a mere arena in which other interests fought. Its forms and activities were not simply a reflection of prevailing modes of production. In fact, only if we were prepared to 'take the state seriously as a macro-structure' (p. 29) – in other words, as a set of organizations collecting taxes, using coercion and otherwise administrating the population – could we understand its central place in social revolutions. The state might, in certain circumstances, pursue its own interests in opposition to those of the dominant class. Its capacity to pursue these interests hinged not upon the extent of its popular legitimacy, but rather upon its capacity to organize coercion, and its relationship to other powerful interests within and beyond national borders.

These three core assumptions were applied to the analysis of 'social revolutions'. By this term Skocpol meant 'rapid, basic transformations of a society's state and class structures, accompanied and in part carried through by class-based revolts from below' (p. 33). Her basic argument was that the social revolutions in late eighteenth-century France, early twentieth-century Russia, and between 1911 and 1949 in China, had certain features in common.

In all three cases, the revolutions occurred in 'wealthy and politically ambitious agrarian states' which had avoided colonial domination. The 'old regimes' were 'proto-bureaucratic autocracies'. In other words, the state and the landed aristocracy shared (and squabbled over) the fruits obtained by exploiting the peasantry – who had to bear the dual burden of taxes and rents. In each case, the old regime suddenly faced a challenge from more developed foreign rivals with greater economic and military strength.

In these circumstances, the threatened old regime found its capacity to respond to the challenge was radically undermined by two factors. These were, first, the institutional relationship between the state bureaucracy and the landed aristocracy and, second, the way dominant establishments were related to the agrarian economy. This will be expanded shortly, but the immediate point is that, faced with the external threat, yet embedded in these contradictory relationships, a revolutionary conjuncture was produced which had three elements.

First, the central state apparatus of the old regime was largely incapacitated. Second, there were widespread lower-class rebellions, especially among the peasantry. Third, attempts were made by 'mass-mobilizing political leaderships to consolidate revolutionary state power' (p. 41). The processes just described were examined in the first part of the book, on 'causes of social revolutions in France, Russia and China' (p. 47). Its two chapters were devoted, respectively, to the contradictory relations focused upon old-regime states, and the interplay of state bureaucracy, landed aristocracy and peasantry within agrarian structures.

Skocpol showed, for example, that in both pre-revolutionary France and Imperial China, landed interests (in alliance with commercial groups) were able to entrench themselves within local assemblies. In this way they could resist the ambitions of the central administration. This was especially important when the state tried to introduce reforms following, respectively, the Seven Years' War between France and England and the Sino-Japanese War. The resulting disruption of the central state helped in each case to bring about the collapse of the old regime.

By contrast, in Tsarist Russia, where the central state was more dominant over the nobility, an extensive programme of reform had been carried out before the Revolution. The task of modernizing Russian agriculture was enormous, and progress very slow. Nevertheless, it took a far greater foreign threat than occurred in France or China – in fact, nothing less than 'massive defeat in total war' (p. 94) – to overturn the Russian old regime.

With respect to their agrarian structures, France and Russia were more similar to each other than to China. Both French and Russian peasant villages managed their own local affairs. They maintained considerable autonomy under the supervision of the imperial bureaucracy. When the central state bureaucracy broke down, aristocratic landowners were left almost completely defenceless against uprisings springing from peasant villages wiwth a high degree of social solidarity.

By contrast, in China local villages were to a much greater extent dominated by local landowners closely connected to the imperial bureacracy. They exercised great influence in the villages through clan networks. Although the breakdown of the central state administration resulted in widespread agrarian disorder in China, there was no spontaneous uprising by the peasantry. The Chinese peasant revolution came later. It is discussed by Skocpol in the second part of her book on the outcomes of the three revolutions.

In each case, the outcome was 'a centralized, bureaucratic, and mass-incorporating nation-state with enhanced great-power potential in the international arena' (p. 41). More specifically, agrarian class relations were transformed, and aristocratic influence was eradicated in central government and over the peasantry. As a result, bureacratic regulation from above and popular participation from below both increased. The new political leaderships faced major challenges from opponents at home and abroad. They were able to successfully consolidate the revolution by mobilizing subordinate groups which had previously been excluded from politics. The new regimes which resulted were more centralized and rationalized than their predecessors.

Very briefly, the French Revolution resulted in a symbiosis between a centralized, professional-bureaucratic state and a social order dominated by property-owners. The new regime did not pursue extensive social-structural change, but created conditions for industrial capitalism. As in France, the Russian new regime needed to build up the state's strength against its foes, including discontented peasants. The challenge of economic backwardness was greater in the Russian case. So was the technological and organizational capacity it could draw upon. The Chinese new regime, unlike the other two, established its base in the peasant villages rather than the cities, mobilizing the peasantry against its old masters. Under communist leadership the peasantry became a powerful instrument of state-building.

Comparing and explaining

There is an important difference between Skocpol and her mentor, Barrington Moore, in the way they applied comparisons between societies. Moore used comparison as a way of testing (and often rejecting) potential empirical generalizations which might explain specific cases. He tested them by confronting them with data that were difficult for them to handle. Two main tactics were adopted in *Social Origin*. First, he sometimes compared examples in which a hypothesized cause is present but which differ with regard to the outcome he wants to explain. For example, he compared relations between industrialists and large landowners in Germany and the United States during the early and mid-nineteenth century. Any explanation which argued that civil war was the 'inevitable' outcome in the latter case must also take account of the former, where it did not occur.

Second, Moore sometimes compared cases in which the relevant outcome was indeed shared, but various potential causal factors were found only in some cases and not in others. He applied this strategy in comparing France and England in the seventeenth century, asking the question: why is it that, despite very different antecedent conditions,

Both books:

- treat the state as having potential autonomy;
- trace ·the outcomes of structural tensions within agro-bureaucratic societies;
- pay attention to conflicts between the state and the great landowners as they compete to exploit the peasantry;
- look at tendencies towards solidarity and division within peasant communities as an indication of their propensity to take part in organized resistance to oppression.

Differences include the following:

- Moore focuses on the impact of commercialization and state bureaucratization on class solidarities and on alliances and conflicts between leading interests (including the state). By contrast, Skocpol focuses on the way structural contradictions are pushed to the point of crisis under the impact of foreign pressures.
- Moore argues that a wide variety of national trajectories led towards a more limited range of political outcomes. By contrast, Skocpol argues that a single form of socio-political transformation led towards more than one political outcome.
- Unlike Moore, Skocpol does not engage in moral evaluation.

Figure 3.4 Convergences and divergences between *Social Origins* and
States and Social Revolutions

democracy developed in both societies? (Smith, 1984c; for other divergences and convergences between Moore and Skocpol, see figure 3.4).

Skocpol did not test her cases in this way. Instead, she argued that they tended to support 'causal, explanatory hypotheses' about social revolutions through the application of the 'method of agreement' and the 'method of difference', terms borrowed from John Stuart Mill. First, despite many dissimilarities between her three cases – for example, in their levels of technological development – they had in common the phenomenon whose occurrence she was trying to explain and a set of causal factors she was able to identify. This was an illustration of the 'method of agreement'.

Second, she used the 'method of difference'. This consisted in identifying societies which did not experience social revolutions, but which were in almost all respects similar to those in which social revolutions did occur, and showing that the societies which failed to produce social revolutions also lacked a crucial causal factor. For example, there was no peasant uprising during the English Civil War, and no obstructive landed aristocracy in nineteenth-century Prussia or Japan. These last-named cases underwent either political revolutions, or abortive social revolutions which failed.

The 'method of difference' only brings into play cases where both social revolution and the hypothesized causes of social revolution are absent. In other words, unlike the procedures adopted by Moore, this particular comparative method allows no chance of encountering data which contradict the initial thesis. Turning to the 'method of agreement', the cases of France and Russia seem much more similar to each other than to China. In fact, this last case poses more general problems.

It is difficult to reconcile the gap of four decades between the collapse of Imperial China and the installation of the communist regime in Peking with the definition of a 'social revolution' as a 'rapid, basic transformation'. Furthermore, the intensive political work by party cadres to mobilize the Chinese peasantry suggests that, contrary to the claims made for the 'structuralist' approach, an important place does have to be given to the intentions of revolutionary elites and, more generally, human agency.[28] Skocpol presented the political campaigns among the peasantry as one of the outcomes of the Chinese social revolution, but perhaps they should have been treated as one of the causes.

A challenge with respect to the role of revolutionary elites was posed by the Iranian Revolution, which 'burst upon the world in 1979, just as my book was published, surprising all observers including myself' (Skocpol, 1989, p. 68). The Shah's regime became unstable as a result of intense, sustained and organized internal opposition. Here was a revolution which 'did not just happen; it was deliberately and coherently made' (Skocpol, 1982, p. 267). In her analysis of the Iranian Revolution, Skocpol presented a supplementary thesis: 'if a historical conjuncture arises in which a vulnerable state faces oppositionally inclined social groups possessing solidarity, autonomy, and independent economic resources, then the sorts of moral symbols and forms of social communication offered by Shi'a Islam in Iran can sustain the self-conscious making of a revolution' (1982, p. 275).[29] A similar proposition, suitably adapted, would also apply to Russia and France. Political weakness at the centre and effective revolutionary forces were co-present in both cases. This still leaves unresolved the question of what conditions produce the 'historical conjuncture' common to France, Russia and Iran: in other words, a vulnerable old regime *and* a revolutionary movement able to take over.

In *States and Social Revolutions*, Skocpol provided convincing answers to two questions: what caused the fall of agro-bureaucratic old regimes in France, Russia and China? (answer: overwhelming international pressures, plus effective peasant uprisings), and what were the institutional outcomes of the installation of new regimes? (answer: state-building processes by mass-mobilizing leaderships who developed and exploited increasingly powerful, centralized, bureaucratized and mass-incorporating nation-states). However, as has just been implied, Skocpol did not pay much attention to the equally vital question which links the two just posed: what are the causes of the successful installation of revolutionary new regimes? This question is relevant because, to take one example, following the breakdown of the Russian old regime, at least three alternative possibilities were on the cards: conquest by a foreign aggressor, colonial subordination, or a Russian Revolution. In practice, the third possibility was, at least in part, 'made' by Lenin and his colleagues.[30]

Skocpol, Trotsky and Eisenstadt

Michael Burawoy has recently argued that factors central to Skocpol's argument – especially, politico-military crises of domination, the emergence as opposed to the 'making' of revolutionary situations, the unevenness of capitalists development, the part played by international economic relations and state-systems, advances in organization and ideology over world historical time, and the potential autonomy of the state – are also to be found in work by Leon Trotsky (Burawoy, 1989).

An important difference between Trotsky and Skocpol, in Burawoy's view, is that the former was committed to a 'research program', drawing on tacit skills flowing from a strong research tradition, while the latter relied on a more rigidly defined strategy of induction through comparison. Burawoy prefers Trotsky's 'research program' to Skocpol's strategy of induction. However, in his view, Skocpol, *'rises above her method'* which is 'the scientific mode' and produces a 'simple, new and powerful unifying idea'. This idea, anticipated in part by Trotsky, is her 'insight into the structural determinants of revolution' (pp. 763, 768; emphasis in original).

Skocpol was obviously perfectly familiar with Trotsky's work at the time of writing *States and Social Revolutions* (e.g. Skocpol, 1979, pp. 94, 367). However, Burawoy's reference to 'the scientific mode' suggests yet another intellectual precursor, much closer at hand, whose approach anticipated her own. The reference is to S. N. Eisenstadt's analysis of historical bureaucratic empires (Eisenstadt, 1963). Both Eisenstadt and Skocpol locate their data in terms of an over-arching model which emphasizes endemic structural conflicts between the ruling power and 'traditional' interests. In both cases, control over 'free-floating resources' (especially cash rent and tax revenue) is at issue. In both cases, these conflicts are only alleviated following a 'total' change which produces a much more thorough interpenetration of state and society; for example, greater centralization and bureaucratization of the state, and more complete political incorporation of the lower orders. Skocpol and Eisenstadt both make a large point – the first by precept, the latter by example – of not devoting attention to the volitional or motivational aspects of social processes. Both present their findings within a quasi-experimental framework. In each case, the implication is that the logic of their method of empirical enquiry, rather than (more correctly) the elegance of their models of structural conflict, gives plausibility to their work.

The politics of social policy

Before turning to Charles Tilly, brief mention should be made of the leading role Theda Skocpol has played since the early 1980s in research into the development of social policy in the United States. Much of this work has been carried out under the aegis of the Project on the Federal Social Role, directed by Forrest Chisman and Alan Pifer. More specifically, it has focused on the network around the Center for the Study of Industrial Societies at the University of Chicago. Much of Skocpol's published work in this area has concentrated on the long-term impact of New Deal legislation upon the development of social provision in the United States.[31]

Although Skocpol's full-length study in this area has not yet been published, it is worth briefly outlining the general approach which informs the overall programme. The 'institutional-political process' perspective which she shares with others including Margaret Weir and Ann Shola Orloff, draws attention to three interconnected aspects of American social politics. These are: first, the peculiarities of American state formation; second, the ways classes as well as regional, ethnic, racial and other interests have intersected with the organization of political parties and the state; and third, the feedback of past policies on subsequent politics (see figure 3.5).

In the nineteenth century, American state formation processes produced a polity of 'courts and parties' (Weir, Orloff and Skocpol, 1988,

---

State formation

- Electoral democratization preceded state bureaucratization;
- bureaucratic–professional transformations greatest and earliest at local levels;
- regional bifurcation between two-part democracy and one-party racial oligarchy.

Institutional leverage

- Federal polity inhibits unified national action by labour or capital;
- social policy breakthroughs occurred in widely separated heterogeneous 'clusters';
- state/party system magnified capacities of southern agricultural elites and northern organized labour.

Policy feedbacks

- Growth of federal spending and employment after New Deal;
- post World War II policy innovations from 'within the state';
- incorporation of Blacks during 1960s occurred within system bifurcated between 'social security' and 'welfare'.

Figure 3.5 The institutional–political process perspective: the American case

p. 18). Private property rights were the disputed province of lawyers. Patronage-driven political parties struggled for the votes of white males. Early in the next century, sovereignty remained fragmented as bureaucratic and professionalized government made most headway at municipal and state levels. Decentralization and division were sustained by the strong local roots of elected representatives in Washington, and the split between the South, dominated by a single party wedded to segregation, and the rest of the country where two-party democracy prevailed.

These characteristics of state formation made a difference to social provision. For example, the close involvement of patronage politics in the distribution of benefits to veterans of the Civil War made respectable reformers reluctant to give the national state responsibility for pensions and social insurance. This allowed local and regional variations in benefit levels and entitlement to persist, with specially disadvantageous consequences for Southern Blacks. Mobilization for World War II expanded the fiscal powers of the federal state, but did not allow it to match the British governent's capacity for intervention in the national economy.

Three aspects of the historical development of institutional leverage stand out. First, regional and ethnic divisions were institutionalized in a manner that prevented either labour or capital from organizing on a class basis nationally, or even, in most cases, locally. Second, the virtual absence of 'unified, persistent class politics' (p. 22) meant that when a national crisis calling for positive action was acknowledged, as in the 1930s and 1960s, a cluster of disparate measures were passed at the behest of a temporary coalition of special interests. These measures were very vulnerable to subsequent conservative backlashes.

Third, the pattern of decentralized political parties, without integrated programmes, meant that well-organized local interests could federate and win great influence within the polity. Great leverage was achieved in this way by the South, especially its agricultural interests. The socially regressive attitudes of a sharecropper system dominated by landlords inhibited the development of national social policy. The legislative advances of the New Deal were aided by the rise of a more favourable ramp based on organized labour in the North.

Finally, policy feedbacks included innovations sponsored from within the growing federal state, such as the extension of contributory old-age insurance, and – more disastrously – the persistence of a clear division between 'social security' for the employed majority, and the far less respectable 'welfare' provided for the poor. As American Blacks became more fully incorporated into the polity during the 1960s, the new programmes from which they benefited were labelled as 'welfare', and were highly vulnerable to cutbacks in later years.

Counter-revolution

Charles Tilly's work is open-ended and open-minded. Like Barrington Moore, he treats historical sociology as a process of never-ending exploration. Like Moore, his texts are spattered with question marks. His conclusions are rarely dogmatic, usually provisional, and almost always point towards further enquiry. Tilly is interested in conflict and collective action, especially in relationship to 'two master processes'. These are 'the expansion of capitalism and the growth of national states and systems of states' (1981, p. 44). Tilly's contributions on state-building in *The Formation of National States in Western Europe* (1975) have now been overtaken by his more recent work, entitled *Coercion, Capital, and European States, AD 990–1900* (1990). This latter work will be discussed at the end of this chapter.

Tilly does not disguise his dislike of the misleading assumptions contained in the structural-functionalist approach to history, as exemplified by Neil Smelser and others. Tilly objects to three structural-functionalist propositions: first, that the breakdown of traditional social control in small-scale groups under the impact of increased differentiation necessarily leads to an increase in conflict; second, that the degree of social disorder is positively correlated with the rate of social change; and third, that all forms of disorder – e.g. crimes against property, strikes, suicide and violent conflicts – were closely associated, and fluctuated in the same way (Tilly, 1981, pp. 104–8).

Tilly's own distinctive approach was already taking shape in *The Vendée* (1964), his first major work.[32] This was a study of contrasting regions in Southern Anjou in Western France during the period immediately before the counter-revolutionary uprising of 1793. He compared Mauges, a district of subsistence agriculture and textiles, and Val-Saumurois, a more prosperous area including large-scale wheat farming and viniculture. Mauges, unlike Val-Saumurois, was deeply involved in the uprising. It was 'the chosen land of the counter-revolution' (p. 36).

One of Tilly's main findings was that in the century before the French Revolution, Mauges had been greatly disrupted by the impact of urbanization. In particular, as the local textile industry had expanded, it had had a large impact on the countryside. This led to great tension and rivalry between town and country, producing very sharp political divisions. Val-Saumurois – whose residents were less opposed to the Revolution – differed from Mauges in many ways. More of its people owned property. Settlements were less dispersed. It was involved in wider French society to a much greater extent than Mauges. Money and market position mattered more there in determining where you stood in the social order. Religious practice was less intense.

The Vendée was a specific case study focused on the background conditions of a dramatic instance of collective action in the aftermath of a revolution. In later work, Tilly has been concerned with the frequency and forms of many types of collective action, including violence.

Collective action

Tilly has distinguished between three forms of collective action. They are 'competitive', 'reactive' and 'proactive'. In the early stages of industrialization, urbanization, and state-formation, the most common form was 'competitive' collective action, directed against the lives, property or reputations of rivals or enemies. 'Reactive' collective action occurred when a threatened group resisted a claim made by another group (e.g. public officials) to its resources. The food riots described by E. P. Thompson come under this heading. Finally, 'proactive' collective action was the means by which a group laid claim to a resource it did not already control. Campaigns for the extension of citizenship rights (cf. Marshall, 1963d) were examples of this.

The long-run tendency of collective action was from competitive in pre-industrial Europe, via reactive in the nineteenth century, to proactive in the twentieth. A key process stimulating reactive collective action was state formation. State officials tried to enforce their assumed powers of taxation and conscription. They also organized national markets to keep the military and urban populations supplied with essentials such as food. In doing this they met organized resistance of a reactive kind from local communities and competing establishments, including large landowners.

Through proactive movements, people attempted to establish claims in the new state structures then coming into being. Such movements represented the interests of new solidarities and associations fostered by industrialization and urbanization, including class-based organizations.

Tilly allied himself with 'solidarity' theories of collective action, including Marxian approaches, and against 'breakdown' theories. His opponents included the structural-functionalists, as already seen. They also included Ted Gurr. In his *Whey Men Rebel* (1970), Gurr argued that rebellious collective action was liable to occur in a society undergoing rapid change if two conditions applied: if large numbers of people experienced intense relative deprivation, through comparison of their lot with a reference group consisting of the most rapidly gaining groups; and if the discontented population had their hopes of reducing this relative deprivation first raised, then disappointed.[33] In criticizing this analysis, Tilly argued that it laid too much stress on individual attitudes, and paid too little attention to changes in the structure and dynamics of political power, including such variables as the repressiveness of the regime and the organizational capacity of proactive groups. Tilly and his co-authors preferred the following formula:

> the relative effectiveness of collective action with a high risk of violence declines as the political system approaches a situation in which any segment of the population involved in that system which articulates a claim has a recognized right to a share of all resources in the system, a share proportionate to the group's size. (Tilly, Tilly and Tilly, 1975, p. 287)

The key phrase is 'recognized right'. Violent collective action is unlikely if rights are recognized. In a democracy, these rights depend upon a sub-population's size rather than its power. And all resources in the system are available for distribution. This formula has a family resemblance to W. G. Runciman's proposed strategy for alleviating social injustice as set out in his *Relative Deprivation and Social Justice* (1966). To para-phrase, Runciman proposed that the needy should be able to treat the whole of society as their reference group when making their claim for help; and the richest should not be excluded from contributing their share towards meeting this claim.

Runciman was concerned with the appropriate criteria for social justice, applicable even in cases where reference groups were narrow, relative deprivation relatively weak, and active protest well within manageable limits. Tilly, by contrast, was envisaging a situation in which reference groups were widening, relative deprivation increasing, and aggrieved interest groups organized to take collective action. Runci-man was concerned, morally, that justice should be done. Tilly descri-bed a situation in which, politically, justice had to be seen to be done. However, their formulae were similar. Incidentally, the passage in *The Rebellious Century* just discussed was followed by a section entitled 'Back to political theory' (p. 298). Like Moore, Tilly combines hard-headed realism with a concern for the moral, philosophical and evalua-tive dimensions of society.

Tilly's interpretation of long-term tendencies in collective action assimilates aspects of E. P. Thompson, Reinhard Bendix, T. H. Mar-shall and W. G. Runciman. It acknowledges (à la Thompson) that violent collective action in the early phases of industrialization embodies a protest against what the system is doing to the people (exploitation, repression), and not simply a complaint against exclusion from the system itself (as non-voters, non-property owners). But it also assumes that reactive collective action will tend to be succeeded by proactive collective action within the system, as protesting interests are gradually incorporated (à la Bendix) as citizens within the nation-state.

However, the stability and coherence of the system are at risk (à la Marshall) from collective bargaining and (going beyond Marshall) other forms of potentially violent collective action which challenge the sys-tem's operating principles. Such challenges are best met by the imple-mentation of distributive arrangements embodying social justice (à la Runciman).

Coercion, capital and European states

In *Coercion, Capital and European States AD 900–1990* (1990) Tilly entered into implicit debate with other researchers such as Perry Anderson, Immanuel Wallerstein, Fernand Braudel and Michael Mann, although he made few explicit references to them. Unlike Immanuel Wallerstein and Fernand Braudel who, as will be seen, placed capital – especially mercantile capital – at the centre of their arguments, Tilly focused upon the men who controlled concentrated means of coercion such as armies, navies and so forth. In Tilly's interpretation, powerful leaders used coercion to conquer populations and capture resources, fighting those who resisted. If successful, they became rulers with stable control over, and ready access to, their captured assets. However, rulers had to accept territorial limits to their power. Other rulers were rivals and, possibly, allies. The military capacity of warlike rulers forced neighbouring powers to be ready to either submit or defend themselves. The demands of war-making led rulers to extract resources from an unwilling population (see figure 3.6).

Struggle and bargaining over extraction shaped the central organizational structures of states. Tilly argued that 'The organization of major social classes within a state's territory, and their relations with the state, significantly affected the strategies rulers employed to extract resources, the resistance they met, the struggle that resulted, the sorts of durable organization that extraction and struggle laid down, and therefore the efficiency of resource extraction' (p. 15). Key variables were the extent to which capital and the means of coercion, respectively, were accumulated and concentrated in specific territories. The way the classes were organized and their relation to the state varied between coercion-intensive regions and capital-intensive regions. In the former, there were few cities and coercive forms of agricultural labour prevailed. In the latter, there were many cities, thriving commercial interests, lively trade, and an emphasis on production for the market. This obviously affected which of the major classes made the most pressing demands on the state. (The influence of Moore's contrast between areas of aristocratic and bourgeois predominance is evident here.)

The background conditions just sketched out conditioned which extractive strategies the rulers used and how successful the various alternative strategies were likely to be. These factors were reflected in the particular trajectories followed by the organizational development of specific states. For example, where accumulation and concentration of capital was high relative to coercive capacities, systems of fragmented sovereignty developed, often taking the form of city-states. Where the

Key variables are levels of
accumulation and concentration of:

Capital and **Coercion**

(= city-based exploitation) (= state-based domination)

Initial forms of indirect rule are:

Fragmented and **Tribute**
sovereignty **taking**

Movement towards direct rule:

shaped by exigencies of war,
interstate system and organization of classes.
Follows three main paths:

Capital-intensive **Capitalized** **Coercion-intensive**
coercion
e.g. Venice e.g. Britain e.g. Russia

Paths towards direct rule typically include the stages of:

Patrimonialism (up to *c*.1500); *Brokerage* (*c*.1400–*c*.1700);
Nationalization (*c*.1700–*c*.1850); *Specialization* (since *c*.1850)

The expanding activities of the state:

State-making, war-making and protection require *extraction* (= tribute,
rent, taxation of cash flows, stocks and income) leading to increased state
involvement in adjudication, distribution and production, and increases in
surveillance, homogenization and civilianization.

Figure 3.6 Tilly on capital, coercion and European states

balance of advantage lay with coercion as opposed to capital, extensive
tribute-taking empires often developed. Both were forms of indirect
rule, requiring the ruler to rely upon the cooperation of relatively
autonomous local powers.

The increasing scale of war and the increasing integration of the
European state system, especially after about 1500, meant that a military advantage was obtained by national states. These could support
large standing armies and combine the capacities of large agricultural

populations, capitalists and commercialized economies. Tilly prefered the term 'national state' to 'nation-state'; in his view, the latter term describes a legitimating ideal of cultural unity which few national states actually achieve. The competitive advantage of the national state led European states to converge upon this form. This meant a shift from indirect to direct rule, allowing the ruler more direct access to and command over the population and resources within the national territory.

In regions of fragmented sovereignty, a capital-intensive path towards greater direct rule was appropriate. By contrast, tribute-taking empires made the journey via a coercion-intensive route. A few societies such as Britain and France were able to combine advantages from both by adopting a path of capitalized coercion. In other words, they combined relatively strong state apparatuses, confident aristocracies, thriving market-orientated economies, and a vigorous commercial class. These societies made the transition to direct rule within a national state relatively early. Capital-intensive regions such as Italy and coercion-intensive regions such as Eastern Europe approached this point more slowly.

Tilly argued that a retrospective analysis explaining the origins of existing national states misses much of the story told by a prospective analysis beginning one thousand years ago. For example, a prospective analysis takes account of the fact that, as late as the mid-sixteenth century, empires (e.g. the Habsburg Empire) and federations of cities and adjacent territories (e.g. the Dutch Republic) were both holding their own. It was by no means clear at that stage that the national state would become the dominant form. However, pressure to shift towards direct rule and the national state gradually prevailed throughout Europe. This took polities through the successive stages of patrimonialism, brokerage, nationalization, and specialization.

Patrimonialism (mainly up to about 1500) combined the use of customary forces such as feudal levies and the extraction of rent and tribute from land and people under the ruler's immediate control. In the era of brokerage (*c.*1400–*c.*1700), rulers relied on mercenaries, tax-farmers, and independent bankers willing to make loans. During the phase of nationalization (*c.*1700–*c.*1850), rulers took direct control of the task of raising large military forces and tax revenues from the national population. The age of specialization (*c.*1850 onward) entailed the creation of distinct professionalized armies, navies, police forces and fiscal administration.

The resource-extracting ambitions of rulers grew under the intense pressures of foreign conflict. The collection of tribute and rent was increasingly accompanied or displaced by the taxation of cash transactions, stocks (e.g. land and property) and incomes. As this occurred, the state was drawn into bargaining with the unwilling and often powerful victims of these predations. Confronted with protests and collective action in various forms, rulers yielded a variety of rights to the population and accepted a widening range of tasks.

State officials became increasingly involved in adjudicating disputes over rights, and taking responsibility for economic distribution and even aspects of production. At the same time the apparatus of state surveillance grew in scope. As the population became increasingly subject to the unifying influence of the state and the national market, it became more homogeneous than before. Ironically, the increased efficiency and specialization of the military within the state meant there was a greater separation of armed forces from the mass of the population and, as a consequence, a civilianization of the latter.

Could Tilly's model, or an adapted version of it, cope with the example of the United States? Presumably this society would fall within the category defined by 'fragmented sovereignty' and a 'capital intensive' path – but the constant pressure imposed by warfare within the inter-state system in Europe since AD 900 had no equivalent in nineteenth-century America, unless you modify the approach to take account of the Civil War. Detailed consideration of the American case in the light of Tilly's model would produce insights with respect to both. How, for example, do we account for the particular pattern of federal involvement in adjudication, distribution and production in American society? or the tensions surrounding surveillance, homogenization and civilianization? In exploring these issues, the contributions of Skocpol and her colleagues would obviously be highly relevant.

4 Soaring High

History from above

The breakdown of the cold-war global order has liberated historical sociology in an extraordinary way. A remarkable surge in collective self-confidence occurred in the mid-1970s. The almost simultaneous publication in 1974 of large works by Perry Anderson and Immanuel Wallerstein – one analysis pan-European, the other global – is a convenient point from which to date the third phase of post-war historical sociology. Both works mobilized an enormous amount of empirical material to support their wide-ranging arguments. Within two years the gauntlet had also been thrown down in the arena of theory, by Randall Collins and Anthony Giddens (Collins 1975; Giddens 1976).

By the mid-1980s major contributions had also been made by Fernand Braudel, Michael Mann and W. G. Runciman. Along with Giddens's recent books, this work marks a movement away from the Marxian emphases of Anderson and Wallerstein.

This chapter focuses on all six writers just mentioned. Taken together, they have been remarkably ambitious in the wide range of societies covered, the long periods of historical time encompassed, and the detailed attention given to the empirical complexities of specific cases.[1] These are examples of global historical sociology written from a towering height, scanning centuries and continents.

Two Marxian perspectives: Anderson and Wallerstein

Perry Anderson and Immanuel Wallerstein both work within the tradition of Marxism. Their empirical concerns overlap to a great extent, but they disagree on at least four fundamental and closely-related issues: the way modes of production and social formations shape each other; the relative significance of economic and non-economic forms of coercion within and between societies; the interpretation of variations in the strength and functions of state apparatuses; and the way feudalism and capitalism are related to each other. Let us turn to Anderson first.

Passages From Antiquity to Feudalism (*Passages*) and *Lineages of the Absolutist State* (*Lineages*) both appeared in 1974.[2] The same year, Perry Anderson was writing the extended essay he later published as *Considerations on Western Marxism* (1976). This coincidence is relevant, because Anderson believed the practice of historical sociology had major implications for the development of Marxist theory (and vice versa).

In his view, the dominant tendency within Marxist theory has to be reversed. After the failures of proletarian revolutions in capitalist Europe following World War I, western Marxism – from Gramsci to Althusser – became increasingly pessimistic. It cut itself off from the real world and retreated into aesthetics, hermeneutics, and abstract metaphysics. Anderson thought pessimism was not justified in 1974. He looked back to 1968 as 'a profound historical turning point' when 'For the first time in nearly 50 years, a massive revolutionary upsurge occurred within advanced capitalism' (p. 95).

Anderson disliked the 'contraction of [Marxist] theory from economics and politics into philosophy' (1976, p. 93). He wanted to turn back to the tradition of classical Marxism – Marx, Lenin, Trotsky – and take up issues they had failed to answer or even formulate, such as:

> What is the constitutive nature of bourgeois democracy? What is the function and future of the nation-state? What is the real character of imperialism as a system? What is the historical meaning of a workers' state without workers' democracy? How can a socialist revolution be made in the advanced capitalist countries? How can internationalism be made a genuine practice, not merely a pious ideal? How can the fate of previous revolutions in comparable conditions be avoided in the ex-colonial countries? How can established systems of bureaucratic privilege and oppression be attacked and abolished? What would be the structure of an authentic socialist democracy? (1976, p. 121)

Passages and *Lineages*, which are concerned with human history from classical antiquity to European absolutism, prepared the ground for answers to these questions. A more direct consideration of them may be expected in two further works, not yet published. These 'will deal specifically, in turn, with the chain of great bourgeois revolutions, from the Revolt of the Netherlands to the Unification of Germany; and with the structure of the contemporary capitalist states that eventually, after a long period of ulterior evolution, emerged from them' (1974b, p. 11).

In these studies Anderson has been putting into practice his belief that the balance between 'history' and 'theory', currently favouring the latter, should be 'redressed in any Marxist culture of the future' (1976, p. 112). Historical investigations and theoretical generalizations should be closely related in terms of methodology. After all, the 'mechanisms of single events' and the 'laws of motion of whole structures' are 'equally amenable to adequate knowledge of their causality'. Both should help to increase Marxism's 'capacity for rational and controllable theory in the domain of history' (1974b, p. 8).

Anderson wants 'totalizing' history, capable of understanding 'dialectical movements' and 'contradictory possibilities' (1964, p. 27). One attempt at this is his essay, 'Origins of the present crisis', dealing with English society between the seventeenth and twentieth centuries (1964). Two of his conclusions were, first, that the seventeenth-century revolution was 'the least pure bourgeois revolution of any major European country' (p. 28) and, second, that the English proletariat came into being in highly unfavourable circumstances.

The English Revolution helped create a dynamic capitalist agriculture and a vigorous mercantile imperialism. However, unlike the French Revolution, it left no distinctive ideological legacy. English capitalism accepted the old aristocracy alongside the new bourgeoisie: there was 'no fundamental, antagonistic contradiction' between them. Also, the earliest proletariat came into being 'when socialist theory was least formed and available' (p. 31).

E. P. Thompson parodied this position. He thought it came from the belief that '*other* countries . . . do – we are sorry to be obliged to say it – in Every Respect Better. Their Bourgeois Revolutions have been Mature. Their Class Struggles have been Sanguinary and Unequivocal. Their Intelligentsia have been Autonomous and Integrated Vertically. Their Morphology has been Typologically Concrete. Their Proletariat has been Hegemonic' (1978b, p. 37; emphasis in original).[3]

Anderson's response to Thompson can be found in *Arguments Within English Marxism* (Anderson, 1980). He praised Thompson as 'our finest socialist writer today' (1980, p. 1) but questioned his treatment, as a historian, of human agency and human experience. Thompson's definition of class was 'far too voluntarist and subjectivist' (p. 40). Compared to Barrington Moore in his discussion of the German working class in *Injustice*, Thompson paid too little attention to the 'objective coordinates' of class formation and failed to treat 'the whole historical process' (p. 33). Perry Anderson has recently returned to questions of class formation and state formation in Britain (Anderson, 1987). This contribution is best considered as part of the global vision developed in *Passages* and *Lineages*.

From ancient Greece to absolutist monarchy

In these two volumes Anderson aimed to identify the distinctive characteristics of historical development in Western Europe, explaining why the capitalist mode of production originated there. Elsewhere, capitalism was imposed or introduced from outside. In carrying out his analysis, Anderson paid particular attention to contacts *between* social formations, including states, and the co-existence of multiple modes of production *within* specific social formations.

In *Passages*, four modes of production were relevant to the argument. First, the slave mode of production, in which individuals captured on military campaigns were made to work on large rural estates. In social formations dominated by this mode of production, slavery, material production, and physical labour became practically synonymous. They all shared low status in the eyes of the free urban citizenry supported by the surplus generated by slave labour.

Second, the primitive communal mode of production in which peasant farmers worked their own household plots but cooperated with fellow villagers to provide communal defence and justice. Military organization was based upon extended kinship ties – although there was a tendency for powerful chiefs to emerge, rewarding their warrior retinues with tribute extracted from the peasantry.

Third, the nomadic mode of production in which geographically mobile pastoralists exploited arid steppeland. Although herds were owned by individuals, nomadic peoples, organized in hierarchical clans, collectively appropriated pasture. Their discipline and riding skills were intermittently used to dominate farming societies based upon the primitive communal mode of production. This enabled the pastoralists to acquire artisans, military conscripts and tribute. However, these empires of conquest were short-lived. Pastoral nomadism operated within strict demographic limits and had no potential for settled urban development.

The fourth variant, the feudal mode of production, was characterized by vassalage and the manorial economic regime. Vassals were granted control over territories (fiefs) by their lord (for example, the king) to enable them to bear the expense of military service. The relationship between the vassal and his superior had a contractual element: in theory at least, protection and privilege were granted in return for loyal service (and vice versa). Vassals were lords of the manor within their fiefs. As such, they extracted labour from their serfs by extra-economic means, including the threat of physical coercion. Anderson's discussion of these modes of production in *Passages* will be discussed shortly.

In *Lineages*, Anderson turned to the absolutist state. In his view, this came about when market relationships and notions of absolute property rights took the place of feudal obligations at the level of the fief. As this happened, the power of the feudal nobility was reduced. Its conditions of existence were transformed. In spite of this, Anderson still regarded the absolutist state as 'feudal'. The point is that the absolutist ruler protected the class interest of the feudal nobility by making sure it continued to benefit from the surplus produced by the peasantry. The task of imposing extra-economic coercion on the labour force moved upward from the local feudal lord with his manorial court to the central state apparatus of the absolutist ruler. Sovereignty became more centralized.

In these two books, Anderson had two consecutive objects of explanation. In *Passages*, his object was a mode of production; specifically, the feudal mode of production as it developed within social formations which also included non-feudal elements such as the towns and the Church. In *Lineages*, his object was a form of the state; specifically, the absolutist state as it developed within social formations dominated, in his view, by the feudal mode of production. In each case Anderson was concerned with three aspects: the historical origins of his *explicandum*, its structural logic, and its implications for the development of the capitalist mode of production. As will be seen, in each case, his empirical analysis located specific societies or regions within a typology distinguishing, implicitly at least, between 'archetypal' cases and a range of other instances.

In *Passages*, Anderson first considered the slavery-based polities of classical antiquity (see figure 4.1). Athenian participatory citizenship was, in the end, incompatible with imperial expansion, although the latter was necessary for maintaining the supply of slaves. By contrast, Roman imperialism prospered under oligarchic rule by landowners, both Roman and non-Roman. Greek-style participatory citizenship was a casualty of this arrangement. However, the Roman polity was undermined by several factors. These included conflict between landowners and military commanders, the burden of supporting the expanding bureaucracy of the Christian Church, and the increasing difficulty of obtaining captives for enslavement.

The eastern part of the Roman Empire finally broke away. Byzantium was not based upon the slave mode of production, so it was not subject to the contradictions of the Western empire. The latter, however, became increasingly rural and decentralized. Law and order deteriorated. Border raids by neighbouring Germanic tribes became commonplace. In the face of these onslaughts, the weak sought protection on the estates of local large landowners. The strong built up armed gangs of sworn followers.

In Anderson's view, the feudal mode of production in Western Europe was the product of a Roman-Germanic synthesis. This brought together a collapsing slave mode of production and the primitive communal mode of production of the empire's adversaries – the Germanic barbarians. A 'balanced' synthesis (1974a, p. 155) was achieved in France and, following the Norman invasion, in England. By contrast, Italy and Spain were more heavily influenced by the Roman inheritance of urban commerce and canon law. Germany leaned in the other direction. It retained strong vestiges of the old retinue nobility and a peasantry wedded to communal traditions.

Elsewhere in Europe, the pattern varied widely but systematically. In the north west, beyond the reach of Rome, slave-based Viking society belatedly adopted feudalism. This followed military failures against neighbouring German rivals with a primitive communal inheritance. By contrast, in the south east, interaction between a native primitive communal peasant tradition and Byzantium, the Roman Empire of the East, completely failed to generate the feudal mode. The missing ingredient was agricultural slavery. In Eastern Europe, there were repeated encounters between the primitive communal and the nomadic modes of production. This did not lead to feudalism, but a series of temporary empires run by mounted warriors.

The East/West contrast is central to the arguments of both *Passages* and *Lineages*. It provides a link between them. In the West, dynamic class conflict between peasants and feudal landlords for control of the agricultural surplus had reached a critical stage by the late fourteenth century. Then, a combined economic and demographic crisis permitted the peasantry, aided by strong towns, to throw off their serfdom. Things happened very differently in the East. There, a similar crisis, arriving later, both encouraged and allowed the state and larger landowners to impose serfdom on the peasantry for the first time. In the East, unlike the West, the towns were weak and could not provide support for the peasantry. These structural changes laid the foundation for the emergence of the absolutist state.

The absolutist state developed between the Renaissance and the eighteenth century. The warrior nobility resisted at first, but eventually

---

North-western Europe (Scandinavia)	*Eastern Europe* (east of Elbe)
FMP partially developed, though beyond influence of Roman Empire (displaced PCMP plus slave labour).	FMP failed to develop because of the predominance of a fragile symbiosis between NMP and PCMP.

Western Europe		*South-eastern Europe* (south of Danube)
SMP (Roman)	Italy Spain	FMP failed to develop, in spite of interaction between PCMP and the Eastern Roman Empire (without SMP).
SMP/PCMP (balanced synthesis)	England France	
PCMP (German)	Germany	

FMP   – feudal mode of production
SMP   – slave mode of production
PCMP – primitive communal mode of production
NMP   – nomadic mode of production

Figure 4.1   Anderson on modes of production in Europe

accepted it, to become a class of courtiers with great influence in the state bureaucracy. The feudal mode of production remained dominant in the absolutist state. However, bourgeois interests were helped by a legal-political superstructure which guaranteed absolute property rights and a uniform body of law.

As has been seen, absolutism had a complex classical-feudal inheritance. This helped to prepare the ground for the capitalist mode of production. The development of rival absolutist states out of the earlier decentralized feudal forms also helped bring into being the structural counterpart of capitalism: the multi-nation state system in Europe. Absolutism strengthened ideas of absolute private property and sovereignty which had been preserved from classical times, mainly by townspeople and clerics. In time, bourgeois revolutions within absolutist states would eliminate their feudal characteristics, especially the use of political coercion in the economic sphere.

These remarks apply to absolutism in Western Europe. In the East the story was different. Here the state was strengthened, where possible. But this was not a means of protecting an aristocracy undermined by the end of serfdom. Instead, as already seen, it was a way of imposing serfdom upon the peasantry. The aristocracy resisted at first, then acquiesced as the state imposed its control from above – over nobles as well as peasants.

In fact, increases in solidarity and central coordination benefited not just the ruler, but also the newly-compliant 'service nobility' (1974b, p. 218). After all, the imposition of serfdom meant it was easier to extract the material surplus. Also, a strong state apparatus closely linked to a disciplined upper class was essential in view of the increased military threat from absolutist states in the West.

Anderson's discussion of absolutism in the West and the East contains an implicit typology of societies (see figure 4.2). Firstly, the transformations undergone in Eastern and Western Europe were distinguished from those in India, China, Japan and the Ottoman Empire. The latter cases did not experience the feudalism-absolutism-capitalism sequence. Nor could they 'be reduced to a uniform residual category, left over after the canons of European evolution have been established' (1974b, pp. 548–9).

Secondly, within both Eastern and Western Europe the societies studied by Anderson fell into three groups: examples of archetypal absolutism, examples of incomplete or defective absolutism, and cases where attempts to install absolutism failed. The archetypal case in the west was France; here the contradictions of absolutism eventually brought revolution. Its counterpart in the east was Prussia, with its well-organized state, strong nobility, weak towns and servile peasantry; eventually, Prussia transformed itself into a western capitalist state.

Incomplete or defective cases in the west included Spain, which failed to exploit its American treasure, and Sweden with its weak towns but

	Archetypes	*Defective*	*Failed*
W. Europe	France	Spain Sweden	England
E. Europe	Prussia	Russia Austria	Poland

Figure 4.2   Anderson's implicit typology of European absolutism

far-from-servile peasantry. Eastern examples were Austria, with its independent and divided nobility, and Russia which was unable to follow the modernizing road taken by Prussia.

Turning to the third group, absolutism failed in the urban enclaves in Italy and Germany. Other examples of failure included Poland in the east and England in the west. Poland established itself as an aristocratic commonwealth but in the process weakened the state's defences against foreign aggressors. Attempts to impose absolutism in England were inhibited by the lack of a standing army and the control exercised by the commercialized aristocracy and gentry over local administration.

The figures of descent

Anderson took his analysis of the British case further in 'The figures of descent' (1987). This paper also makes reference to the development of the capitalist mode of production in other societies. For example, he argues that the dominant position of the landed aristocracy in England as late as the twentieth century was mirrored in other industrializing societies. However, the English aristocracy outstripped their foreign competitors and, even more so, the English bourgeoisie, in terms of wealth, experience and self-confidence. Under aristocratic influence the English state remained small and wedded to minimalism. Following Geoffrey Ingham and W. D. Rubinstein, Anderson stressed the division of capital between a financial sector oriented to empire and international trade, and a weaker domestic manufacturing sector (Ingham, 1984; Rubenstein, 1981).

England's 1689 revolution was incomplete; it left the job unfinished. Unlike the other major capitalist powers, Britain has not experienced 'a modern "second revolution", abruptly or radically remoulding the state inherited from the first' (Anderson, 1987, p. 47). Modernization was incomplete. No 'independent bourgeois representation' flourished (p. 39). The dominant ruling bloc which had crystallized by World War I trained its offspring to exercise gentlemanly rule, not engage in trade. After this war, the Labour movement stepped into the breach vacated by the Liberal party, and took over policies advocated by the liberal intellectuals, Keynes and Beveridge. Labour politicians were unable to bring about fundamental change. The defensive capacity of organized labour was a powerful obstacle to large-scale reconstruction of industrial capital by Labour politicians in government. So was the power of the international market.

Other capitalist societies had successfully taken corrective measures to make themselves more efficient. The French used a highly trained technocracy. German reform was coordinated by the banking system. Japan had an effective interventionist state. In Sweden and Austria, mass trade-union and party organization provided a strong base allowing Labour to take the leading role. The British government in the 1980s chose to rely upon the logic of the market. Unfortunately, this could not provide a solution. On the contrary, the market-led behaviour of particular capitals was, in Anderson's view, responsible for the structural problems confronting Britain.

The levers for change used by France, Germany, Japan, Sweden and Austria were not available in Britain. Nor, indeed, in the United States. This was relevant because, despite the much greater influence of industrial capital in the United States, it was beginning to encounter similar difficulties to Britain. This was not the end of it. The 'radical internationalization' of the forces of production and circulation occurring in the late twentieth century meant, perhaps, that the structural problems of uneven development encountered in Britain would be generalized 'throughout the advanced capitalist world' (p. 77).[4] This is a good place to turn to the second writer discussed in this chapter, since the globalization of uneven development has been one of his major preoccupations.

The capitalist world-economy

Immanuel Wallerstein, like Anderson, has tried to produce work which combines scholarly objectivity and political relevance. Wallerstein argues that in making this attempt he stands in the tradition of the Enlightenment: 'I myself feel that I am being thoroughly consistent and that my concern with history, with social science, and with politics is not a matter of engaging in three separate, even if related activities, but is a *single* concern, informed by the belief that the strands cannot be separated, nor should they if they could' (Wallerstein, 1979, p. vii; emphasis in original). Like Anderson, Wallerstein responded enthusiastically to the events of 1968. He gave active support to student radicals at Columbia University, where he belonged to the sociology faculty. At the time he published a book showing the links between turmoil on the campus, broader changes in the United States, and shifts at the global level.[5] Two decades later, he returned to the theme in a book, written with two colleagues, entitled *Antisystemic Movements* (Arrighi, Hopkins and Wallerstein, 1989) and a paper '1968, Revolution in the world-system' (Wallerstein, 1989b).

In the intervening period Wallerstein developed in great detail his interpretation of the rise and 'future demise' of the world capitalist system (Wallerstein, 1979, p. 1). Three volumes on the capitalist world-economy have appeared so far, covering its development from the 1450s to the 1840s (Wallerstein, 1974; Wallerstein, 1980; Wallerstein, 1989a). Wallerstein's views on antisystemic movements and the 'Revolution of 1968' (Wallerstein, 1989b, p. 431) are best considered in the context of this major enterprise, still incomplete.

Wallerstein has rejected the Western theory of development, which assumes that each society passes through the same series of determinate stages, moving from tradition to modernity. He also dismisses the 'Marxist embrace of an evolutionary model of progress' (Wallerstein, 1983, p. 98). In fact, historical capitalism has brought 'in both material and psychic terms . . . absolute immiseration' (p. 104) within its sphere. This sphere is the capitalist world-economy. Some definitions are required. A world-economy and a world-empire are types of world-system. The other kind of system is a minisystem. World-systems and minisystems both incorporate a division of labour amongst specialized parts which depend upon economic exchange with each other. Minisystems – such as a hunting and gathering band – are small and have a single culture. Few, if any, have survived. By contrast, world systems are much larger and include several cultures. Within a world-empire – such as the Roman Empire – economic exchange is to a considerable extent guided by a central political bureaucracy. As late as the early sixteenth century, attempts were still being made, unsuccessfully, to recreate this form in Europe. By the 1560s, however, world-empires had given place to world-economics.

Exchange within world-economies is not contained within a single empire, but traverses several polities. The modern world-system is a capitalist world-economy. Its 'essential feature . . . is production for sale in a market in which the object is to realize the maximum profit' (1979, p. 15). Such a world-economy can incorporate production systems based upon 'feudal' forms of extra-economic coercion, and also 'socialist' national economies which do not recognize private ownership: in both cases, the goods and services produced become commodities within an international market driven by profit-seeking. The rules and constraints operating in this market result from:

> . . . the complex interplay of four major sets of institutions: the multiple states linked in an interstate system; the multiple 'nations', whether fully recognized or struggling for such public definition (and including those sub-nations, the 'ethnic groups'), in uneasy and uncertain relation to the

states; the classes, in evolving occupational contour and in oscillating degrees of consciousness; and the income-pooling units engaged in common householding, combining multiple persons engaged in multiple forms of labour and obtaining income from multiple sources, in uneasy relationship to the classes. (Wallerstein, 1983, p. 64)

Despite all this unease and uncertainty, the capitalist world-economy maintains its stability as a social system due to three mechanisms: the concentration of military strength in the hands of dominant forces within 'core' societies; the ideological commitment of the cadres who run the system; and the division of the exploited majority into two tiers of subordinate societies – a larger lower tier (or 'periphery') and a smaller middle tier (or 'semiperiphery'). The bourgeoisie within core societies exploit members of societies in the periphery. The economic role of the semiperiphery varies at different stages of the capitalist world-economy. Its chief function is political, its presence weakening potential opposition to the core.

The main actors within the system are classes and 'ethno-nations' (1979, p. 24), two overlapping or alternative identities adopted by social groups. The bourgeoisie – including entrepreneurs, 'nouveaux riches' and 'coasters' (p. 287) – pursues capital accumulation. Its ruling ideology is universalism, the regime of scientific rationality. By contrast, the proletariat have been shaped by 'the ethnicization of the world workforce' (1983, p. 77). Strong ethnic identities contribute to the effective reproduction, socialization and hierarchical ranking of the proletariat.

Historically, the market has been modified in two ways within the commodity chains and production activities binding bourgeois exploiters to the labouring population. First, the commodification of labour has been limited by the persistence of non-waged work within households. Proletarianization is a continuing but incomplete process. Second, this largely *semi*-proletarian workforce has been managed within global structures with a high degree of vertical integration, such as chartered companies, merchant houses and transnational corporations. Bureaucracy, politics, and various forms of bullying have modified the free play of supply and demand within the open market place. Furthermore, unequal exchange – between bourgeoisie and workforce, between core and periphery – has been enforced through the hidden or overt exercise of state power; in particular, the power of strong state apparatuses in core societies.

In the course of competition between state apparatuses and bourgeoisies located in different polities, the capitalist world-economy undergoes repeated geographical restructuring and continual expansion. In fact, it was originally born from processes of restructuring and expansion within medieval Europe. In the wake of the economic, ecological and demographic crisis of feudalism, a search for exploitable land and labour was under way by the fifteenth century. This search was untrammelled by the restrictions of centralized bureaucracy which so inhibited contemporary Chinese explorers. It eventually brought into being a new transatlantic and pan-European market.

Differentiation within the capitalist world-economy was aided by territorial extension. Also by inflation, which distributed profits unevenly between participants. The structural logic of this modern world-system was expressed in the forms taken by the division of labour and modes of domination within the rural and urban sectors of core, peripheral and semi-peripheral societies. During the sixteenth century the core of the modern world-system was located in England, the Netherlands and Northern France. The semiperiphery centred on the Mediterranean, including Italy, Southern France and Spain. America and Eastern Europe belonged to the periphery. Figure 4.3 summarizes some aspects of the capitalist world-economy with particular reference to this first phase.

1   *Struggle in the core*   For over three centuries, leadership within the core of the modern world-system was disputed between the French and the English. During the sixteenth century the French were hampered by internal conflicts. Their society was tugged in several directions at once: was it a Mediterranean or an Atlantic power? Maritime or land-based? Under the dominant influence of Paris or Lyons? Capitalist development was more favoured in England, with its uniform and centralized legal system, larger estates and weaker feudal residues. The English benefited from competition between France and Spain, the long-term increase in Atlantic trade, and the existence of the Tudor state – strong enough to resist foreign invasion, but too weak to rake off commercial profits made by its own subjects.

In the early seventeenth century the French state overrode centrifugal tendencies with the help of a prestigious royal court. The French bourgeoisie was feudalized. By contrast, the English aristocracy had long been bourgeois. Centralized but not absolutist, the English state served the interests of the powerful London-based mercantile establishment. Unfortunately, political centralization in France was to the disadvantage of native commercial enterprise since the latter was most vigorous in the provinces.

Economic contraction and political restructuring during the period of the Thirty Years' War (1618–48) led to consolidation and, subse-

	State	Rural	Urban
C o r e	Strong state (compared to periphery).	Free waged labour. Tenant farmers. Early shift to pastoral agriculture on large estates.	Free waged labour. Strong urban bourgeoisie.
S e m i – p e r i p h e r y	Strength of state varies. Stronger if seeking promotion to core status.	Share-cropping. Specialized agriculture (e.g. viticulture) on smallholdings. Moderate levels of skill and supervision.	Strong urban occupational associations (e.g. guilds) inhibit innovation.
P e r i p h e r y	Weak state (compared to core).	Slavery and serfdom. Monoculture. Low levels of skill and supervision. Low productivity.	Weak native urban bourgeoisie dominated by powerful foreign bourgeoisie.

Figure 4.3 Wallerstein's capitalist world-economy

quently, further expansion of the capitalist world-economy. Although the Dutch gained a medium-term advantage, they were elbowed out by the French and English in the new phase of mercantilist inter-state struggle during the late seventeenth and eighteenth centuries. By this time, the conflict extended throughout the colonial periphery.

The Treaty of Paris in 1763 sealed British victory in that conflict. A new phase began during which specialization increased throughout the system, while mechanization advanced in the core. Industrialization in Britain and revolution in France contributed to the final victory of the former over the latter. By the early nineteenth century 'Britain was finally truly hegemonic in the world-system' (Wallerstein, 1989a, p. 122). This position however, was soon challenged by other societies struggling to rise from the periphery and semiperiphery.

2   *Periphery and semiperiphery*   The economic recession of the early seventeenth-century led to an intensification of labour repression in the serf-based regimes of Eastern Europe. Where, as in Poland, the state remained weak, this resulted in serious internal conflict and social disruption. Elsewhere in the periphery, in the Americas, a reduction in the volume of trade with core societies allowed local manufacturing interests to become more powerful.

From the mid-eighteenth century Russia, the Ottoman Empire, India and West Africa were incorporated in the periphery as the system expanded. Ironically, one effect of including African mini-systems was that the social disruption imposed by the slave trade could no longer be externalized. In due course this trade ceased. By that time the American colonies were becoming independent states and were competing to enter the semiperiphery. When the modern world-system came into existence the semiperiphery included the commercial heartland of medieval Europe – North Italy, Southern Germany and Flanders – and the two Iberian societies. Spain and Portugal had failed to establish themselves as core societies. Instead, during the seventeenth-century Spain came to be 'at best a rather passive conveyor belt between the core countries and Spain's colonies' (Wallerstein, 1980, p. 185).

A typical approach of would-be entrants to the semiperiphery was to strengthen the state apparatus, protect home industry and exploit local monopolies to the full. Sweden, in alliance with the Dutch, effectively adopted this strategy during the late seventeenth and early eighteenth centuries. Even more successful was Prussia, with its strong alliance between the *junkers* and the state bureaucracy. By the late nineteenth century the German Empire and the United States were both mounting a strong challenge to British hegemony from within the semiperiphery. In both cases, manufacturing interests had established dominance over 'peripheral' agricultural sectors. Russia and Japan had also entered the semiperiphery by this time.

3   *Consolidation and challenge*   Since World War II, following a period of American hegemony, the principal members of the core have become the United States, USSR, Japan and the EEC. Wallerstein

argued that socialist republics such as Poland and Hungary belonged to the semiperiphery. The Third World constituted the periphery. However, this arrangement has been undermined by conflicts whose origins lie at least as far back as the French Revolution. Proletarianization, urbanization, industrialization and the reinforcement of organizational structures have undermined established hierarchies in various ways. For example, urbanization has made it easier to organize opponents of the power structures. Industrialization has undermined the political and economic justifications for inequality. Bureaucracies have become top-heavy and cumbersome.

Antisystemic movements asserting the rights of oppressed classes, nations and ethnic groups grew stronger throughout the nineteenth and early twentieth centuries. By 1848, 'as good a symbolic date as any' (Arrighi *et al.*, 1989, p. 30), such movements had begun to create continuing organizations with specific political objectives. Their chief objective was to capture the state apparatus. By the mid-twentieth century social democratic movements, communist movements, and national liberation movements had achieved this objective to an impressive degree.

However, the achievement of state power resulted in little redistribution, disappointing rates of economic growth, and 'a very widespread sense of unfulfilled revolution' (p. 34). The sovereignty of the state was hedged about with *de facto* limitations, including the power of multinational firms managing a global division of labour. The old antisystemic movements failed to represent the interests of the young, the old, females, migrant workers, ethnic minorities, and workforces in the semiperiphery. Or to overcome the contradictions between the systemic demands of capitalism and the claims of welfarism and human rights. Furthermore, their westernized assumptions were subject to increasing criticism.

The year 1968 signalled a 'Revolution in the world-system' (Wallerstein, 1989b, p. 431). It drew energy from destalinization, anti-colonial wars and minority protests. The revolution embodied a protest against the system of alliances and stylized conflict associated with American hegemony. It also expressed disappointment with the old antisystemic movements. The central images promoted by these movements – their visions of the urban industrial proletariat and the oppressed nation – had become crude clichés, insensitive to complex realities. Racial, sexual and other minorities were no longer prepared to take second place. They set about creating their own 'rainbow coalitions'.

In Wallerstein's view, the key debate of the late twentieth century is under way. Its protagonists are the old and new antisystemic movements, and it concerns '*the fundamental strategy of social transforma-tion*' (p. 440; emphasis in original). Six movements are in play: the western 'old left'; new social movements in the West concerned with women, 'green' issues, ethnic minorities and so on; the traditional communist parties of the socialist bloc; new movements for human rights and against bureaucratic rule in the socialist bloc; traditional national liberation movements in the Third World; and anti-western Third World movements, often taking religious forms.

The mutual suspicion of these six movements has diminished since the late 1960s as they have begun to debate the desirability and relevance of seeking state power, and the value of egalitarianism. A number of queries dominate the agenda, according to Wallerstein. For example: can significant political change be achieved not by taking state power directly, but by increasing civil society's control over the state? How can the dangers and limitations of bureaucratic organization as a way of seeking change be overcome?

Furthermore, is it possible to overcome short-run disagreements among antisystemic movements and achieve cooperation in transform-ing the capitalist world-economy as a whole? How can we reconcile the tensions between universalist appeals to liberty and equality on the one hand and, on the other, the particularist demands of ethnicity and gender? And, finally, how can we resolve the conflict between the demand for economic growth and the need to protect the global ecol-ogy?

How these issues are resolved will be influenced by the outcome of the latest of 'those periodic downturns, or contractions, or crises that the capitalist world-economy has known with regularity since its origins in Europe in the sixteenth century' (Wallerstein, 1979, p. 95). In an article initially published in 1976, Wallerstein looked forward as follows:

> The heyday of US world hegemony is over . . . The unity of what was a bloc of socialist nations is more or less definitely broken, and the USSR and China are both challenging each other's socialist credentials . . . One of the most important consequences . . . is the destruction of the myth about the monopoly of party and state in socialist countries . . . We are now forced to take seriously the reality of continuing internal class struggle *within* socialist countries. . . At the end of this present downturn (which may not come until 1990) there will probably be a new inter*state* political alignment of forces at the world level, reflecting a new phase in the economic history of the capitalist world-economy. (pp. 95–6; emph-asis in original)

This must have appeared a very bold statement in 1976. In retrospect, it appears remarkably prescient.[6]

Comparing Wallerstein and Anderson

No attempt will be made to synthesize or adjudicate between Wallerstein and Anderson. However, some systematic differences between them may be summarized. For example, the passage just quoted indicates once more the close connection made by Wallerstein between class struggle and inter-societal relations. The state plays an important mediating role. As far as Wallerstein is concerned, both the strength of a state apparatus and its function are mainly understandable in terms of its location within the capitalist world-economy: is it in the core, periphery or semiperiphery? What part does it play in the management of unequal exchange relationships between societies through the market? Is it seeking to maintain or alter the position held by the society in which it is located within this system of relationships?

By contrast, for Anderson the strength and function of the state apparatus within a society are mainly understandable in terms of the contribution it makes to maintaining the dominant mode of production within that society. Interstate relations are relevant to his argument, especially in explaining the transmission of the absolutist state to Eastern Europe. But Anderson treats the sphere of contact between competing polities as a crucible helping to stimulate change *within* specific societies at particular times, not as a system whose cycles and processes are all-determining.

Perry Anderson and Immanuel Wallerstein both acknowledge that Western Europe's feudal heritage made a decisive contribution to the development of capitalism. For Wallerstein, the crisis of feudalism was the stimulus for the transatlantic discoveries which made the capitalist world-economy possible; and – by virtue of its decentralized character – feudalism raised no bureaucratic obstacles to the vast movements of labour and capital entailed. In other words, its contribution was largely negative.

By contrast, Anderson believes that feudal social formations not only carried the seeds of capitalist relations of production, transmitted from classical times, but also provided the basis for a decentralized Europe of competing nation-states. Furthermore, in Anderson's view, feudalism remained dominant, in some European societies at least, for up to three centuries after the sixteenth century – by which time, according to Wallerstein, it had been eclipsed by capitalism.

Wallerstein accepted that 'feudal' forms of labour control entailing extra-economic coercion continued to exist after the fifteenth century. However, they were subsumed within the *capitalist* world-economy. This view may be contrasted with Anderson's perspective on the absolutist state: although there were relatively powerful capitalist interests within absolutist states benefiting from a legal system protecting market transactions and guaranteeing absolute property rights, these interests were subsumed within a social formation dominated by the *feudal* mode of production.[7]

Finally, there are a couple of strategic differences between the approaches taken by the two scholars. Firstly, Wallerstein focuses upon exploitative relationships between societies primarily mediated by the market; Anderson upon exploitative relationships within societies primarily mediated by physical coercion in military and judicial guises. Secondly, Anderson concentrates upon the complex articulation of multiple modes of production within a specific social formation (e.g. French or English society); Wallerstein upon the complex articulation of multiple social formations within a specific mode of production (i.e. the capitalist world-economy).

Both Anderson and Wallerstein have occupied solid institutional bases from which to transmit their ideas. Anderson has his stake in the *New Left Review*. Since 1970, Wallerstein has been employed in the State University of New York at Binghampton, where he is director of the Fernand Braudel Center for the Study of Economies, Historical Systems and Civilizations. The second volume of *The Modern World-System* (Wallerstein, 1980) is dedicated to Fernand Braudel. The regard has been mutual. In his own trilogy entitled *Civilization and Capitalism 15th–18th Centuries* (Braudel, 1981–4), especially in the third volume *The Perspective of the World* (1984), Braudel makes occasional use of a world-system perspective. For all these reasons, Braudel should be the next scholar to be considered. As will be seen, his work has some surprising convergences with Michael Mann's approach.

Infrastructures of power: Braudel and Mann

In a paper published in 1972 Fernand Braudel wrote:

> I was born in 1902 . . . in a little village . . . whose roots go back for centuries . . . Things that others had to learn from books I knew all along from first-hand experience . . . I was in the beginning and remain now a historian of peasant stock. I could name the plants and trees of this village of Eastern France: I knew each of its inhabitants; I watched them at work: the blacksmith, the cartwright, the occasional woodcutters, the '*bouquillons*'. I observed the yearly rotation of the crops on the village lands which today produce nothing but grass for grazing herds. I watched the turning wheel of the old mill which was, I believe, built long ago for the local lord by an ancestor of mine. And because all this countryside of

eastern France is full of military recollections, I was, through my family, a
child at Napoleon's side at Austerlitz . . .. (1972, p. 449)

This portrait of a young 'savage mind' naming the local plants, trees and
country folk would no doubt have appealed to Claude Lévi-Strauss. The
author of *Structural Anthropology* (1963–77) was Braudel's colleague at
the École des Hautes Études during the 1950s and 1960s. To borrow
another of Lévi-Strauss's terms, Braudel's contribution to historical
scholarship was a sustained exercise in *bricolage*. It was an impressive
feat of individual craftsmanship, drawing on a vast warehouse of accumulated facts, welding them together, and making them 'work'.

Braudel produced three very big books. His best-known work,
appearing in two large volumes, is *The Mediterranean and the Mediterranean World in the Age of Philip II* (1972a; henceforth *The Mediterranean*), originally published in 1949. Even more ambitious is Braudel's
trilogy *Civilization and Capitalism 15th–18th Centuries* (1981–4; originally published in 1979; henceforth *Civilization and Capitalism*). At the
time of his death in 1985 he was working on *The Identity of France* and
had produced two of the projected four volumes. The first appeared in
1988.

The first words of the preface to the first volume of Braudel's first
major work are 'I have loved the Mediterranean with passion' (1972a, p.
17). His last major book begins with the statement: 'Let me start by
saying once and for all that I love France with the same demanding and
complicated passion as did Jules Michelet' (1988, p. 15). These are clear
indications of the very strong attachment Braudel felt to the empirical
subjects of his research. Like any ardent lover, his main objective was to
get to grips with 'the real thing', rather than spend too much time
theorizing about it.

Braudel relied upon relatively simple models, accepting ambiguity or
vagueness as the price of flexibility. He was sceptical of complex
theoretical constructs since, in his view, they were liable to depart from
social reality. Lévi-Strauss went too far in that direction for his taste. So
did another colleague, the sociologist George Gurvitch. In fact,
although they had important differences, Braudel had great respect for
Gurvitch, and happily borrowed elements from his approach.[8]

Evolution and discontinuity (1)

Gurvitch treated social structure as an intermediary between, on the
one hand, spontaneous, unorganized phenomena and, on the other
hand, institutionalized social interaction, subject to regularized coordi-

nation and control. Structuration maintained, at best, 'a precarious equilibrium, constantly being renewed'. It was 'composed of a multiplicity of hierarchies at the heart of a total social phenomenon'. This equilibrium was 'fortified and cemented by the patterns, signs, symbols, regular and habitual social roles, values and ideas – in brief, by the cultural works which are proper to these structures' (Gurvitch, 1958, p. 214). However, equilibrium was always liable to be disrupted by human beings exercising their liberty in an unexpected way. Social phenomena were constantly subject to processes of 'structuration', 'de-structuration' and 're-structuration' (1958, p. 19) in the course of which 'groups and societies are at once creating and being created, changing and being changed' (p. 20). In some respects, Gurvitch anticipated the approach later developed by Anthony Giddens, although there are differences between them.

Braudel happily accepted the intellectual usefulness of models, and in particular the idea of structure (Braudel, 1958b, p. 90). However, he could not identify with Gurvitch's special interest in the creative potential of personal encounters, or his enthusiasm for microsociological 'sociodrama'. Such a preoccupation with circumscribed events furnished a very inadequate basis for 'global history', and was no way to discover humanity in its 'true social form' (Braudel, 1953, p. 360). There was more significant drama – 'tensions, antimonies, contradictions' – to be found in the 'slow history' of the 'long term' (p. 355).[9] At this point a further point of contention arose between Gurvitch and Braudel.

Gurvitch objected to the way Auguste Comte, like Hegel, had 'identified historical reality with development, with evolution, with a unilinear progress which was spiritual and material at the same time' (1957, p. 75). It was necessary to get beyond these metaphysical dogmatics. In fact, there were radical discontinuities between, say 'archaic' societies (e.g. bands, tribes) and 'Promethean' societies: including charismatic theocracies, patriarchal societies, city-states becoming empires, enlightened despotisms, liberal capitalist democracies, fully-developed organized capitalist societies, techno-bureaucratic fascist polities, state collectivist societies, and pluralist collectivist societies (1955).

These Promethean societies were distinguished from each other by their division of labour, economic and political hierarchies, dominant cultural activities and forms of sociability, and the perceptions of social time operative within them (cf. Gurvitch, 1964). Archaic societies were confined within the limits of tradition or 'collective memory'. By contrast, the Promethean societies had 'historical memory', a capacity to reflect upon history and perceive the possibility of changing it by active human intervention' (1957, pp. 78–9).

In general terms, then, Gurvitch believed sociologists should identify the interpenetrating tensions and conflicts below the surface in each type of society. In fact,

> The object of sociology is the typology of total social phenomena: the microsociological types, the types of groupings, the types of social classes, and the types of global societies. (It studies them) in their movements of structuration and destructuration at the interior of these various types located in time segments which are reconstructed (by the sociologist) according to their discontinuity. (1956, p. 15)

Braudel made use of Gurvitch's distinctions between global types (at one extreme), microsociology (at the other) and various kinds of social groupings (e.g. classes); especially the last aspect. However, he objected to the cavalier way in which Gurvitch, having dispensed with the false god of unilinear evolutionism, then subdivided time into a host of temporalities – the 'longue durée', cyclical time, time running ahead of itself, time running late, explosive time and so on. Gurvitch had created a wide range of 'colours' but it was impossible for him to reconstitute them as 'unitary white light'.

In other words, Gurvitch could not cope with 'historical time – this reality which remains violent even if one tries to arrange and diversify it, this constraint which the historian never escapes' (Braudel, 1958b, pp. 96–7). The sociologist was prepared only too well by philosophy – which is 'where he comes from and where he remains' – to ignore this 'concrete necessity of history' and focus on the immediate, the current. As far as Braudel was concerned, the test of a model was how successfully it could be reinserted in the real world. He repeatedly compared models to seacraft. He asked: 'Doesn't every ship have to be launched into its element? Is George Gurvitch's "model" living, does it float?' (Braudel, 1953, pp. 352–3). Would it 'navigate the waters of the *longue durée*'? (1958b, p. 96).[10] Despite its useful aspects, Gurvitch's model was static: 'History is absent from it' (1958b, p. 96).

The longue durée

In 1923, after graduating in history from the Sorbonne, Braudel went as a schoolmaster to Algeria, where he was to be based for a decade. In the same year he began work on a study of Philip II's Mediterranean policy. Gradually, the sea became more interesting to him than the monarch. The next quarter of a century was spent producing a thesis, successfully defended at the Sorbonne in 1947 and published two years later as *The Mediterranean*. Thousands of hours were passed in many archives, including those at Simancas in Spain where Braudel 'aroused envy and admiration among the archivists and *buscadores* . . . by taking 2,000–3,000 photos a day and rolling some thirty meters of film' (1972b, pp. 451–2).

A brief period working in the faculty at São Paulo in Brazil during the mid-1930s was followed by appointment to the École des Hautes Études in Paris. The main outlines of *The Mediterranean* were composed during 1939, just before war broke out. Braudel wrote the first draft of the text between 1940 and 1945, without his notes, as a prisoner of war in Germany. He later recollected that during these years:

> . . . my vision took on its definitive form without my being entirely aware of it, partly as a direct intellectual response to a spectacle – the Mediterranean – which no traditional account seemed to me capable of encompassing, and partly as a direct existential response to the tragic times I was passing through. All these occurrences which poured in upon us from the radio and the newspapers of our enemies, or even the news from London which our clandestine receivers gave us – I had to outdistance, reject, deny them. Down with occurrences, especially vexing ones! I had to believe that history, destiny, was written at a much more profound level. Choosing a long time scale to observe from was choosing the position of God the Father as a refuge. (1972, p. 454)

Braudel fixed his attention on the massive, slow-moving structures of geography, climate, habit and custom, rather than the happenings that fill daily experience. He had little sympathy with the Sartrian view that human beings acquire meaningful existence by the way they act and participate in events.

In fact, personal biography and intellectual methodology were closely intertwined for both Fernand Braudel and Jean-Paul Sartre. J. H. Hexter has pointed out the stark contrast between their respective lives in the period immediately following the 'strange defeat' of France in 1940. While Braudel was stuck in prison, Sartre was in the Parisian Resistance risking his neck, making life-and-death decisions every day. Coping with this 'made him the person he was and required him to remake himself every day in the face of them' (Hexter, 1972, p. 509).

Three years after the first edition of *The Mediterranean* was published, Braudel was working on a second, even larger project at the invitation of his colleague and mentor, Lucien Febvre. Another quarter of a century of research produced *Civilization and Capitalism*, which appeared in 1979. Although it placed Europe at the centre, this work covered the whole globe in the period between 1400 and 1800. Meanwhile, its author advanced to the top of his profession. When Febvre died in 1956, Braudel succeeded him as head of the Sixth section of the École des Hautes Études and editor of *Annales*. In 1962 he became chief administrator at the Maison des Sciences de l'Homme. Apart from these duties, Braudel also revised and expanded *The Mediterranean*, bringing out a second edition in 1966 (translated in 1972). With great optimism, at the age of 77 he set out on his third great venture, *The Identity of France*. This unfinished work will not be examined here.

This chronology indicates that for well over a decade, during the 1950s and early 1960s, Braudel was working simultaneously on *The Mediterranean* and *Civilization and Capitalism*. It is not surprising that, although the latter work broadens out the focus from a particular region to the world as a whole, it forms a close sequel to the former.

Both works have a tripartite organization (see figure 4.4). The first part of *The Mediterranean* is devoted to 'man in his relationship to the environment', seen from the perspective of the long term or '*long duree*' (1972a, pp. 20, 23). It is dominated by geography, and emphasizes the

	The Mediterranean	*Civilization and Capitalism*
Vol I: *Structures*	Humankind and the environment: land/sea, mountains/plains, cities/countryside, East/West, North/South in geographical time.	Material life and everyday human activity.
Vol II: *Structures* *and* *Conjunctures*	Groups, collective destinies and trends in social time.	Choices and strategies within the market economy and merchant capitalism: economies, social hierarchies, states, civilizations.
Vol III: *Conjunctures* *(Events)*	Political and military events in individual time.	Economic and cultural conjunctures including the rise and fall of specific world-economies.

Figure 4.4 Structure and conjuncture in Braudel

role of 'structure' in history. The second part focuses upon human beings and 'the history of groups, collective destinies, and general trends' (p. 353). This part of the argument 'combines . . . *structure* and *conjuncture*, the permanent and the ephermeral, the slow-moving and the fast' (p. 353). The third part of the text deals with the history of events. Having traversed 'geographical time' and 'social time', it arrives at 'individual time' (p. 21).

Turning to *Civilization and Capitalism*, the first volume of this work – like the first part of *The Mediterranean* – is preoccupied with structures seen from a long-term perspective. Entitled *The Structures of Everyday Life* (Braudel, 1981), it deals with 'material civilization' as expressed in the daily lives or ordinary people, changing only very slowly over several generations. There is an important difference from the earlier work. Although Braudel regards structures as a product of extended interaction between nature and humankind, in *The Mediterranean* the analysis leans towards 'the role of the environment', to quote the title of part one. By contrast, in *The Structures of Everyday Life* it focuses more heavily upon patterns of human activity.

The second volume of *Civilization and Capitalism*, whose title is *The Wheels of Commerce* (1982), examines in detail the market economy rising upon the base of material civilization. It also considers the choices and strategies available at a still higher level, that of merchant capitalism. Like the second part of *The Mediterranean*, *The Wheels of Commerce* straddles the realms of structure and conjuncture. In both the earlier and later works, Braudel moves from a treatment of the economy to a consideration of social hierarchies, civilizations and states.

The third volume of *Civilization and Capitalism*, *The Perspective of the World* (1984), is concerned with the 'rhythms of the . . . conjuncture' (p. 71) as expressed in the fluctuating fortunes of successive world-economies, from the eleventh century to the 1970s. Like part three of *The Mediterranean*, it deals with the rise and fall of distinct interests. However, the nature of the interests is different in the two cases.

In the earlier book these interests are mainly political and military. Braudel's account culminates in the Battle of Lepanto between Christians and Turks in 1570 and the death of Philip II in 1598. By contrast, in *The Perspective of the World*, the relevant interests are mainly economic ('capitalism') and cultural ('civilization'). In this third volume Braudel bursts out of his self-imposed chronological limits and takes the argument up to the world oil crisis of the early 1970s.

It would obviously be misleading to suppose that the three volumes of *Civilization and Capitalism* correspond directly in content to the three parts of *The Mediterranean*. Differences in this respect have already been noticed. In fact, *Civilization and Capitalism* is a large-scale elaboration of themes central to the second part of *The Mediterranean*. This is concerned with structural and conjunctural aspects of economic life, social hierarchies, states and civilizations in the 'Greater Mediterranean' (1972a, p. 168) during the sixteenth century. In *Civilization and Capitalism*, the spatial and temporal framework is greatly extended, but the themes just mentioned remain at the heart of Braudel's argument. This argument will be explored shortly.

Running through the earlier and the latter works is an unresolved tension in Braudel's approach – or, rather, a gradual shift of perception. On the one hand, he has a powerful sense of the shaping and constraining power of enduring historical structures. On the other, especially in his later work, he sees that interests at the summit of social hierarchies greatly influence the pattern of rules and resources within institutions, as well as their survival chances. In the preface to the first edition of *The Mediterranean*, Braudel dismissed most previous research. Its concern was 'not the grand movement of Mediterranean life, but the actions of a few princes and rich men, the trivia of the past, bearing little relation to the slow and powerful march of history which is our subject' (1972a, p. 18).

Contrast the following remark, published thirty years later in the conclusion to *Civilization and Capitalism*:

> In short, the chief privilege of capitalism, today as in the past, remains the ability to *choose* – a privilege resulting at once from its dominant social position, from the weight of its capital resources, its borrowing capacity, its communication network, and, no less, from the links which create between the members of a powerful minority – however divided it may be by competition – a series of unwritten rules and personal contacts. Its sphere of action has undoubtedly widened, since all sectors of the economy are now open to it and in particular it has very largely penetrated that of production. (1984, p. 622; italics in original)

The actions of 'rich men' and 'princes' (especially merchant princes) were evidently more than 'trivia', after all.

The Mediterranean world

The Mediterranean is exhilerating and exasperating. The first part is a marvellous journey across mountain tops and valleys, finding sheep trails and trade routes, tracking migrants, smugglers and pirates, hopping between Naples and Nuremberg, Lyons and London, Ragusa and the Red Sea. By contrast, the second part is intriguing but confusing, a dazzling stream of imperfectly-related topics, featuring American silver, Portuguese pepper, Ottoman slaves, Flemish sailors, Spanish *hidalgos*, bandits, baroque cathedrals, and ransom notes. Its immanent logic emerges more clearly in the later *Civilization and Capitalism*. Finally, part three of *The Mediterranean* is thoroughly boring and almost unreadable. The sharp contrast with the previous parts could almost be intentional.[11]

Braudel set out to 'create a history that could be different from the history our masters taught us'; in other words, a study that looked 'beyond the diplomatic files, to real life' (1972a, pp. 19, 20). Part one of his book was a challenging restatement of priorities – his first subheading was 'Mountains come first' (p. 25). Successive chapters were devoted to the mountains, plateaux and plains of 'the peninsulas', the seas and coasts at 'the heart of the Mediterranean' (p. 103), the boundaries of the Greater Mediterranean extending across the Sahara, Northern Europe and the Indian and Atlantic Oceans, the impact of climate upon Mediterranean life, and the way urban life and transport patterns helped shape the Mediterranean 'as a human unit' (p. 276).

The Mediterranean world was like 'an electric or magnetic field' (p. 168) whose boundaries were difficult to specify. Climate provided one criterion. Throughout the Mediterranean could be found 'the same eternal trinity: wheat, olives and wine' (p. 236). All the coastal areas, Christian or Muslim, produced wax, wool and skins. However, there were key internal divisions: in part ecological, in part a consequence of the impact made by human beings upon their environment, in part an expression of the biases within contrasting civilizations and political orders.

At least six such divisions can be extracted from these early chapters. The first is between the land masses (or 'peninsulas') surrounding the Mediterranean and the maritime world of coastal shipping and longer, more dangerous crossings. The peninsulas – Iberia, Italy, North Africa, the Balkans, Anatolia, and so on – were by turns conquerors and conquered. Meanwhile, large seaports like Barcelona, Marseilles, Genoa and Ragusa (now Dubrovnik) passed at different periods through a life cycle of prosperity and decline: 'the seashore provinces, always short of men, could not survive for long what we would call periods of prosperity, and which were in fact periods of hard work and strain. To a very great extent, maritime life was a proletarian life, which wealth and the accompanying inactivity regularly corrupted' (p. 147).

A second division was between the mountains and the plains. High places allowed refuge from feudal subjugation. As they became overpopulated, they spilled their human surplus on to the plateaux and into the valleys. Down on the lower ground, different rules applied. For example, human management of nature often took the form of vast irrigation schemes demanding a high degree of collective discipline. The necessary investment typically came from large urban settlements such as Venice and Seville, with their large trading profits and hungry populations.

These considerations have already introduced a third division, between city and countryside – the latter supplying food and people for the former, the former sometimes bringing investment and government to the latter. Closely related to all three distinctions made so far is a fourth; between settled or fixed capital and labour on the one hand, and mobile goods and people on the other. There is conflict between the two, as when farmers and herdsmen clash, or respectable townsfolk look out for thieving vagrants. However, there is also complementarity. Cities and roads needed each other. For example, in Spain 'a road system . . . links Medina del Campo, Valladolid, Burgos and Bilbao, four outstandingly active cities: the great fair-centre; the court of Philip II (until 1560); the headquarters of the wool trade; and lastly, the seaport with its sailors and carriers. The road passed through them like an assembly line, distributing tasks' (p. 316).

Two further divisions cut across all those already noticed. They are between East and West, and between North and South. The two great basins of the Mediterranean tended to organize themselves into 'closed circuits' (p. 136), despite the links between them. All attempts by East to dominate the West, or vice versa, were short-lived or followed by a severance of links between the conquerors and their base (as, for example, occurred in Muslim Spain, and the Latin kingdom of Jerusalem). During the sixteenth century East and West were dominated by, respectively, the Turkish and Spanish empires: 'Politics merely followed the outline of an underlying reality' (p. 137).

The gradual rise of the West at the expense of the East was complemented by the steady advance of the North at the expense of the South. In the latter respect, the crucial boundary lay along a line from Lyons to Lvov. South of this line was the land of vineyards, olive groves, and mule trains. North lay a different Europe, with its breweries, forests and wheeled traffic. This was the 'new' Europe of the Reformation, which captured the Atlantic while Spain hesitated. Despite the shift of power from South to North, the decline of the South was not rapid: 'On the contrary, the Mediterranean shaped the Atlantic and impressed its own image on the Spanish New World' (p. 226).

Part one of *The Mediterranean* produces a kind of mental intoxication. This carries us through the second part, where interesting detail makes up for fuzziness in the overall analysis. However, at the start of part three the law of gravity reasserts itself. We come down with a bump. Titles like '1550–1559: war and peace in Europe', 'The last six years of Turkish supremacy: 1559–1565' and 'Origins of the Holy League: 1556–1570' promise (and deliver) little more than competent but pedestrian diplomatic and military history. Nor does Braudel's first sentence offer much in the way of encouragement. It appears he published the third part 'only after much hesitation'. In his view, 'Events are the ephemera of history', which 'pass across its stage like fireflies' (1972b, p. 901).

In fact, part three is integrated even less closely than part two into the analytical framework established in the first part. Why did Braudel leave it like this, even in his heavily revised second edition? Perhaps because it provided a dramatic illustration that intellectual liveliness and new growth in historical scholarship were to be found not in the dry-as-dust practices of his mentors, but in the study of 'that other, submerged, history . . . which is little touched by the obstinate erosion of time' (1972a, p. 16). Braudel wanted to turn the world of historical scholarship on its head. As a practical move in this direction he had an upside-down map of the world printed in his third chapter (1972a, p. 169).

If this interpretation is correct, Braudel's message was conveyed at the expense of any sustained attempt to trace systematically the interactions between structures and conjunctures, between the long-term and the relatively fleeting. However, a more serious attempt to do this was made in *Civilization and Capitalism*.

Civilization and capitalism

It is convenient to divide Braudel's argument in this work into three pairs of themes: civilizations and societies; cities and states; and merchants and world-economies. For Braudel, a civilization is rooted in earth:

> Man lives from choice in the framework of his own experience, trapped in his former achievements for generations on end. When we say man, we mean the group to which he belongs: individuals leave it and others are incorporated, but the group remains attached to a given space and to familiar land. It takes root there. (1981, p. 56)

The simpler societies, from hunter-gatherers, through nomads to hoe-users, were classified as 'cultures'. However, by AD 1500 there was a handful of 'civilizations', identifiable by their ploughs, domesticated animals, carts, and 'above all, towns'. They formed 'a narrow belt of wells, tilled fields and dense populations' (p. 57) around the whole of the Old World, from Japan to Northern Europe.

Each civilization was 'a world of "things and words"' (p. 333). During the fifteenth century, human beings were enslaved within them, trapped by the tyrannical demands of material life and the constraints imposed by language itself. However, a struggle to slip free of these bonds and establish mastery was under way. Complete escape from the constraints of time, space and culture was impossible. However, there were some remarkable achievements with stretched their limits. The most spectacular success was the conquest of the Atlantic by the West. The skills of northern and southern Europeans were combined in this enterprise, which required considerable self-mastery by those involved. Indeed, 'the greatest difficulty was to conquer one's fear of the unknown' (p. 409).

Other advances gave the West an edge over its rivals: for example, the conquest of empty lands on the outskirts of Europe. In the sixteenth century, Russia pushed east into Siberia and south towards the Volga, Don and Dniester. The Cossacks helped colonize the steppes and, in the process, set up a barrier against Islamic nomads, especially the Tartars from the Crimea.

By the following century, the containment of internal threats to bourgeois thrift and order was also well under way in the West. The indigent and the incompetent were driven into hospitals, workhouses and prisons: 'This "great enclosure" of the poor, mad and delinquent- . . . was one psychological aspect of seventeenth-century society, relentless in its rationality' (p. 77). Other conquests – the spread of birth control, the gradual defeat of the plague, and major technological breakthroughs – had to wait until the eighteenth century.

'Civilization' and 'the long term' were closely related. However, 'these major categories call for a supplementary classification, based on the notion of *society*' (p. 561; emphasis in original). In Braudel's view, society was 'not a single container'. It was 'a set of sets' including economic aspects, the social hierarchy, politics and culture. No single sector (e.g. economic or political) could achieve 'permanent superiority over another'. Furthermore, the border-lines between categories or classes had 'the fluidity of water'. And every society contained 'obstinate relics of the past' (1982, pp. 458–61).

Finally, at the level of civilizations (as opposed to simpler cultures), societies contained competing hierarchies. They took the form of 'diversified pluralities . . . divided against themselves'. Following the examples of Marc Bloch and Georges Gurvitch, Braudel characterized 'feudal society' as a combination of five 'societies': seigneurial, theocratic, the ties of vassalage, the territorial state and, 'to us the most important of all . . . the towns' (pp. 464–5). This last comment directs us to the second pair of themes in Braudel's argument: cities and states:

> Towns are like electric transformers. They increase tension, accelerate the rhythm of exchange and constantly recharge human life. They were born of the oldest and most revolutionary division of labour: between work in the fields on the one hand and activities described as urban on the other. (1981, p. 479)

This division of labour was between unequals. For here is yet another conquest, the town's mastery of its rural hinterland. In fact, towns were always associated with 'power, protective or coercive' (p. 481). Their self-consciousness was expressed and reinforced by their ramparts. City walls provided security and, in some societies (e.g. China), a means of monitoring and controlling the urban population. Everywhere, towns were active within communications networks (local and long-distance), drawing in people and goods, competing with rivals.

In the West the towns had won an unparalleled degree of independence by the thirteenth century, especially in Italy, Flanders and Germany, where the territorial state was slow to develop. This disjuncture between city and state was vital, since it allowed the former 'to try the experiment of leading a completely separate life for quite a long time. This was a colossal event' (p. 511), a conjuncture with major structural consequences. Towns created a new form of civilization – riven with class struggles, yet united by local patriotism; systematically calculating, but also attuned to gambling and risk. Braudel described them as 'outposts of modernity' (p. 512).

Three basic types of city could be identified. First, the open towns. These were largely non-industrial, and blended into the surrounding countryside – such towns were inherited from the Roman Empire. Second, there were the closed cities. These were self-governing, bourgeois and exclusive – city-states such as Venice were extreme examples. Third, there were the subjugated towns. These had fallen under the thumb of the territorial state. Broadly speaking, the three types also represented three phases through which urban life passed (although this was not an iron rule: for example, Russian towns passed from the first directly to the third phase).

Those large urban centres which became capital cities – London, Paris and so on – 'produced the national markets, without which the modern state would be a pure fiction' (p. 527). Control of economic life within this market was one of the state's tasks. It needed a regular supply of money, which it siphoned from the wealth in circulation in the form of taxation, loans and, as sophistication increased, the device of the national debt. Two other tasks were the maintenance of order and careful monitoring of cultural movements.

Although the territorial state borrowed and extended institutional forms developed earlier within city-states, rulers were not 'bourgeois': they did not live within their means, and their courts were attuned to display rather than modesty. Braudel recalled the argument of Norbert Elias that royalty in the West was marked by its feudal origins. Kings fought the aristocracy, imprisoned it within the royal court and cut it off from its rural roots. But rulers remained tied to the class from which they came. Instead of destroying it, 'the Crown had to take the nobility under its wing' (1982, p. 550).

Rulers could not achieve a similar degree of control over capitalism, since the latter 'always wore seven-league boots' taking it beyond national boundaries (p. 554). This brings us to Braudel's third pair of themes: merchants and world-economies. Merchants, small and grand, were specialists in the language of money and credit, the means of economic exchange. At the lower end their circuits included local markets, shops, farms and workshops. Higher up they first operated through international credit fairs, later basing themselves in warehouses and exchanges located in key entrepôt cities. The object was to buy cheap and sell dear, a feat often requiring lengthy travel; in fact, long-distance trade was the source of the larger profits. Networks of merchants, linked by kin and ethnic origin, cooperated and competed along intercontinental trade routes.

As markets became more complex and extensive, they played a crucial intermediary role between the other two layers of human activity. The market economy, the world of supply and demand, bit deep into the layer below, the zone of 'material civilization' sanctified by custom and tradition. Households and communities producing mainly for use were bludgeoned into producing mainly for sale. These pressures were usually resisted, in the short run at least. Meanwhile, the settled routines of the market place were themselves, in turn, subject to raids from the layer above, occupied by the very large global operators.

This 'zone of the anti-market, where the great predators roam and the law of the jungle operates . . . is the real home of capitalism' (p. 230). Windfall gains were to be had not by trading in a regular way on well-established markets, but by using the power coming from great wealth to force your way into new areas, or to shift existing terms of trade in your own favour. The largest capitalists could get hold of useful information before their competitors. They had special influence with the territorial power.

These predators were very slow to move directly into the sphere of production. They bought grain from Eastern European estates, but were not prepared to undermine the seigneurial regime, there or elsewhere, until very late in the day. Similarly, they left most industrial production in the hands of artisans and local merchants, stepping in at the point where the finished articles came on to the market. Capitalism was originally rooted in trade, not production.

Furthermore, capitalism's arena was not the city or the kingdom, but the world-economy. Braudel introduced this concept into the argument of *The Mediterranean* (1972a, pp. 387ff., 418ff.). It was less elaborate than Wallerstein's later version. However, Braudel's idea of a world-economy was similar in emphasizing the differentiating and integrating function of markets transcending political boundaries. In *The Perspective of the World* (the third volume of *Civilization and Capitalism*), Braudel focused his argument upon this concept, frequently referring to Wallerstein while noting that 'I do not always agree with him' (1984, p. 634).

In Braudel's version, world-economies cut across states, societies and cultures, interacting with them but by no means governing them or determining their shape. Each world-economy had a distinctive centre, identifiable boundaries, and an internal hierarchy of zones. At the centre would always be found a dominant capitalist city and an exceptional state apparatus. Cities took it in turn to take the lead, as did Venice, Antwerp, Genoa, Amsterdam, and London in the West. The principal instruments of domination varied, including (in different cases), shipping, trade, industry, credit, and political power or violence (p. 35).

However, the infrastructure of 'basic distances, routes, delays, production, merchandise and stopping places' remained almost unchanged, despite alterations at the centre:

> At ground level and sea level so to speak, the networks of local regional markets were built up over century after century. It was the destiny of this local economy, with its self-contained routines, to be from time to time absorbed and made part of a 'rational' order in the interest of a dominant city or zone, for perhaps one or two centuries, until another 'organizing centre' emerged. (p. 36)

Braudel shared Wallerstein's interest in the effects of slow-moving economic cycles and their contribution to the 'rhythms of the "conjuncture" ' (p. 71). However, he thought Wallerstein 'a little too systematic, perhaps' (p. 70). Two differences between them are worth emphasizing.

First, Braudel disputed Wallerstein's assumption that capitalism first appeared in the sixteenth century. He preferred to locate its origins in thirteenth-century Italy. This leads directly to the second difference, which is the much greater sensitivity of Braudel to the pioneering role of city-states. Cities like Venice were driven to batten on to larger states, such as the Byzantine and Turkish empires, in order to gain access to the markets they needed. The shift from city-centred world-economies to world-economies focused on national states (still driven by the dynamism of their cities) did not begin before the mid-fifteenth century.

National integration took several generations. For most of the four centuries (1400–1800) covered by Braudel's trilogy, there was 'a gulf between nation-states on the one hand, the locus of *power*, and urban centres on the other, the locus of *wealth*' (p. 288; emphasis in original). Not until the crystallization of national markets during the eighteenth century were capitalist wealth, political power and military capacity woven closely together within territorial states. In fact, 'Real life capitalism, the form of economy that actually triumphed for a time over Europe and the whole globe, actually presupposed, and embedded within itself, other forms of power, especially military and political power.' The last quotation, which apparently gels so neatly with Braudel's argument, actually comes from Michael Mann's *The Sources of Social Power* (1986, p. 495). A comparison between the work of Braudel and Mann is surprisingly relevant.

Braudel's long career ended with his death the year before Mann's book appeared. Mann makes only fleeting reference to the work of Braudel (Mann, 1986, pp. 205, 445). There are, in fact, important differences between the two writers. For example, Mann pays attention to four major sources of social power, over a historical span beginning before 5000 BC, while Braudel concentrates on the economic sphere and restricts himself to a mere four centuries. Furthermore, while Braudel traces a sequence of world-economies linked primarily through the market, Mann's treatment of the same period emphasizes the gradual formation of a multistate system whose principal actors are governments wielding military power. Finally, while Braudel is sympathetic to a broadly evolutionist approach (e.g. Braudel, 1972a, p. 379; 1972b, p. 681; 1982, pp. 466, 600), Mann asserts that '*No general social evolution occurred beyond the rank societies of early, settled neolithic societies*' (Mann, 1986, pp. 69–70; emphasis in original). This last topic will be taken up at the end of this chapter.

Nevertheless, Mann and Braudel have a very similar 'feel' for society and history. For example, both emphasized that power is polymorphous; in other words, that the coercive and creative capacities of men and women dominating social hierarchies can take a variety of forms. The leading part may be taken by economic, political, military or cultural/ideological means of power, depending upon the broader world-historical setting. Mann has shared Braudel's keen interest in the infrastructure and logistics of power, especially the limits imposed by time, space and technological capacity. Also in the way people adapt to these limits, whether they are rulers collecting taxes, military commanders putting down provincial revolts, merchants working the spice routes, or peasants ploughing the fields.

Either writer could have composed the following passages, which actually come from Braudel:

> Between the fifteenth and eighteenth centuries . . . the state was far from occupying the entire social stage; it did not possess the 'diabolical' power of penetration attributed to it today; in the past, the means were simply lacking. (1984, p. 51)

> . . . the *power apparatus*, the might that pervades and permeates every structure, is something more than the state. It is the sum of the political, social, economic and cultural hierarchies. (1982, pp. 554–5; emphasis in original)

> . . . total society can only be a sum of living realities, *whether or not* these are related to each other: . . . it is not a single container, but several containers – and their contents. (1982, pp. 458–9; emphasis in original)

> Of the various social hierarchies – the hierarchies of wealth, of state power or of culture, that oppose yet support each other – which is the most important? The answer is . . . that it may depend upon the time, the place and who is speaking. (1984, p. 623)

Finally, in his analysis of the spatial dimension of social relations, Braudel made creative use of Von Thunen's theory of concentric rings around an imagined city: in successive rings, moving out from the city, will be found market gardening, dairy production, cereals and livestock (Braudel, 1984, p. 38; Von Thunen, 1966). In the same spirit, Mann draws upon Owen Lattimore's theory of concentric rings around a political centre: moving from the inner to the outer circle, successive rings mark the limits of economic integration, civil administration, and military action (Mann, 1986, p. 9; Lattimore, 1962).

The sources of social power

Michael Mann began as an 'empirical sociologist in the regular British mould' (Anderson, 1990, p. 57), critical of both Parsonian and Marxist approaches to consciousness and values.[12] However, during the 1970s his ambition increased considerably. *The Sources of Social Power* (1986) is the first major product of this new phase in his career. In it, Mann set out to trace the 'leading edge' of social power through time and space from Mesopotamia before 5000 BC, to the formation of national and international capitalism in north-west Europe during the late seventeenth to early nineteenth centuries. By social power he meant 'the capacity to integrate peoples and spaces into dominant configurations' (p. 31). In his view, societies consisted of the multiple, overlapping sociospatial networks resulting from the exercise of these capacities. More briefly, they were 'organized power networks' (p. 1).

Mann identified four main sources of social power: economic, ideological, political and military. The last two of these, combined in intersocietal relations, constitute 'geopolitical' power (Mann, 1988, p. ix). None of these four sources of social power has ultimate primacy. Which of them predominates has varied according to the world-historical context. At different times, they have all acted as 'tracklaying vehicles', providing 'social concentration, organization and direction' (p. 28).

Three of Mann's objectives were: first, to trace the logistical capacities of the four sources of social power (in other words, what could be done with them and how); second, to identity 'power jumps' (p. 525), where power capacities have increased sharply, perhaps by more effective organization of 'intersitial' (p. 16) processes and networks not fully recognized or exploited in existing institutions; and third, to explore the development of the most powerful human society, modern western civilization.

Mann stepped into this arena armed with a number of sensitizing ideas about power. The main ones will be briefly listed. Power may be distributive (A's power over B), collective (the shared power A and B acquire if they cooperate with each other) or, presumably, both (the power of A and B over C). Power may be either extensive or intensive. Extensive power means the ability to produce at least minimal compliance over a large population and a large territory. Intensive power is the capacity generated by high commitment and tight organization within a group. Neither implies the other.

Power may also be either authoritative or diffused. Authoritative power is expressed through command and obedience, stemming from the enforced will of a specific institution or group. Diffused power derives from widespread acquiescence in social practices (e.g. those of the capitalist market) on the grounds that they are natural, proper or inevitable. Again, neither implies the other.

Military power has both an intensive (mainly defensive) aspect and an extensive (aggressive) aspect. Both aspects rely on the use of 'concentrated coercion' (p. 520), one form of which is the authoritative enforcement of 'compulsory cooperation' (p. 521) upon subject labour. Ideological power may be either immanent (e.g. as intensively expressed in the collective morale of a class or nation) or transcendent (e.g. as extensively and diffusely expressed in a universalistic religion throughout a whole region or continent).

Political power takes the form of centralized state regulation of social relations within a bounded territory – although the claims of the political elite may not be matched by the penetrative powers of the political infrastructure. The state has a dual role: regulation of civil society is complemented by geopolitical diplomacy within the multistate system.

Finally, economic power integrates (intensive) productive labour and (extensive) networks of exchange and consumption within 'circuits of praxis' (p. 520; see figure 4.5).

Military	*Ideological*
Intensive–defensive	Immanent (intensive)
	Transcendent (diffused, extensive)
Extensive–aggressive	
(concentrated coercion; compulsory cooperation)	
Political	*Economic*
Regulation of civil society; maintenance of territorial boundedness.	Productive labour (intensive)
	Exchange and consumption (extensive)
Geopolitical activity within multi-state system.	(Circuits of praxis)

Figure 4.5   Mann's four sources of social power

All four sources of social power are implicated in the distinction between two types of configuration which recur throughout history:

1 *Empires of domination* combined military concentrated coercion with an attempt at state territorial centralization and geopolitical hegemony. So they also combined intensive authoritative powers along the narrow routes of penetration of which the army was capable, with weaker, but still authoritative and far more extensive, power wielded over the whole empire and neighbouring clients by its central state. The principal reorganizing role is here played by a mixture of military and political power, with the former predominating.

2 In *multi-power-actor civilizations*, decentralized power actors competed with one another within an overall framework of normative regulation. Here extensive powers were diffuse, belonging to the overall culture rather than to any authoritative power organization. Intensive powers were possessed by a variety of small, local power actors, sometimes states in a multistate civilization, sometimes classes and fractions of classes, usually mixtures of all of these. The predominant reorganizing forces were here economic and ideological, though in varied combinations and often with political and geopolitical help. (Mann, 1986, p. 534)

A classic example of the former was the Roman Empire, and of the latter, the Greek city-states of classical times. Mann suggests there is some evidence for 'repeated creative interplay' (p. 535) between the two types. In empires of domination, collective social powers created by authoritative power tended to slip beyond state control and into civil society; for example, private property and literacy skills became diffused in this way. This decentralizing and fragmenting process in empires of domination was complemented by an opposite dynamic in multi-power-actor civilizations. In this latter case, there was a tendency towards greater hegemonic centralization. A key role was played by marcher lords protecting the flanks of multi-power-actor civilizations. These military guardians of the hinterlands were able to combine the fighting strengths of agriculturalists and pastoralists, using both as the basis of new empires of domination.

This 'modest' (p. 535) theorizing about change processes was matched by an empirical generalization. There was, Mann pointed out, a steady drift towards the north-west by the leading edge of social power, from Phoenicia, Greece and Rome towards the North Sea and the Atlantic. For example, the Scandinavians were opening up the Baltic just as Rome collapsed.

This process was encouraged by the existence of desert to the south, and Islam to the east, while in the north and west there were the ecological opportunities offered by 'heavier, wetter, deeper, richer, rain-watered soils and the navigable varied coastlines of the Mediterranean, Baltic, North and Atlantic seas'. In sum, the drift towards the north-west was the result of 'a gigantic series of accidents of nature linked to an equally monstrous series of historical coincidences' (p. 540).

Greece and Rome

The transition from general social evolution to specific local histories occurred, in Mann's view, after the Neolithic Revolution; in other words, after human beings had learned to grow crops and rear animals. In particular, the shift towards stratification, the state and civilization was certainly not inevitable, natural or widespread. On the contrary, although decisive it was a rare and abnormal occurrence. In most cases, it was difficult to advance beyond the village and/or the chiefdom as modes of social organization.

On the one hand, 'delayed return labour investments' (p. 44) – in land, livestock, tools, production teams and exchange relationships – tended to increase social fixity and constraint. On the other hand, it was technically difficult to turn networks into 'cages'. There were no means of imposing central rule upon large numbers of people over extensive areas with a high degree of ecological specialization.

Outside the village, social interaction typically occurred within a 'broader exchanging, diffusing network' (p. 46). People were unwilling to see an advance in collective power become the basis of permanent distributive power over themselves. If elders and chiefs became too oppressive, villagers preferred to depose them or move away. In recurrent cycles, integration was followed by fission, and centralization by decentralization.

However, these cycles were broken in a number of cases – Mesopotamia being a key example – where alluvial agriculture and irrigation predominated (from about 5000 BC). Fertile soil produced large surpluses, but it was limited in supply, fixed in space, and required intensive management. Private property, literacy, grain stores and urban centres became viable, as did trade between a dominant alluvial core and a periphery of pastoralists, miners, fishermen and so on. Moving away was no longer a viable option.

Civilization, stratification and the state – in other words, permanent distributive power of the few over the many – arrived on the scene. At first, small city-states embodying authoritative power and strong territoriality operated within a much wider region of 'extensive, diffused, and "transcendent" ideological and geopolitical organization' (p. 127). At a later phase, the inner and outer power networks of these multi-power-actor civilizations merged, mainly through military means, producing empires of domination.

The first empires of domination in the Near East (from about 2500 BC) were pioneered by marcher lords. Federal and fragile, these early empires had to live within their logistical means. There was a 30 kilometres a day limit upon unsupported military advances over land. 'Compulsory cooperation', or militarized economic organization, spread such benefits as pacification, communications, and literacy. However, this was typically followed by greater decentralization of power into the hands of local elites. Centralized state power and decentralized private property were outcrops of the same infrastructure.

The early empires confronted challenges, first, from nomadic warriors (*c*.1800–*c*.1400 BC) and, subsequently, from the economic and military power of iron-using peasant farmers (*c*.1200–*c*.800 BC). Both challenges came from the north. The advance of the first disrupted centralized political controls, without being able to impose an alternative. Successes by the latter gave positive strength to decentralizing tendencies. The northern ploughlands produced household surpluses which fed directly into trading networks. Villages supplied infantrymen to safeguard these resources. These challenges produced two responses.

The first response was the multi-power-actor civilizations of Greece and Phoenicia (*c*.800–*c*.300 BC). The second was the revitalization of empires of domination (*c*.1000 BC onwards), including the Assyrian, Persian and Roman empires. Mann paid most attention to the Greeks and Romans. The Greek city-states combined profitable plough-based agriculture and cheap sea transport. They traded in wine, oil, slaves and mercenaries. Military and economic power shaped a symmetrical and politicized class struggle between rich and poor.

The consciousness of the common citizenry was sharpened by service in the infantry. Over time, these divisions within the *polis* were overlaid by stratification of the city-states in terms of military power and economic wealth. Imperialist tendencies and increased reliance on mercenary soldiers undermined democracy within the *polis*.

Unlike the Greek city-states, Roman society managed to combine widespread citizenship, social stratification, tribal loyalties, and a sense of shared ethnicity. Militarism was central. Roman success was based upon extensive power networks created and dominated by its legionaries – serving as soldiers, administrators and civil engineers. This was matched by a willingness to extend citizenship to incorporated territories and to give membership of the Roman upper class to conquered elites.

Far from following Perry Anderson's argument that the weakening of slavery fatally undermined Rome, Mann argued that the blurring of free and slave statuses in the category of *colonus* (dependent cultivator) provided a means of extracting further surplus from the peasantry. In fact, the fatal weakness lay in the chronic conflict between the upper class on their provincial estates and the military in control of the state apparatus at the centre. State and upper class could not cooperate to make the shared sacrifices necessary to pay for effective defence against the empire's enemies (cf. Skocpol on the causes of social revolutions). As a consequence, the fiscal-military system broke down. This was disastrous for the economy and, ultimately, for the empire itself.

A major legacy of the Roman empire was the transcendent ideological force of Christianity, embodying the ideal of 'a universalistic, egalitarian, decentralized, civilizing community – an *ecumene*' (Mann, 1986, p. 307). Like the other world religions, Christianity was a 'tracklayer', even though it compromised in many ways with particularism, hierarchy and centralizing rulers. Building on the universalizing capacities of literacy and trade, it extended awareness of personal identity, acquired great influence over the family life cycle, and mobilized the people into a normative community. The key world historical moment for Christianity was the period between the fall of Rome and the dynamic revival of Europe.

The European dynamic

After AD 800 Christianity became thoroughly incorporated into the chivalric culture of medieval Europe. In fact, its influence spread throughout society, providing normative regulation of economic and political activity. It wielded an 'unseen hand, not Adam Smith's but Jesus Christ's (p. 398). Beneficiaries of this framework of rules included the owners of private property successfully 'hidden' (p. 399) from state, ecclesiastical or baronial control. They were able to exploit intensive techniques of economic production. Dynamism was greatest along the commercial corridor between Northern Italy and Flanders, where kings, bishops and feudal lords were weakest.

By 1500, extensive power networks were rapidly developing, not only in trade but also in the political and military spheres. Gradually, national states took over from Christendom the task of normative pacification. During the sixteenth century, the rapid diffusion of technical advances in navigation, printing and the instruments of land war increased the interdependence of capitalism and the national state. As the financial costs imposed by the geopolitical commitments of states became greater, considerable pressures were exerted upon states to increase their coordinating role within civil society, regulating and taxing its members.

As interpenetration of civil society and state increased, the relationship became more organic. The Protestant Reformation and the establishment of national churches helped bind the constituents closer together. Monarchy became more 'public' (p. 459). The nobility and bourgeoisie increasingly acquired collective organization as classes in the course of managing their relationship to the state. To a considerable degree, they became part of the state, serving as its officers. At the same time, the state developed its infrastructural powers (e.g. its ability to collect taxes and enforce laws), enhancing its capacity to get its way within civil society.

In practice, cooperation with the major landowners was inescapable. In constitutional regimes such as England and Holland, taxes were collected from rich households in city and countryside, with their consent. By contrast, in absolutist regimes such as Spain and France, taxes were imposed upon the poor peasantry and rich tradespeople with the forceful backing of the rich landed class. Despite the despotic claims of the rulers of absolutist regimes, their infrastructural capacities were less well developed. Absolutist states had more internal divisions among the rich, and were less organic than constitutional societies. The organic character of the latter was enhanced by processes of class development within the centralized and bounded territoriality of the nation.

By the eighteenth century, in England a 'class-nation' had developed 'stretching across and whole country [and] comprising gentry, nobility, burghers and political "placemen" ' (pp. 459–60). It was part of a larger entity: 'Modern Europe has been integrated by four interrelated, secular institutions: (1) by the capitalist mode of production, which soon took the form of (2) industrialism, both of which have been normatively and geographically channelled by (3) a national state within (4) a multistate, geopolitical, diplomatic civilization' (p. 471). The leading edge of social power had once more been embodied within a multi-power-actor civilization.

Classes, nations, states and warfare

In Mann's view, classes, nations, states and warfare are bound closely together. For example, classes and nations depend on the same diffused practices, sentiments and identities. Before the development of class-nations in Europe, class solidarities were grounded in the infrastructure provided by Christianity. Class remained latent until this infrastructure came into being with the spread of literacy, trade and coinage.

As the infrastructure developed, extensive class organization and consciousness took shape, first among the upper class, where it often took the form of class-based political control. The penetration of the market into the countryside and the growth of national identity ensured that the lower class also developed organization and consciousness (cf. E. P. Thompson). As a consequence, extensive political and symmetrical classes appeared within state boundaries.

Centralizing territorial states structured the social spaces into which social classes – including the bourgeoisie and, at a later date, the proletariat – entered. States benefited from the realizable and taxable wealth generated by capitalism. The symbiosis between states and capitalist interests hardened national boundaries even further. With industrialism, class consciousness and national consciousness 'rose up together' (1988, p. 142). The development of mass citizenship was closely associated with mass mobilization for warfare. This leads directly to Mann's critique of T. H. Marshall's approach to citizenship.

Mann criticized Marshall's 'Anglophile and evolutionary model' (p. 189) of the development of citizenship. In fact, the British pattern represents only one possibility from among several actually pursued by advanced industrial countries (see figure 4.6). In each case, head-on collisions between 'massive, antagonistic classes' (p. 190) were converted into more limited, complex and institutionalized conflicts. A key part in this was played by ruling-class strategies. These were shaped not so much by industrialization, as by structural transformations within old regimes and the impact of geopolitics.

In Mann's view, Katznelson's work (Katznelson, 1981b) helps explain how American labour was absorbed into a liberal regime. This regime permitted conflicts between narrowly-defined special interests exercising their civil and political rights, but denied legitimacy to class-based organizations. The rights and privileges associated with citizenship and class membership did not come on to the agenda of industrial confrontation. One consequence was relatively weak pressure from below for the enhancement of social citizenship.

In the case of Britain, the second main example of a constitutional regime, the struggle for political citizenship brought class-based organizations fully into the arena. The state veered between a non-interventionist liberal strategy and active reformism. One consequence was to provide more substantial rights of social citizenship than in the United States.

In several countries, constitutionalist and absolutist tendencies were in contention. In Scandinavia, mutual accommodation and merging occurred early on. Sufficient of the absolutist tendency remained to buttress a corporatist state committed to reformism, corresponding more closely than Britain to Marshall's vision. By contrast, in France, Spain and Italy, anarchist, revolutionary and socialist ideologies flourished, as the battle over citizenship continued until after World War II.

The most striking aspect of Mann's argument is his assertion that the authoritarian forms of modernization stemming from absolutist regimes were relatively stable, and liable to endure – had it not been for military defeats inflicted by alliances of liberal and reformist regimes. More specifically, by use of divide-and-rule tactics, skilful politicians such as Bismarck were able to develop a mix of full civil citizenship and limited political and social citizenship which kept effective power in the hands of authoritarian regimes. Authoritarian monarchy 'could probably have

Industrializing regime	Ruling-class strategy	Principal examples
Constitutional	Liberal Liberal/reformist	United States Britain
Contested (= constituional *vs.* absolutist)	Authoritarian monarchy leading (eventually) to liberal/reformist	France, Spain, Italy
Merged (= Constitutional *plus* absolutist)	Authoritarian monarchy leading to reformist	Scandinavia
Absolutist	Authoritarian monarchy leading to fascism	Germany, Austria, Japan
	Authoritarian monarchy leading to authoritarian socialism	Russia

Figure 4.6 Mann on ruling-class strategies and citizenship

survived into advanced, post-industrial society' (p. 203). However, World War I was fatal for such regimes. In its aftermath, social citizenship was extended further under fascism, which failed not on account of its internal policies but, again, for geopolitical reasons. Soviet Russia, born during World War I, differed from Germany and Japan in being on the winning side in World War II. Mann concluded that 'the stability of the fifth solution, authoritarian socialism, cannot be in doubt' (p. 204). This was, of course, written before the events of 1989.

The presentation of empirical materials takes priority in Mann's major work on social power. However, he is also quite explicitly concerned with the formulation and presentation of a general theory. It is therefore quite appropriate to follow discussion of his work by turning directly to two scholars who have placed theory construction at the top of their list of priorities.

Constructing theories: Runciman and Giddens

Grand theory is back – and it takes history seriously. The historical dimension of society has been a major preoccupation of (for example) Randall Collins, W. G. Runciman, Anthony Giddens and Ernest Gellner.[13] Generally speaking, they use empirical cases to illustrate the relevant theory's capacity to make specific socio-historical phenomena meaningful or significant. But their principal purpose is not to provide ordered and detailed surveys of huge tracts of human history. By contrast, Anderson, Wallerstein and Braudel devote relatively little space to expounding in an abstract way the theories and models which inform their work.

The shift of emphasis between the two approaches may be illustrated by contrasting the way Mann and Runciman have organized their respective trilogies. The first two volumes of Mann's *The Sources of Social Power* are 'histories', dealing, respectively, with 'power from the beginning to AD 1760' and 'power in industrial societies'. Not until these histories have been absorbed will the reader be given a third volume, entitled 'A Theory of Power'. By contrast, the first two volumes of Runciman's *A Treatise on Social Theory* (hereafter *Treatise*) deal, in turn, with 'the methodology of social theory' and 'substantive social theory'. Only in the third volume will this social theory be applied at length to a specific empirical case, twentieth-century England.

After *Relative Deprivation and Social Justice*, which appeared in 1966, Runciman undertook an 'exercise in self-education' which helped him 'to see not only why Weber's methodology would not quite do but also how it might be put right' (1989b, p. 7).[14] This self-education culminated in the *Treatise*. After the first methodological volume, the second volume contains a lengthy exposition, historical and comparative, of a social theory based upon the idea of evolution. At its centre is an emphasis upon the competitive selection of practices. Runciman's third volume, as yet unpublished, will cover a similar historical period to *Relative Deprivation*. (For an early indication of the third volume's approach, see Runciman, 1990). His object is to 'do for the study of societies what Darwin and his successors have done for the study of species' (1989b, pp. 12–13).

At the beginning of the second volume Runciman stated that its aim was 'primarily explanatory' (1989e, p. 4). He was referring back to distinctions made in the first volume between reportage, explanation, description and evaluation as operations carried out by sociologists and other observers of human behaviour. These distinctions will be briefly explored.

The methodology of social theory

In Runciman's view, 'explanation' is one of three modes of understanding. Reportage leads to primary understanding. Explanation or the identification of causes leads to secondary understanding. Tertiary understanding is based upon description, a term used to mean giving an account of what it is like to participate in a specific situation which has been (or might be) the object of reportage and explanation. Reportage (e.g. on a specific kinship system) raises questions of explanation: why is it this kind of system and not another? Explanation, in turn, raises the issue of description: what is this kind of system like for people brought up within its rules? Finally, description raises issues of evaluation: what is good or bad about this system?

Briefly, Runciman argued that reportage involves 'recovering the constitutive intentions and beliefs' (p. 70) of actors, a process that typically entails paying attention to the social, political and historical contexts that give specific intentions and actions their meaning. If it is to withstand potential criticism from rival observers, especially those with competing theoretical orientations, reportage in specific cases has to avoid pre-empting explanation, description or evaluation of those cases. Some terms often used in reportage do pre-empt explanatory or evaluative positions: for example, 'social class' and 'exploitation', respectively. However, this need not render all such accounts invalid as reportage. Rival observers with different explanatory strategies or evaluative dispositions may, in some cases, be able to transpose into their own frameworks empirical data initially reported in terms they do not accept.

In Runciman's view, the mode of reasoning most appropriate for explanation is 'quasi-experimental'. More specifically, 'practising sociologists should normally be looking neither for regularities nor for probabilities but for suggestive contrasts' (p. 168), capable of testing or extending theories about specific ranges of social phenomena. They would find it most rewarding to concentrate on hypotheses which history provided the empirical means to test in a quasi-experimental way, for example through comparison.[15] However, practical limits were imposed on the possible scope of generalization by the diversity of causal influences at work; often, any one of them is contingently sufficient if the others are held constant.

A reasonable objective is to devise quasi-experiments which prevent rival theorists talking past each other. Runciman recommended, as did Skocpol, the methods of similarity and difference set out by J. S. Mill. A decisive controlled comparison varying antecedent and initial conditions may be impractical in a specific case. However, thinking through what would be required in such a quasi-experiment makes it possible to see at what level rival theories differ – presupposition, theory, model or hypothesis – and whether such differences are reconcilable.

Description (or tertiary understanding) is liable to lapse into 'misapprehension' or 'mystification' (p. 244). Misapprehension may involve incompleteness, oversimplification, or ahistoricity. Mystification may take the form of exaggeration, ethnocentricity, or the suppression of relevant information. Description and evaluation are closely related in practice. This may lead to pejorative, hagiographical, or romanticized accounts being given. Many valid descriptions of the same experience are possible. The only test of whether or not such a description avoids the dangers stated, and therefore enlarges the reader's tertiary understanding, is that 'those who had the experience could in principle be brought to agree that it does' (p. 272).

Turning finally to evaluation, Runciman argued that moral, political and aesthetic values were only contingently related to the values of science. Value judgements could always be 'sifted out' (p. 303). In practice, all scholars shared 'some sort of tacit, if unspecific commitment to the value of benevolence'. They would tend to support whatever 'promoted the well-being as they interpret it themselves of the members of the society under study' and would be hostile to 'rulers who can be shown to have permitted, encouraged or even actively promoted avoidable hardship or distress for its own sake (p. 304).[16] In Runciman's view, in so far as scholars could 'properly submit to their readers' this 'one limited kind of evaluation' (p. 333), then explanation and description could, to that extent, be subordinated to it. The presumption of benevolence could be built into theoretical terms as long as explanations and description passed tests of validity.

Furthermore, there was nothing wrong with scholars with particular political biases trying to persuade readers of the validity of specific reports, explanations and descriptions which, if accepted, tended to support their point of view. However, they were at fault if they 'have chosen their reports, explanations and descriptions to illustrate rather than to test an answer to which they are pre-emptively committed in advance' (p. 324).

Social evolution

Turning to Runciman's second volume, he concentrated on two questions: what kinds of society – i.e. 'what modes and sub-types of the distribution of the means of production, persuasion and coercion' (1989e, p. xi) – were possible at given stages of evolution; and why did any given society evolve into one mode or sub-type rather than another?

The key actors in any society are, in Runciman's view, role-incumbents who actually pursue their 'systactic interests' (p. 38). The term 'systact' was invented by Runciman. It refers to a group or category – e.g. a class, status group, caste or faction – which contains people in roles which have 'a distinguishable and more than transiently similar location and, on that account, a common interest' (p. 20). Competition for power among the key actors determines how their societies work and evolve. At any point in time each society is the outcome of a process of competitive selection. The process selects not societies, groups or ideas, but *practices* – functionally defined units of reciprocal action informed by the mutually recognized intentions and beliefs of designated persons about their respective capacity to influence each other's behaviour by virtue of their roles' (p. 41; emphasis in original). Examples of practices include, say, share-cropping, or the use of firearms.

Practices carried out by incumbents of specific roles have, under specific conditions, a survival value deriving from a power advantage gained in terms of production and/or persuasion and/or coercion. The systacts and institutions in which these roles are located are the beneficiaries. In each case, the question 'which particular practices gives those systacts or institutions a power advantage?' has to be argued by testing hypothetical explanations through quasi-experimental contrasts between specific societies, institutions, systacts, roles and practices. Careful reportage is essential, paying attention to the wider context in which practices occur.

Institutions in two societies may be homologous (i.e. similar in structure) but perform dissimilar functions for the working of the societies, and produce dissimilar consequences for the way power is distributed within them. For example, share-cropping may work to the great landowners' advantage on large latifundia in one society, yet be a means of cooperative risk-sharing by village communities in another (p. 149). To cite another case, slavery produced little dissent in classical Athens, whereas Roman authorities were faced with the Spartacus revolt. Slave soldiers were successfully used in the Ottoman empire but were disastrous when employed by the Portuguese in East Africa (p. 128). By the same token, institutions with different structures may perform similar functions and produce similar outcomes with respect to power (i.e. they may be analogous). For example, in certain circumstances class may be the analogue of caste, in the allocation of people to occupational roles (p. 120).

Reportage and the testing of explanatory theories should be oriented to 'Darwinian' and 'Linnaean' typologies of societies (p. 49). A Darwinian typology locates societies in 'a presumptive evolutionary sequence' (p. 49). A Linnaean typology distinguishes reported societies synchronically with respect to similarities and differences in their modes of production, persuasion, and coercion. Runciman did not accept Michael Mann's separation of military from political power, since that was 'to confuse the different kinds of . . . inducements and sanctions which the incumbents of different roles can bring to bear on one another . . . with the different kinds of institution and forms of organization through which this is done' (pp. 14–15). Runciman's provisional version of a Linnaean typology, admittedly not 'totally rigorous or exhaustive' (p. 58) is summarized in figure 4.7. His proposed Darwinian typology will be indicated shortly.

Runciman's argument had three stages. First, he showed how systacts could be identified with reference to the location of roles and institutions within the modes of production, persuasion and coercion within societies. Second, he looked at these 'systems of social relations in motion' in a number of societies, asking in each case 'how does it work?' (p. 123). Third, he elaborated and tested the theory of competitive selection of practices. These three stages will be examined briefly.

An initial report on a society should pay particular attention to 'standard roles' and 'routine careers' (p. 70), such as those associated with leadership and the exchange of goods and services. Standard roles will, typically, involve practices impinging on all three dimensions of structure (production, persuasion, coercion). These effects are conditioned by a broadly positive correlation between the level of usable resources in a society, the complexity of its social organization, and the distance between roles (pp. 77–8).

The formation of systacts depends upon the existence of a common interest among role-incumbents, whose effects are not diluted or undermined by cross-cutting interests, internal divisions or hazy perceptions. A complex part is played by kinship and geography. Particular attention

---

Mode of production
(i)   Serfdom.
(ii)   Tenancy.
(iii)   Autonomous peasant cultivators.
(iv)   Debtor–creditor relations.
(v)   Indentured or corvée labour.
(vi)   Division of labour and ritual exchange by status group or caste.
(vii)   Wage–labour.
(viii) Slavery.

Mode of persuasion
(i)   Ritual hierarchy of purity and pollution.
(ii)   Hereditary status of king/nobles/commoners.
(iii)   Hierarchy orientated to the sacred.
(iv)   Ethnicity ascribed by birth.
(v)   Age-set ranking.
(vi)   Genealogical ranking by proximity to king, chief or head.
(vii)   Prestige according to functional value attributed to occupational roles.
(viii) Charismatic rank–order by personality/achievement.

Mode of coercion
(i)   Conscript army at disposal of ruler.
(ii)   Warrior aristocracy monopolizing weapons.
(iii)   Republic magistracy and civilian militia.
(iv)   Sovereignty decentralized among local magnates.
(v)   Servile administration and military directly answerable to monarch.
(vi)   Professional administrators and politicians voluntarily recruited.
(vii)   Aliens hired for pay.

Figure 4.7 Runciman's Linnaean typology of modes of production, persuasion and coercion

should be paid to systacts which are capable of engaging in collective action based upon collective consciousness and a sense of relative deprivation. Having identified the principal roles and systacts, in many instances 'there will almost be forced upon observers of all theoretical schools certain initial conclusions . . . broadly speaking, to the effect that there is one institution, or perhaps one set of practices observable in several institutions which is, self-evidently, central to the pattern of social relations as a whole' (p. 113). An example is the pervasiveness of economic sanctions (as distinct from ideological or coercive ones) in the early consumer society of eighteenth-century England.

The second stage of the argument explored how societies 'work'. At this point Runciman introduced his Darwinian typology. Although practices are the object of competitive selection, the typology locates them within the broader structural context which gives them significance. In other words, it is a typology of systactic patterns and modes of the distribution of power. A simplified and schematized version of it is set out in figure 4.8. The typology identifies the following: simple societies based upon generalized reciprocity such as hunter-gatherers in which power is limited; societies, some with specialized political roles (including the Melanesian 'big-men'), in which power cannot be stored but is continually being dissipated, for example through resource transfers to followers; societies (again, sometimes with specialized political roles) in which power is shared approximately equally within a restricted group; societies, such as Hawaiian chiefdoms, with specialized political roles and tribute collection, but where power is obstructed 'at a point just short of statehood' (p. 153); protostates, a category including patrimonial societies, societies (e.g. city-states) based on the distinction between citizens and non-citizens (e.g. slaves), warrior societies (e.g. the Teutonic knights), absolutist societies, feudal societies, and bourgeois societies such as seventeenth-century England; and, finally, industrializing nation-states, including capitalist, socialist, and authoritarian societies.

Using this typology as a framework, Runciman carried out a number of empirical comparisons. This enabled him to note, for example, that within the citizen sub-type of protostate, the classical Greek *polis*, a centre of administration and consumption, was 'an evolutionary dead-end', while the North Italian towns of the twelfth and thirteenth centuries, centres of production and commerce, nurtured mercantile capitalism 'with all the long-term consequences which that turned out to imply' (p. 198). Elsewhere, he suggested the great success of the Roman empire as a 'working absolutism' was due to its combining all four of the major functional alternatives available to that type of protostate: a venal

Limited power	e.g. hunter–gatherer societies	Generalized reciprocity
Dissipated power	e.g. 'big man' societies	How can a usable surplus of power be attached to superordinate roles?
Shared power	e.g. societies dominated by adult male household heads	
Obstructed power	e.g. chiefdoms	
Protostates	e.g. • permanent state apparatus • institutionalized inequality • free-floating resources	How is the surplus to be institutionally distributed and applied?
subtypes:	Patrimonial Citizen Warrior Feudal Bourgeois Absolutist	
Industrializing nation-states	e.g. • wage–labour • secular rationalism • mass political mobilization	How is the surplus to be institutionally distributed and applied?
subtypes:	Capitalist Socialist Authoritarian	

Figure 4.8   Runciman's Darwinian typology of systactic patterns and modes of the distribution of power

bureaucracy, a service nobility, a professional mandarinate and special-ized slaves (pp. 228–30).

In the third stage of his argument, Runciman focused directly on the selective pressures causing societies to evolve, bearing in mind that 'Evolution is, by definition, movement away from rather than towards' (p. 297). He examined processes of regression, possible dead ends and turning points, and examples of rebellion, reform and revolution. Finally, he looked very briefly at a series of 'test cases' (p. 367). Instead of discussing these particular cases here, it will be more interesting to look at the tests Runciman applied to the competing intellectual practi-ces of Perry Anderson, especially in the latter's *Passages* and *Lineages*. Anderson was a worthy subject for this treatment since, like Runciman, he set his 'constructive and illuminating' analysis within a broadly evolutionary framework (Runciman, 1989b, p. 17). Runciman's review of Anderson, initially published in 1980, was reprinted in *Confessions of a Reluctant Theorist* (Runciman, 1989a).

In Runciman's view, Anderson's history 'implicitly recognizes' that the process whereby societies evolve is 'analogous, although by no means equivalent, to natural selection' (p. 203). Furthermore, he paid attention to homologues and analogues between societies. For Runci-man, these institutional and functional variations were evidence of the need for a wide variety of distinctive explanations to account for them. These explanations should be organized in terms of 'explicit and illumi-nating comparisons'. Unfortunately, Anderson diverged from this approach in two ways. First, he preferred to present his argument 'diachronically, case by case'; narrative took precedence over compari-son. Second, instead of exploring in an open-minded way how institu-tions related to their wider structural context and evolved over time, Anderson constrained his account 'within a narrative sequence in which certain sequences are taken to be expected in the absence of special explanation' (p. 194). This criticism of Anderson's approach, inciden-tally, is similar to the case made earlier against Smelser's *Social Change and Industrial Revolution*.

Three of the sequences assumed by Anderson were: first, that an agrarian empire dependent upon slavery faces insuperable internal contradictions, which become critical when imperial expansion ceases; second, that feudalism is a necessary precondition of an endogenous transition to capitalism; and, third, that in Western Europe the transi-tion from feudalism to capitalism was by way of an absolutist phase, during which the domination of the feudal aristocracy was perpetuated. Runciman set out to undermine the assumptions underlying these sequences. He pointed out, for example, that Anderson neglected the possibility that Japan's differences from Europe were at least as significant as its partial similarities in explaining that society's successful transition to capitalism. Likewise, he wrongly categorized England before the Civil War as 'absolutist'. Furthermore, by neglecting the part played by urban businesspeople in absolutist societies, Anderson failed to notice how similar were the French and Russian cases, even though one was western and the other eastern.

A comparison of the Roman empire with the later Han empire, in which slavery was at best marginal, suggested that the power and relative autonomy of large estate owners may have been a much more significant cause of imperial collapse than slavery. The Ottoman empire, with its servile soldiery and free peasantry (the reverse of the Roman situation) provided better material for Anderson's argument. By contrast, the Scandinavian case was less promising. With the end of the Viking conquests, agricultural slavery did not die out. The feudal mode of production was only partially adopted. Yet Sweden went on to develop 'one of the most successful absolutisms in Europe' (p. 206).

Despite his effective critique of Anderson, Runciman has produced no hypotheses of equivalent scope. As Anderson commented, 'Runciman's typology itself lacks any dynamic' (Anderson, 1990, p. 66). However, hovering in the background of volume two of the *Treatise* is the perception that Europe's 'dominance over the period from roughly the fifteenth century AD to the present is an unarguable social fact which has therefore to be explained.' This 'old question', as Weber called it could only be answered by way of appropriate quasi-experimental contrasts. Volume two was not 'directly addressed' at this question (Runciman, 1989e, p. 368). However, the implication seems to be that all such questions will be settled as sociology, anthropology and history move towards the ideal of a classification in which every single society 'has its own "Linnaean" polynomial and its own "Darwinian" niche' (Anderson, 1990, p. 57). This is a convenient point at which to introduce a contrasting approach to historical sociology, incorporating a trenchant rejection of evolutionist theory.

Structuration or evolution?

Anthony Giddens became a fellow of King's College, Cambridge in 1969. This followed a period of eight years as a lecturer in sociology at Leicester University. In the early 1960s Norbert Elias, nearing retirement as a university teacher, was teaching a course on sociological theory at Leicester. Despite their paths crossing in this way as junior and senior colleagues, Giddens's work shows little sign of having been greatly influenced by Elias. On the contrary, Giddens has forged his own distinctive approach to sociology. Ever since the publication of *Capitalism and Modern Social Theory* (1971) and *The Class Structure of the Advanced Societies* (1973), he has pursued the twin objectives of rethinking central problems in social theory and analysing the principal institutional features and tendencies in modern societies.

Giddens indicated the direction in which he was moving in 1976 with the publication of *New Rules of Sociological Method* (henceforth *New Rules*), a critique of 'interpretative sociologies'. This concluded by listing in summary form a series of propositions concerning the nature of society and sociology. The mid-1970s was a time of ambitious projects and manifestos, as has been noticed. However, Giddens modestly produced only nine 'rules', as opposed to the four hundred-plus theoretical propositions generated by Randall Collins the previous year in his *Conflict Sociology*. Collins was in pursuit of causal empirical explanations accounting for variations within and between complex interaction networks. By contrast, Giddens wanted a valid account of sociology, its subject matter and the relationship between them. Collins's conflict sociology 'emphasized the social construction of subjective realities and the dramaturgical qualities of action, while viewing these as based upon an underlying world of historically conditioned material interests' (Collins, 1975, p. 14). Giddens also set out, in a rather different way, to establish links between subjective meaning and the practical involvements of human beings in the material world.

To oversimplify, in *New Rules* Giddens argued that human beings make a meaningful social world by their skilled practical activity, not least in using language. By getting to know this language and the culture ('frames of meaning' and 'mutual knowledge') on which it draws, social scientists can analyse social conduct. Explanations should also take account of the causal conditions of human action, including the way social norms are related to power and the division of labour. For example, routine reflexive monitoring of conduct is expressed as 'intentions' and 'reasons' only when conduct is challenged with reference to moral norms backed by sanctions. When Durkheim and Parsons try to relate action to institutions, they cannot cope with inequalities of power and conflicts of interest. In fact, although human beings do not realize it, when they are constituting the social world through their activity, they depend on resources and conditions brought into being and reproduced through 'modes of *structuration*'. These modes of structuration – assymetrical power relations and forms of meaning and morality – are, in turn, reproduced through the interaction of human subjects (Giddens, 1976, pp. 155–8; emphasis in original).

During the early 1980s Giddens moved into the heart of the academic establishment, becoming a member of the Executive Committee of the British Sociological Association (1983), co-founder of Polity Press (1984) and Professor of Sociology at Cambridge (1985). The two works discussed here – *A Contemporary Critique of Historical Materialism* (1981; henceforth *A Contemporary Critique*) and *The Nation-State and Violence* (1985) – both stem from this period. As in the cases of Anderson, Wallerstein, Runciman and Mann, these books represent only part of an unfinished *magnum opus*. At the centre of both *A Contemporary Critique* and *The Nation-State and Violence* is the distinction between class-divided societies such as agrarian empires, and class societies, especially modern capitalist industrial nation-states. A third volume is to appear dealing with 'the institutional parameters of modernity' and 'the extraordinary dynamism of modern institutions' (Giddens, 1990, p. 305).

The first volume of the trilogy has a strong negative theme: a comprehensive attack on historical materialism, especially in the form of neo-evolutionary Marxism. More positively, Giddens also developed an approach to time-space distanciation, power, surveillance, the city and the state in class-divided societies and class societies. A number of these ideas were developed in the second volume at greater length, in a more integrated way and with more empirical support. Further ideas were also added. The present discussion will move freely between the two books.

It is worth beginning by briefly contrasting the approach to evolutionary theory taken by Giddens with that of Runciman. Giddens had 'some sympathy . . . with what is sometimes called "limited multilinear evolution"' (Giddens, 1981, p. 23) – with one major reservation. His main objection to evolutionary theories was their assumption, as he saw it, that 'adaptation' – essentially understood as the process of mastering the material environment – explained processes of social change. Logically, it did not. In any case, many simple societies (e.g. hunter-gatherers) have deliberately avoided maximizing their productive potential. 'Only with the advent of capitalism is there established a constant emphasis upon, and capacity for, the chronic expansion of the forces of production' (p. 22).[17] Criticism was aimed explicitly at Marx's evolutionary scheme.

In fact, Marx's scheme was also criticized by Runciman, 'because capitalist societies have evolved in a way different from that predicted by it, and for reasons that cannot be accommodated within it' (Runciman, 1983, p. 220). However, Runciman embraced not only the idea of evolution, but also the concept of adaptation. In his view, adaptation is a process occurring at the level of specific roles in response to the competitive selection of practices. Adaptation consists of changes in the practices associated with specific roles as the balance of advantage flowing from particular practices alters (Runciman, 1989e, p. 291). Runciman focused his attention not upon the relationship of whole societies to material environments, but upon the relationship of practices, roles and institutions to modes of production, persuasion and coercion within specific societies. Potential explanations of particular processes of competitive selection and adaptation had to be tested through quasi-experimental contrasts. As developed by Runciman, the idea of evolution did not provide a general explanation of social change, so much as suggestions about which social relationships to explore if you wanted specific explanations of particular changes.

Runciman's approach inevitably leaves gaps. For example, as Anderson pointed out, Runciman's focus upon just one aspect of society, the distribution of power, is 'even more single-minded than Mann's' (Anderson, 1990, p. 66). Furthermore, despite his work on the origins of states in archaic Greece (Runciman, 1989d), Runciman generally paid little attention to the multiple origins of the wide range of competing practices. He showed more interest in the subsequent process of selection. Also, although reportage has, in his view, to take full account of 'the intentions and beliefs constitutive of the agents' observed behaviour' (Runciman, 1983, p. 77), specific explanations of social change through social selection do not: 'Given the initial conditions, it is the practices themselves which are "the" causes of the change, not the state of mind of those performing the actions which constitute them' (1989e, p. 286).

Giddens objected to what he saw as evolutionary theory's neglect of 'the knowledgeability of human subjects' (Giddens, 1981, p. 22). His own theory of structuration postulated knowledgeable human actors who express meanings (embodied in rules) and exercise power (drawing upon resources). Human beings creatively engage in '*situated practices*' which lead to the '*reproduction* of social systems across time-space'. The knowledgeability of these actors is, however, 'always *bounded*, by *unacknowledged conditions* and *unintended consequences* of action' (pp. 27–8; emphasis in original).

Rejecting evolutionary theory does not mean neglecting time as an aspect of society. In fact, the structuration of social systems occurs within at least three time-frames, as expressed in everyday social interaction, the human lifespan, and the generational reproduction and transformation of institutions. Questions of time are closely related to questions of space. Both may be expressed in terms of presence and absence. For example, while hunter-gatherers experience 'high presence-availability', developments in transport and communications permit 'time-space distanciation' (pp. 4–5). Technological advance (in record keeping, time measurement, surveillance capacity, and so on) facilitates the concentration of allocative (material) and authoritative (political or coercive) resources within various forms of 'storage container' (p. 5) or 'power container' (1985, p. 13). Cities and nation-states are two key examples.

The basic logic for classifying social institutions derives from the structural properties of social systems. The principal types of institution are: symbolic orders (and modes of discourse) which express the property of signification; the law (and legal sanctions) which express the property of legitimation; political institutions which express domination through authoritative resources; and economic institutions which express domination through allocative resources. These distinctions apply, in principle, to all societies.

However, with modernity, four 'institutional clusterings' become prominent, of which 'None is wholly reducible to any of the others' (1985, p. 5). These clusterings are associated with heightened surveillance, capitalistic enterprise, industrial production, and consolidated central control of the means of violence. Exploration of these clusterings is part of the task for a 'Discontinuist interpretation of modern history' (p. 31); in other words, one based on the perception that 'originating in the West but becoming more and more global in their impact, there has occurred a series of changes of extraordinary magnitude when compared with other phases of human history' (p. 33).

More specifically, the development of capitalism marked 'a series of fundamental discontinuities with previous history' (Giddens, 1981, p. 81). At first sight, this may seem to refer back to Weber's 'old question' (Runciman, 1989e, p. 368) about the origin and nature of the competitive advantage achieved by European societies since the early modern period. However, Giddens's main point is that analysis of the contrast between the world before and after these great changes is often more illuminating than discussion of the historical continuities which link the two worlds. Understanding the discontinuities helps carry out '*the* task of "sociology" ' which was 'to analyse the nature of that novel world in which, in the late twentieth century, we now find ourselves' (Giddens, 1985, p. 33; emphasis in original).

From class-divided to class societies

The key discontinuity for Giddens is between class-divided societies – which have classes, but whose organizational principles are not based on class – and class societies whose organization is indeed class-based (see

Simple societies	Limited time–-space distanciation: nomadism, kinship, tradition.
Class-divided societies: general	Increased time–space distanciation: • literacy enhances surveillance capacity; • cities as power containers; *But* in agrarian empires cosmpolitan ruling class at centre is superimposed on segmental polity of local villages; no labour market; property inalienable; empires have frontiers, not borders.
Class-divided societies: absolutist states	Increased time–space distanciation: • war and diplomacy within interstate system fosters territoriality, mutual surveillance, improved military technology; • development of sovereignty, rational legal codes, carceral organizations, improved fiscal system and centralized state administration as aspects of enhanced internal surveillance capacity.
Class societies: capitalist societies/ nation-states	Increased time–space distanciation: • nation-state as principal power container within international economic, political, military and symbolic systems; • insulation of economic, political and military spheres within nation-states; • capitalism, industrialism and the nation-state mutually supportive but not reducible to each other; • interplay between nationalism, sovereignty and citizenship; • dialectic between internal pacification and contestation in four key institutional clusters: (a) surveillance (resisted within polyarchic political system); (b) private property (resisted by wage–labour within limits imposed by capitalistic labour contract); (c) commodified urban environment (resisted by ecological social movements); (d) military violence (opposed by peace movements).

Figure 4.9   Giddens on simple, class-divided, and class societies

figure 4.9). A subordinate distinction is made between, on the one hand, class-divided societies such as agrarian empires, city-states and feudal societies and, on the other hand, simple or primitive societies such as hunter-gatherers and settled agricultural communities which do not have classes. Within class-divided societies (sometimes referred to as traditional states) there is an important sub-category: absolutist states.

Time-space distanciation is very restricted in simple band societies. Their nomadism gives them some extension through space. Extension backward in time in mediated by kin relations between the generations, living and dead, and the collective memory embodied in tradition. Kinship and tradition remain powerful in more complex class-divided societies within urban and rural communities. However, rulers in city-states and agrarian empires have two new sources of power. First, the technology of writing provides a means of information storage, surveillance and administrative control. Second, cities are major power containers, concentrating the religious, political and military means to dominate the surrounding countryside from which they derive economic resources through trade and taxation.[18]

Traditional states are segmental and heterogenous. Within them, networks of political and economic life are not closely related to each other. The effective authority of the central state administration over local rural communities is limited and intermittent. There are no labour markets and there is very little alienability of property. Taxation is little more than taking booty by force from unwilling peasants. The military do not so much administer borders as defend frontiers. Internal social control by the ruler is most effective among the bureaucracy. It is only intermittent in the outlying peasant villages. The unified and cosmopolitan cultural world of the ruling class is far removed from the beliefs and practices of local rural communities. No society belonging to any of the categories considered so far existed in isolation. Simple societies typically belonged to local cultures containing other bands or tribes. City-states traded with others. Feudal states fought with others. Agrarian empires threatened their neighbours and were threatened by them. However, a distinctive and highly developed system of interstate relations came into being with the dominance of absolutist states in Europe during the sixteenth and seventeenth centuries.

In the period of absolutism, relations among the ruling classes of competing states, sometimes peaceful, sometimes warlike, became more orderly and rule-bound. Elaborate diplomatic techniques developed in conjunction with increased emphasis upon territoriality, mutual surveillance, the maintenance of precise boundaries between states, and a distinctive ideology of sovereignty. Warmaking provided a strong incentive for concentrating authoritative and allocative resources in the hands of the state. It also stimulated improvement in military technology (e.g. more effective field artillery), rationalization of organization and discipline within the armed forces, and a great advance in naval capacity, including the invention of ships that could sail in all weathers and brave the Atlantic. The great voyages of discovery provided knowledge of the globe as a whole for the first time as well as bringing new wealth to Europe from the New World. However, Giddens commented, 'it would be foolish to press all of this into some sort of functionalist frame' (1985, p. 92).

This last remark was, perhaps, directed against Wallerstein. By contrast, Giddens was more sympathetic to Anderson's approach to absolutism. This sympathy did not extend to Anderson's 'progressivist' desire to locate the modern state's origins in 'a disintegrating medieval order' (p. 83). However, Giddens agreed that absolutist states were hybrids combining 'surface "modernity" ' with 'a subterranean archaism' (p. 93). His own account stressed the relative modernity rather than the continuing archaism. He emphasized three aspects of absolutism: first, expansion and centralization of administrative power, as authority was displaced upward at the expense of great landowners and peasant communities; second, the development of rational legal codes enacted by the state, backed up by carceral organizations designed to enforce social discipline; and, third, reforms in fiscal administration to cope with the enormous strain imposed by military involvements.

As the absolutist state solidified, the market and the cash nexus penetrated into more areas of life. The maxims of Roman law gave increased recognition to a distinct economic sphere and helped define the private rights of those who owned property or sold their labour. Meanwhile, taxation provided the means and incentive for improving the state's capacity to monitor and regulate the population.

The interstate system of European absolutism helped shape the system of nation-states which succeeded it in the modern world. Giddens defined a nation-state as 'a set of institutional forms of governance maintaining an administrative monopoly over a territory with demarcated boundaries, its rule being sanctioned by law and direct control of internal and external violence' (p. 121). The nation-state enabled 'capitalist society' to exist (p. 141). Understanding each helps make sense of the other.

In Giddens's view, capitalism – the form of economic enterprise arising in sixteenth-century Europe – marked a 'massively sharp wrench' (p. 132) away from traditional ways. Capitalism entailed an advance in commodification within social relationships, including the employment of labour power. Capitalist societies, as distinct from capitalism, originated around the beginning of the nineteenth century. To understand them, attention must be paid to the interplay between industrialism (which by itself lacks an inner dynamic), capitalism (which is driven by the pursuit of profit) and the nation-state (which delimits the external borders and key internal boundaries of the capitalist society).

The state's autonomy in a capitalist society is conditional on a process of capital accumulation which is outside its control and which extends beyond its territorial borders. However, the state maintains the insulation between the 'economic' sphere based upon private property and the capitalist labour contract and the 'political' sphere based upon citizenship rights (the franchise) and nationalism. This insulation is intrinsic to the character of capitalist societies as class societies.

The relationship between commodified wage-labour and the private ownership of capital is the basis of class conflict which plays a much more central and dynamic role than in class-divided societies. However, as already mentioned, the institutions shaping class conflict are closely tied to three other clusterings, all of which express the interplay between capitalism, industrialism and nation-state. These are: institutions radically increasing surveillance capacity within the political and economic spheres (including the workplace); institutions through which industrial capitalism transforms the connections between social life and the material world, producing a 'created environment' (p. 146), especially in the form of modern urbanism; and, finally, institutions mediating the control of violence, especially military power.

This leads to Giddens's central thesis, which is as follows:

> In industrial capitalism there develops a novel type of class system, one in which class struggle is rife but also in which the dominant class – those who own and control large capital assets – do not have or require direct access to the means of violence to sustain their rule. Unlike previous systems of class domination, production involves close and continuous relations between the major class groupings. This presumes a 'doubling up' of surveillance, modes of surveillance becoming a key feature of economic organizations and of the state itself. (pp. 159–60)

Surveillance and citizenship

As administrative coordination by the state increased with the transition from absolutism to the nation-state, internal pacification occurred. The new industrial order was stabilized, nationally and internationally, by a concentration of authoritative resources. More specifically,

> . . . the correlate of the internally pacified state – class relationships that rest upon a mixture of 'dull economic compulsion' and supervisory techniques of labour management – is the professionalized standing army. The process of internal pacification . . . is only possible because of the heightened administrative unity that distinguishes the nation-state from previous state forms. On the other hand, this very administrative unity depends upon the 'infrastructural' transformations brought into play by the development of industrial capitalism, which help finally to dissolve the segmental character of class-divided societies. (p. 160)

Infrastructural transformations brought about by mechanized transport, the electronic media, computerization and so on were complemented by the systematic collection of statistical and other data, allowing a 'vast expansion of the reflexive monitoring of social reproduction that is an integral feature of the state' (p. 181). As the term implies, internal pacification largely eradicated the means and habit of violence, both from the streets and from the labour contract. As violence diminished, there was an expansion of 'disciplinary power' (Foucault's term), for example through new forms of 'sequestration', such as lunatic asylums.

Total institutions of this kind provided locales in which a high degree of supervisory control could be exercised. Intense monitoring and strict regulation were techniques applied not only by the state to 'deviants' in total institutions, but also, as far as possible, by private employers to their employees in the work place. The latter, of course, had more opportunity to exercise countervailing power as part of a 'dialectic of control' (p. 186).

Internal pacification was complemented by 'regionalization' (p. 193), in other words, the multiplication of heterogenous locales due to uneven development, the complex intersection of product, labour and housing markets, and so on. This process of fragmentation was, in turn, compounded by the relocation 'behind the scenes' of basic human events such as birth and death, excluding them from daily life and so suppressing the existential contradictions which give moral life its depth and meaning. The ensuing psychological emptiness prepared the ground in which nationalism took root in the industrial capitalist nation-state.

In Giddens's view, nationalism has to be understood in the broader context of class, sovereignty and citizenship. 'Polyarchy' (p. 199), or rule by the many, is generic to the nation-state. Citizenship rights are the counterpart of the state's sovereignty. The irreducible interdependence between rulers and the population at large allowed the latter to bargain forcefully for rights. To borrow T. H. Marshall's tripartite distinction, they pursued civil rights to limit police powers, political rights to monitor state administration, and economic rights to counter-act their disadvantageous position in the sphere of production.

Ironically, the enactment of citizenship rights to some extent facili-tated class domination through surveillance. As already noted, the key site was the capitalist labour contract. It excluded workers from influence over the organization of the workplace. This exclusion was a manifestation of 'bourgeois' civil rights protecting the rights of private property. Only in the political sphere could workers exercise a franchise denied them within the workplace. Within both the political and the economic spheres, citizenship rights have been 'a *focus* of class conflict' (Giddens, 1982, p. 174; italics in original).

Civil, political and economic (i.e. social) rights were 'three arenas of *contestation* or *conflict*' (Giddens, 1985, p. 205; emphasis in original), each with its distinctive form of surveillance. Struggles over civil rights were focused upon the law court and entailed police surveillance. Political rights resolved around parliamentary institutions and the 'refle-xive monitoring of state administrative power' (p. 206). Economic rights were fought over at the workplace and in the context of managerial surveillance of production.

Giddens emphasized the active struggles by individuals and social classes over citizenship rights, the fact that successes were potentially reversible, and the significance of international relations, especially war, in shaping outcomes. In contrast, Marshall stressed the rhythm and 'logic' of the historical process through which citizenship rights had been realized in Britain. Giddens drew attention to differences between his own and Marshall's account. However, they were not as far apart as he implied.

For example, Giddens noted that civil and political rights developed together. In other words, the separate spheres of the economic and the political appeared at the same time rather than being 'as Marshall describes them, successive steps in the expansion of "citizenship" in general' (Giddens, 1982, p. 173). This oversimplified Marshall's posi-tion. In fact, Marshall acknowledged that a distinct political sphere with its characteristic form of political citizenship appeared as early as the eighteenth century (in this context, 1689–1832), during the 'formative period' of civil rights.

In Marshall's view, the nineteenth century saw more people entering the public sphere through 'the granting of old rights to new sections of the population. In the eighteenth century political rights were defective not in content, but in distribution' (Marshall, 1963b, p. 80). Marshall emphasized the gradual process of empowerment of the mass of the citizenry in the political sphere as industrial capitalism developed. By contrast, Giddens laid stress on the restriction of workers' rights in the economic sphere. However, both acknowledged the existence of separate spheres, and observed that working-class pressure for increased social/economic rights became strong in the economic sphere through the agency of trade unions. Both agreed that a regime of social/ economic rights would contradict at many points a social order governed by the market and the capitalist labour contract.

It is true that Giddens stressed the different and conflicting roles played by the bourgeoisie and the working class in achieving and implementing these rights. He also speculated about the implications of his analysis for a theory of socialism. However, this analysis was not incompatible with Marshall's account, despite the latter's evident political preference for the vigorous individual rather than the obstructive collectivity clogging up the market. Even here there is some similarity of tone. Giddens sounded a distinctly Marshallian note in the following comment: '[Union] power has turned out, in some circumstances and contexts at least, to be quite formidable. But as sheerly negative power it almost inevitably tends to be obstructive – and often is obstructive – to those who actually form policies either in industry or government' (1982, p. 174).

Although Giddens very usefully located citizenship in the context of power struggles involving the state, capital and surveillance strategies, in one respect, at least, Marshall's was the more sophisticated account. He brought the education system into his analysis as an institutional order at least as relevant to social rights as the sphere of economic production. Both in the schoolroom and on the shop floor, expectations about social rights challenged the dictates of *laissez-faire*. Unions made demands which took little account of the employers' market position. School-leavers thought their grades should get them the jobs they 'deserved', irrespective of supply and demand. The education system does not figure very largely in Giddens's discussion of citizenship.

Giddens and Marshall are closer together, intellectually, than they are to some more recent commentators. Both were preoccupied with the relationship between citizenship and social class. By contrast, Bryan S. Turner and David Held have been more interested in the use of civil and political rights to assert specific social rights within contexts other than social class: for example, gender, race, ethnicity, the family and the environment.[19] They raise, but do not resolve, the question of whether gains on these fronts are transforming the relationship between labour and capital or, instead, are 'permitted' because they occur in a segregated political sphere which leaves the economic sphere untouched.

However, the relationship between citizenship and social class remains central to the debate. Citizenship is negotiated with and through the state; social class is shaped by the market. As Ira Katznelson has noted, markets cannot reproduce themselves unaided: 'From the outset, therefore, state intervention to secure the functioning of markets and to mitigate their outcomes defined a *contested* terrain of discourse and policy with regard to capitalism, the state and citizenship'. Tensions result throughout the welfare state: between clientship and citizenship; between autonomy and subjection to therapy; between universalism and ascriptive identities; between 'equal' opportunity and unequal outcomes; between needs and deserts; between free exchange and planning; and so on (Katznelson, 1988, pp. 523, 528–9; italics in original).

Nationalism

Giddens argues that the ideology of nationalism supplies a patina of tradition and allows dominant classes to define and appeal to 'the national interest'. In some nation-states, nationalism may provide a means of linking together the universalistic, centralized administrative organization of the state with a wide variety of localized cultures whose legitimacy is acknowledged. In others, however, it might constrict citizenship rights and emphasize the people's duty to obey national leaders controlling the state, to advance the nation's cause against its rivals. This leads to a consideration of the external face of the nation-state.

The internal pacification of nation-states in Europe during the nineteenth century occurred in the context of increasingly industrialized warfare, drawing upon and stimulating science and technology. For example, Britain participated in fifty major colonial wars between 1803 and 1901. A major outcome of World War I was international recognition that nationhood and the nation-state should be the norm. A system of mutual surveillance was established through international organizations such as the League of Nations and, later, the United Nations.

Military service by conscripted soldiers during that war strengthened the connection between national sovereignty and citizenship rights. More generally, the two world wars have had a large influence upon the development of class struggles within participating nation-states, for example through the displacement of existing ruling classes (in Germany and Japan) and by enabling large social security programmes to be pushed through (as in Britain).

The importance of military aspects of the nation-state does not imply they are ruled (as C. Wright Mills suggested) by a 'military-industrial complex' (Mills, 1956, p. 247). In fact, the separation between the 'economic' and 'political' is matched by insulation between the 'political' and the 'military'. The existence of military governments in the Third World is an indication that the states concerned are relatively underdeveloped in terms of centralized administrative coordination; they have not yet become proper nation-states.

Giddens distinguished among nation-states according to their geopolitical locations within a bipolar world state system – focal/hegemonic, adjacent/subsidiary, central/aligned, central/non-aligned, peripheral/aligned or peripheral/non-aligned (1985, p. 267) – and modes of original state formation (p. 269): classical (e.g. France), colonized (e.g. United States), post-colonial (e.g. Nigeria), or modernizing (e.g. Japan). The complexities expressed in distinctions of this kind showed up the limitations of an analysis giving too much prominence to the 'world capitalist economy'. On the one hand, Wallerstein's analysis overemphasized exchange relationships at the expense of the global spread of capitalist production; on the other hand, economic institutions were interwoven with political institutions (the nation-state system), symbolic orders (the global information system) and international laws and other sanctions (enforced through the world military order).

Giddens's analysis of the modern nation-state led him towards moral and philosophical issues. At the end of *A Contemporary Critique* he argued that 'A philosophical anthropology relevant to socialism' must come to terms not only with the 'empty routines of everyday life' in the world created by capitalism but also with 'the shadow of possible destruction' (1981, pp. 251–2). *The Nation-State and Violence* concluded by recognizing the difficulty of reconciling the state's monopoly of violence with received political ideas about the 'good society'. The potential for totalitarian rule is inscribed in the nation-state's capacity for surveillance and terror, especially if linked to nationalism. Furthermore, tensions, struggles and social movements centre upon each of the four institutional clusters.

People organize to defend democratic freedoms against surveillance, advance labour's claims against capital, demand global peace in the face of military power, and defend ecological interests against the harm done through the 'created environment'. These and other movements 'exist in the same "arenas of historicity" as the organizations they oppose, seek to modify or create' (p. 318). The actors involved have self-consciously reflected on history and, as a consequence, seek to alter it.

Giddens concluded that rights are always liable to erosion, and need defending, especially against the state. A normative political theory of control of the use of violence within and between nation-states is needed. So is a critical theory which builds on historical understanding to show how institutions can be transformed. At this point the sociologist must turn towards philosophy. Similar concerns have been expressed by a philosopher who has turned to sociology:

> It is the sphere of coercion, of politics, which is now crucial . . . [The] political order can neither be diminished and consigned to the dog-house, nor will it wither away. A new kind of need for coercion or enforcement of decisions has arisen. The new affluent economy requires an enormous and largely lumpy, indivisible infrastructure. Strategic decisions concerning its deployment and form affect enormous populations for long periods and often do so irreversibly. This infrastructure is not, and cannot be, spontaneously generated, but needs constant attention and servicing. The state is now largely the name for the cluster of agencies that perform this role. How it is to be organized and checked, in conditions simultaneously of moral premiss-lessness [sic] and of great economic leeway – that is the question. (Gellner, 1988, p. 278)

This question is taken up, indirectly at least, in the final chapter. In the mean time, there is one final aspect of the third phase worth discussing briefly.

Evolution and discontinuity (2)

In the third phase of post-war historical sociology, the distinction between evolutionist and discontinuist approaches has become more visible. This distinction is obviously not a recent one. Giddens in *A Contemporary Critique of Historical Materialism* (1981) and Mann in *The Sources of Social Power* (1986) – both discontinuists – were anticipated, in important respects, by Gellner in *Thought and Change* (1965) and Foucault in *The Archaeology of Knowledge* (1972; see Poster, 1984, pp. 74–8). As has been seen, Bendix was issuing warnings in the 1950s and 1960s about the evolutionism implicit in structural-functionalist vocabulary. On the other side, the line stretches back from Runciman (1989e) and Anderson (1974a; 1974b) to include (for example) Lenski (1966), the later Parsons (1966; 1971) and Marshall (1963d).

It is important that differences of approach should not become battle lines – that would obscure the many overlaps that exist. For example, discontinuists oppose the idea that, as a society adapts to its environment, endogenous mutations are stimulated which pass through a determined sequence of stages. But so do Runciman and Anderson.[20] Discontinuists concentrate on identifying discourses, structures, tensions and contradictions intrinsic to specific totalities such as civilizations, cultures and epochs. However, a writer like T. H. Marshall who expounded the unfolding logic of citizenship was also able to make a major contribution to our understanding of the self-contradicting discourses of modernity, a contribution that is, in principle at least, detachable from his evolutionist tendencies. To take another example, in his discussion of the absolutist state, Anthony Giddens feels able to draw upon Perry Anderson, albeit critically, to buttress parts of his own case (e.g. Giddens 1985, pp. 93, 97). John Hall, who develops arguments from both Mann and Gellner in *Powers and Liberties*, happily presented himself as an evolutionist (1985, pp. 17–19, 249).

Discontinuist accounts do not depend upon assumptions about whether or how totalities are causally related to each other in the flow of history. However, they do not exclude, and sometimes incorporate, accounts of the way particular totalities came, or might have come, into existence.[21] Furthermore, they may observe secular tendencies within totalities; for example, Bloch's account of the transition from the first to the second feudal ages.[22]

This is obviously not a new debate. Nor was it new four decades ago, when Fernand Braudel commented in a review of George Gurvitch's *La Vocation Actuelle de la Sociologie* (1950) that 'Some dead things have to be killed twice'. Braudel was referring to Gurvitch's enthusiastic attack on unilinear evolutionism. Braudel recalled that before World War II Bloch dissented from the 'sacrosanct principle of continuity' at a meeting of modern French historians – and received a frosty reception for his pains (Braudel, 1953, p. 348). However, Braudel feared that Gurvitch would go too far. In the course of his vigorous critique of evolutionism as a philosophy of history he might make it impossible for sociologists to use the past. They would become isolated in the 'brief living present' (p. 349).

Like Gurvitch, Braudel rejected unilinear evolutionism. Furthermore, as has been seen, he happily incorporated aspects of Gurvitch's anti-evolutionist theory. However, Braudel felt perfectly comfortable writing about (for example) the way each society in its own zone within the world-economy 'was responding to a different economic obligation and found itself caught by its very adaptation, incapable of escaping quickly from these structures once they had been created', although (he added) this adaptation 'had nothing of the foregone or mechanical conclusion about it' (1984, pp. 63–3).

Elsewhere, he argued that his empirical research had shown, inside and outside Europe, 'the same sequence of events, the same creative evolution', proving that 'the market economy, the same everywhere with only minor variations, was the necessary, spontaneously-developing and in fact normal base of any society over a certain size' (1982, p. 600). In fact, Braudel found room for cycles, long waves, world-economies and human choice as well as evolutionist ideas in his work. He depended utterly on none of them. As has been seen, the result was an interpretation of capitalism and civilization which had many convergences with Mann's discontinuist approach.

The debate between the two approaches has caught fire again in recent years.[23] The worst outcome of such a debate would be that all evolutionist vocabulary – e.g. adaptation, competitive selection – was stigmatized as entailing a unilinear, teleological view of history, and all discontinuist thinking condemned as ahistorical.

5   Historical Sociology in the 1990s

Historical sociology as an intellectual field

Historical sociologists can draw on a long tradition. It was all but killed off in the 1930s, and the 'second growth', from the 1950s onward, is still young. However, its internal dynamics are complex and it thrives in an ecological environment which is rich, complex and relatively uncontrolled. It is not easy to pick your way through it.[1] Eighteen historical sociologists have been considered at some length in this work – more precisely, thirteen sociologists (Parsons, Smelser, Eisenstadt, Bendix, Skocpol, Lipset, Moore, Wallerstein, Marshall, Runciman, Giddens, Mann and Elias), four historians (Thompson, Anderson, Bloch and Braudel), and one sociologist-cum-historian (Tilly). Although the selection has inevitable biases, the people and issues dealt with are central, representing a strategically important part of historical sociology as an intellectual field, one which can be further explored as a way of increasing our understanding of this field.

I will not be able to provide a comprehensive map of historical sociology as a dynamic configuration of individuals and groups in different positions within power balances, competing to define what is legitimate, prestigious and so on. In fact, the methodological and theoretical implications of such an exercise are the subject of lively dispute.[2] However, it is certainly possible to make a provisional assessment of 'the historical sociologist' as '*homo academicus*' (Bourdieu, 1988). The relevant issues are: first, whether historical sociologists have operated as 'outsiders', or as members of the relevant 'establishment'; second, the way they handle problems of involvement and detachment; third, their orientations towards theory, empirical generalization and primary exploration of historical data; and, fourth, the strategies of explanation they adopt.

Established and outsiders

One theme which must enter into any analysis of historical sociology as an intellectual field is the respective roles of established and outsider groups. It is closely related to the second theme, the management of involvement and detachment, to be discussed shortly. The issues are complex and resist easy formulation. Some examples will be explored, but first it must be stressed that insider/outsider distinctions are not just a matter of ethnicity (or race) and class. The strength of a scholar's identification with his or her nation is a significant variable, though not straightforward. For example, Bloch and Lipset are both strong patriots, but this factor enters much more evidently into Lipset's academic practice than Bloch's. Also, as already seen, there is a strong convergence between Bloch and Elias as historical sociologists, in spite of Elias's sceptical view of patriotism. The fight of female academics against the disadvantaged situation of women is another factor which is hard to assess (cf. Skocpol, 1988a). Here, however, the argument will be restricted to ethnicity and class, dealing only with a few of the more easily classifiable cases.

The major contribution of Jewish scholars, some of them exiles from continental Europe, or the American offspring of recent European immigrants, is very evident. So is the part played by the progeny of very comfortably-off, high-status families. A number of the scholars discussed in this book come from patrician or establishment backgrounds, including W. G. Runciman, Perry Anderson, Barrington Moore, and T. H. Marshall. First, however, let us take the cases of Reinhard Bendix and Norbert Elias. Both were brilliant emigré German Jews. However, Elias did not achieve in British sociology the secure position Bendix had carved out for himself in the United States by the mid-1960s. Even though Bendix could write, as late as 1990, 'I cannot be sure how American a sociologist I have become' (Bendix, 1990, p. 474), he nevertheless served on the council of the American Sociological Association and became its president. By contrast, Elias had to wait until long after he had reached retirement age for international recognition on a wide scale. Even though he spent most of his working life after World War II in the English-speaking academic world, his reputation even now is much higher in France and Germany than in the United States and Britain. For most of his life he was only marginally attached to academic institutions.

The relevant point is that no simple equation links marginality (or 'outsider' status) and capacity for detachment. What matters is not whether you are, or have been, an 'outsider' or a member of the

	Achieved	Ascribed
Outsiders	Barrington Moore Perry Anderson	Norbert Elias
Insiders	Reinhard Bendix S. M. Lipset	T. H. Marshall W. G. Runciman

Figure 5.1   Insiders and outsiders: some examples

'establishment' but, rather, how you are able or choose to deal with the experience available from either vantage point. It is possible, for example, to distinguish between the following categories: scholars who live most of their lives as 'ascribed outsiders'; scholars with establishment backgrounds who become 'achieved outsiders' by taking a political, intellectual or moral stance at odds with the rest of their class; 'ascribed insiders' who have been socialized into the establishment from an early age and who operate from within its values, broadly speaking; and 'achieved insiders' who have made it to the top from the fringes of the society or the profession. Each situation offers its unique opportunities and pitfalls (see figure 5.1).

Some qualifications should be added. First, 'achieved insider' status is the approved ending of the classic American success story. It is the category in which detachment is hardest to maintain, and requires the most deliberate commitment (compare Bendix and Lipset). Second, there is an evident distinction between outsiders, whether achieved or ascribed, who are genuine 'loners', and those who belong to a close-knit intellectual network providing a shared public identity (compare Moore and Anderson). Third, ascribed insiders vary in the extent to which they take for granted the class position they occupy, as opposed to being prepared to subject it to moral and political scrutiny (compare Marshall and Runciman). Having opened up the topic of involvement and detachment, I now turn to it directly.

Involvement and detachment

In a recent work entitled *Involvement and Detachment* (1987), Norbert Elias retold a story by Edgar Allan Poe about two brothers on a fishing boat. They were caught in a maelstrom. Terrified, they circled in the narrowing funnel of the whirlpool. However, the younger brother collected himself sufficiently to notice

> ... that cylindrical objects went down more slowly than objects of any other shape, and that smaller objects sank more slowly than larger ones. On the basis of this synoptic picture of the regularities in the process in which he was involved, and recognizing their relevance to his own situation, he made the appropriate move. While his brother remained immobilized by fear, he lashed himself to a cask. Vainly encouraging the older man to do the same, he leapt overboard. While the boat, with his brother still in it, descended more rapidly and was, in the end, swallowed by the abyss, the cask to which he had tied himself sank very slowly, so that gradually, as the slope of the funnel's sides became less steep and the water's gyrations less violent, he found himself again at the surface of the ocean and eventually returned to the living. (Elias, 1987a, pp. 45–6)

One of the lessons of this story is that detachment improves your survival chances. As the younger brother found, self-control and intelligent observation of processes made possible a degree of human control within a potentially threatening and rapidly changing situation. The span of control was small, but it was sufficient to save a life. This supreme effort of detachment was urgent and necessary precisely because the man in the story was vitally involved, both physically and emotionally, in the processes he was analysing.

Elias was very sensitive to the vulnerability and emotionality of human beings. In his work he explored our involvement in relations of interdependence with each other and with nature. He argued that fear and shortsightedness could be and, in some aspects of human affairs, had been overcome or alleviated. This occurs when sufficient detachment is developed to allow participants to observe objectively the processes occurring within the configurations to which they belong.

Elias demonstrated that the historical sociologist can be both involved and detached, relative to the subject of analysis: involved in the sense of empathizing with or entering into the human situations being examined; detached in the sense of being able to discount emotion-laden responses with get in the way of clear perception. Historical sociologists with these skills can make distant times, places and people seem alive, important and understandable. They can also make very close and familiar things to which we are comfortably accommodated seem strange, distant and less taken-for-granted.

In *Feudal Society*, Bloch provided a good example of these skills in practice, He made 'doubt . . . an "examiner" ' (Bloch, 1954, p. 81). Like an examining magistrate, he followed the instincts of the scientist and the advocate, using each to modify the excesses of the other. The advocate's interest in human motivation and moral interests was governed by a clinical disinterestedness. At the same time, Bloch resisted the temptation to dissect and manipulate the data by distributing its constituent parts into separate boxes, with a view to producing controlled reactions between them. Instead, he took his data in large lumps and tried to discern or 'listen to' the complex interactions going on within them. He was aware of the way human actions enter into the shaping and reshaping of structure; the way structural constraints and opportunities shape the exercise of choice; and the way these processes, intended and unintended, ramify through time and space.

This marriage of closeness and distance took another form in his use of anecdotes and examples. As a guide, Bloch rarely dwells for long on any single instance. Since his object is to show us the complex structure of feudal Europe as a whole, he has to travel quickly across time and space, scanning the territory. He alights briefly in specific places, giving us a 'feel' for the local topography and atmosphere, but then he moves swiftly on.

One brief illustration concerns the Northmen. There was a large element of control and calculation on the part of the Vikings. They were quite prepared to let certain communities – for example, isolated monasteries – buy themselves immunity from their raids, which brought back gold and prisoners with an exchange value in ransom payments. However, the Vikings inspired enormous panic, and seemed to embody the principle of chaos. This is not difficult to understand since

> ... these warriors of the North were men of strong and brute sensual appetite, with a taste for bloodshed and destruction, which manifested itself at times in great outbreaks partaking of madness, when violence no longer knew any restraint: one such occasion was the famous orgy in 1012, during which the Archbishop of Canterbury, whom till then his captors had carefully guarded with an eye to ransom, was pelted to death with the bones of the animals eaten at the feast. Of an Icelander who had campaigned in the West the saga tells us that he was surnamed 'the children's man', because he refused to impale children on the point of his lance, 'as was the custom among his companions'. All this sufficiently explains the terror spread by the invaders wherever they went. (Bloch, 1961, p. 19)

And having made his point, Bloch pushes on quickly to the next. The reader is drawn into a process of exploration and discovery. Bloch was an impressario, manipulating involvement and detachment, playing each off against the other. The tone is urbane, distancing, drawing on our capacity for empathy, but not indulging it.

It is interesting to assess some of the other writers discussed, in terms of the way they handle the dialectic between involvement and detachment. Compared to Bloch, Neil Smelser in *Social Change and the Industrial Revolution* was insufficiently 'detached' from his model and insufficiently 'involved' with his data. The most important characteristic of his data, from Smelser's point of view as a structural-functionalist, was that it could be organized in terms of the prescribed model. This consideration placed severe limits on which relationships within the data could be explored. The imagination was shut off. Neil Smelser's analysis of the early English textile industry and its workers removed all danger from the past. It underplayed the pervasive vulnerability and uncertainty of the human situation. But if these aspects of life in the early textile towns are more fully taken into consideration, a quite different assessment of the family's 'functions' becomes plausible.

An alternative approach which illustrates this is found in Michael Anderson's *Family Structure in Nineteenth-Century Lancashire* (1971). Anderson was concerned with the consequences for kinship relations of industrialization in the cotton town of Preston in the early and mid-nineteenth century. Like Smelser, he looked at data relating to the family, labour market practices, friendly societies, and poor relief. However, he also considered factors, such as migration patterns and the use of lodging houses, neglected by the former. Anderson and Smelser both looked for the purposes served by social practices, and both emphasized the interdependence between different activities and institutions. However, Anderson did not work from the 'top down' like Smelser, who assumed the family's primary function was socialization and tension management. Instead, he worked from the 'bottom up', exploring the functions which kinship ties fulfilled for individuals in a variety of critical situations stemming from economic fluctuations (e.g. unemployment) and domestic life cycles (e.g. pregnancy).

Smelser emphasized the stabilizing function of collectively-enforced normative controls – apparently assuming that the moral order of the rural village could operate in the 'frontier towns' of the cotton boom. By contrast, Anderson stressed the situational logic implicit in individual calculative behaviour under conditions of insecurity and distrust. Society in the cotton towns was a volatile mix of kinfolk, neighbours and strangers. If you needed help quickly you probably went to a relative first, since he or she might feel a residual sense of obligation – but this was by no means the only option. In Anderson's view, kinship ties were not the basis of a new social equilibrium organized around the family as value-instiller and norm-enforcer, to paraphrase Smelser. On the contrary, Anderson found that in mid-century Preston such ties were merely one part of a 'generalized exchange net' (p. 12), within which individuals made mainly short-term bargains with each other in times of need.

Returning briefly to Smelser, a distinctive feature of *Social Change and Industrial Revolution* was its covert assault upon Marxian historiography and, more generally, left-wing political ideology. This critique was largely implicit, but can be sensed throughout the text. Smelser concentrated on a stretch of history crucial to competing political myths. As you read, the suspicion grows that Smelser's intention was, in effect, to clear away an 'alien' ideology from a disputed strategic redoubt. Unfortunately, these undertones make the historical argument less convincing. They create nagging doubts about the author's objectivity, without actually surfacing as a clear message.

If that interpretation is correct, the 'scientist' and the 'advocate' are once more present in a single work. However, in the case of Smelser, unlike Bloch, they undermine rather than reinforce each other. Smelser comes over as a 'partisan expert witness' rather than an 'examining magistrate'. In this respect, he stands in the middle position on a dimension which has S. N. Eisenstadt, the 'scientist', and Seymour Martin Lipset, 'the advocate', at opposite ends.

In *The Political Systems of Empires*, Eisenstadt brought distant territory on to the cognitive map of social science. He showed that unfamiliar political structures exemplified discoverable regularities. Specific sequences of structural conflict or change were taken from their historical context and relocated, alongside similarly de-contextualized examples from other societies, in the appropriate boxes within his model. Unlike the analyses by Bloch, Elias and Bendix, Eisenstadt's argument takes little account of specific cultural forms, moral frameworks or political languages within different historical societies. Variations of this kind are collapsed into a dichotomy between embedded 'traditional' values and solidarities on the one hand and, on the other, 'autonomous' goals and 'free-floating' resources. Locating a social group or institution within such a dichotomy requires minimal involvement with the situations of individual or collective actors. Eisenstadt's model focuses upon contradictory principles of structure, not upon people coming to terms with dilemmas or engaged in acts of choice. However, these aspects of human action feed into processes of change, pushing them towards one possible option rather than another. The model's power to explain such processes is weakened by ignoring them.

If the uninvolved scientist neglects potentially valuable data about groups and institutions, the over-involved advocate risks becoming too closely identified with the point of view of specific groups and institutions. When, in *The First New Nation*, Lipset referred to a 'world-wide totalitarian conspiracy seeking to upset political and economical development from within' (p. 91), he aligned himself clearly with an identifiable Cold War stance towards left-wing opposition, both inside and outside the United States. It is also significant that in a book preoccupied with egalitarian values, no more than three pages should be devoted to the situation of American Blacks. *The First New Nation* is infused with national pride. As far as Lipset was concerned, 'the fact that this New Nation has succeeded in fostering economic growth and democracy under the aegis of equalitarian values holds out hope for the rest of the world' (1963, p. 343). The book clearly advocates the American model as an ideal to be pursued by later 'new nations'.

To summarize, distinctions have been made between four ways of handling the relationship between involvement (the capacity to empathize with and evoke the situation of particular participants in specific historical situations) and detachment (the capacity to observe processes and relationships objectively, discounting political/moral commitments and emotion-laden responses). Four tendencies have been identified: an 'examining magistrate' is able to achieve a creative balance between involvement and detachment, each complementing the other; by contrast, in the case of the 'partisan expert witness' the author's involvement with a particular viewpoint limits his or her capacity to be detached, and/or the effort to be detached inhibits overt expression or cultivation of that viewpoint; the 'scientist' achieves a high degree of detachment, at the expense of involvement; by contrast, the 'advocate' expresses a high degree of involvement, at the expense of detachment.

At this point it is worth bringing in Bendix and contrasting him with both Eisenstadt and Lipset. Bendix is as sensitive to processes of structural differentiation as Eisenstadt, but has much greater interest in the way groups such as public officials and industrial managers define their situations and adopt strategies to manage them. He is as aware as Lipset of the benefits bestowed by democracy, but absolutely determined to remain uncommitted to political totems.

Bendix emphasized one aspect of western liberalism – belief in the rationality, or potential rationality, of human beings – and used it as a means to question all ideologies, East and West. His most powerful advocacy has been directed against the claims of science as a 'secular theodicy' (1984, p. 125). His most penetrating empirical investigations have been concerned with the ideologies employed by powerful groups to advocate their interests. The deepest empathy felt by Bendix is with the detached reasoner who has a strong concern for human interests combined with a realistic perception of human vulnerability and gullibility. This category includes people like Norbert Elias and himself.

This analysis can be extended to other scholars examined in this book. It can be seen immediately from figure 5.2 that important work has been done by people working from each of the four perspectives just outlined. In fact, it is vital for the vigour of historical sociology as an intellectual field that all four should be represented. None should predominate. According to the analyses carried out in this present

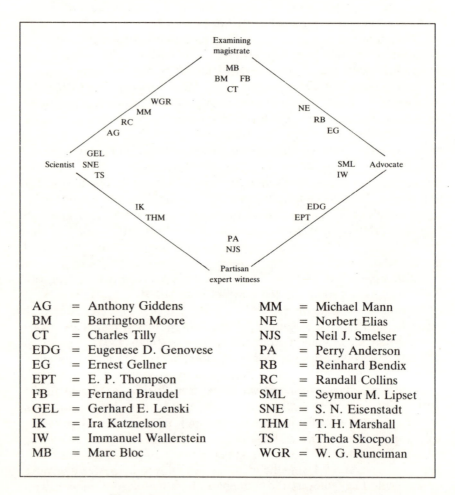

AG	=	Anthony Giddens
BM	=	Barrington Moore
CT	=	Charles Tilly
EDG	=	Eugenese D. Genovese
EG	=	Ernest Gellner
EPT	=	E. P. Thompson
FB	=	Fernand Braudel
GEL	=	Gerhard E. Lenski
IK	=	Ira Katznelson
IW	=	Immanuel Wallerstein
MB	=	Marc Bloc

MM	=	Michael Mann
NE	=	Norbert Elias
NJS	=	Neil J. Smelser
PA	=	Perry Anderson
RB	=	Reinhard Bendix
RC	=	Randall Collins
SML	=	Seymour M. Lipset
SNE	=	S. N. Eisenstadt
THM	=	T. H. Marshall
TS	=	Theda Skocpol
WGR	=	W. G. Runciman

Figure 5.2   Involvement and detachment

work, the clearest examples of 'examining magistrates' are Marc Bloch, Barrington Moore, Charles Tilly, and Fernand Braudel. It is striking that none of them is closely or systematically identified with any single theoretical viewpoint. 'Partisan expert witnesses' are to be found on the left and the right. They include Neil Smelser and Perry Anderson (see, for example, Runciman, 1989c). Three 'scientists' are S. N. Eisenstadt, Gerhard E. Lenski and Theda Skocpol. Two 'advocates' are Seymour Martin Lipset and Immanuel Wallerstein, scholars with very different political commitments.

There are some interesting intermediate cases. E. P. Thompson and Eugene D. Genovese both set their work in an explicitly Marxian framework. In this respect they resemble Anderson. However, both Genovese and Thompson identify strongly with the interests of the subordinate groups they have researched. This gives their work the undertones of advocacy. By contrast, in the cases of T. H. Marshall and Ira Katznelson, what is striking is the extent to which they achieve detachment within roles (respectively, liberal English gentleman and American Marxist intellectual) which impose strong pressures for overt expressions of political and moral commitment.

Norbert Elias, Reinhard Bendix and Ernest Gellner are three 'examining magistrates' whose work also conveys a keen desire to convert readers to a particular philosophical or sociological position which they can then, hopefully, exemplify in their own lives. Gellner is, on the surface at least, the most laid-back. However, works like *Thought and Change* (1965) and *Plough, Sword and Book* (1988) are sprinkled with warnings, advice and implicit invitations to consider political implications. The tone is urbane but urgent. Elias and Bendix are more evangelical. To oversimplify radically, Bendix is promoting reason against ideology, Elias sociology against fear and fantasy.

Finally, Michael Mann, W. G. Runciman, Randall Collins and Anthony Giddens all develop theoretical positions which combine detachment with full recognition of the part played by the perceptions, feelings and meanings of actors within social situations. Their views on methodology locate them with the 'examining magistrates'. However, they rarely deploy 'on the ground' (so to speak) in particular historical analyses the practical skills of combining involvement and detachment displayed by Bloch, Moore, Braudel or Tilly. This is not a comment on their capacity to do so: see, for example, Giddens on public executions, Mann on Tiberius Gracchus, Runciman on life in the Suez Canal Zone, and Collins on status competition in America.[3] It is, rather, a matter of choices made with regard to the use of intellectual energy.

The four 'examining magistrates' have all shown less interest than

Collins, Giddens, Runciman and Mann in developing coherent theoretical approaches. To oversimplify radically once again, Bloch, Moore, Braudel and Tilly have all tried to give coherence to as much empirical complexity as possible. By contrast, Giddens and Collins have tried to conceptualize as many dimensions or aspects of social reality as possible, within coherent theories. So have Mann and Runciman. However, the last-named, each preoccupied with the problem of power in society, have a still more ambitious goal. On the one hand, unlike the four 'examining magistrates', they do not want to sacrifice theoretical coherence to empirical comprehensiveness. On the other hand, unlike Giddens and Collins, they do not want to give up empirical comprehensiveness on behalf of theoretical coherence.

Exploration, generalization and theory

Turning to a further aspect of this intellectual field, it is possible to distinguish within it three activities: primary exploration of specific historical situations which have wider implications for understanding diversity and change; empirical generalizations which draw upon the explorations of others and refer, implicitly or explicitly, to theoretical issues; and systematic theorizing about processes of historical change, drawing upon the results of historical explorations and empirical generalizations to a greater or lesser degree (see figure 5.3).[4]

The interests of some scholars tend to veer towards one of the three points of the triangle, while still being 'in touch' with the aspects of historical sociology represented by the other two points. The work of others oscillates between two points of the triangle.[5]

The line between social theory and historical exploration is the one most ridden with tension. Work in this area is liable to be criticized by historians worried that inappropriate theories will be foisted on them.[6] Residual antagonism between historians and sociologists upon this front 'remains part of the informal academic culture', a guerilla war fought out 'in *sotto voce* comments in university staff bars' (McLennan, 1984, p. 139).[7]

This diffuse clash of academic cultures took a more specific form during the 1970s over the issue of structuralism. Louis Althusser's version of Marxism insisted on the need to cleanse social theory of 'historicism'. It called for a complete separation between the empirical study of phenomena in historical time and the formulation of concepts. It was deeply ironic that the historian E. P. Thompson's attack on Althusser and his supporters within sociology should introduce conflict between two disciplines whose mainstream traditions were both unsympathetic to structuralism.[8]

The historical sociologists examined in this book are spread fairly evenly between the three points of the triangle shown in figure 5.3. The inner triangle includes nine scholars who have incorporated large amounts of all three activities in their work, sometimes with a bias towards one or two of them. The particular location of individuals within these triangles is based only on the works considered in this present book. Almost all the people considered have done important

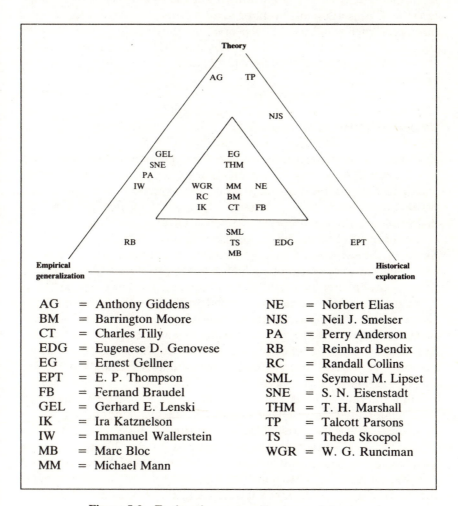

AG	= Anthony Giddens	NE	= Norbert Elias
BM	= Barrington Moore	NJS	= Neil J. Smelser
CT	= Charles Tilly	PA	= Perry Anderson
EDG	= Eugenese D. Genovese	RB	= Reinhard Bendix
EG	= Ernest Gellner	RC	= Randall Collins
EPT	= E. P. Thompson	SML	= Seymour M. Lipset
FB	= Fernand Braudel	SNE	= S. N. Eisenstadt
GEL	= Gerhard E. Lenski	THM	= T. H. Marshall
IK	= Ira Katznelson	TP	= Talcott Parsons
IW	= Immanuel Wallerstein	TS	= Theda Skocpol
MB	= Marc Bloc	WGR	= W. G. Runciman
MM	= Michael Mann		

Figure 5.3 Exploration, generalization and theory

work with other emphases. For example, Giddens has been involved in empirical research on elites (Giddens and Stanworth, 1974). However, such work is not taken into account here.

Not surprisingly, it can be recorded that Anthony Giddens and Talcott Parsons have a marked inclination towards theory construction, Reinhard Bendix towards empirical generalizations, and E. P. Thompson towards historical exploration. Lipset, Skocpol and Bloch all combine empirical generalization and historical exploration in roughly equal measure in their major works. Genovese has been more inclined to undertake empirical generalizations than Thompson. Anderson, Wallerstein, Eisenstadt and Lenski encompass theory and empirical generalization. Smelser's *Social Change and the Industrial Revolution* falls on the axis of theory and historical exploration. The inner triangle includes Braudel, Collins, Elias, Gellner, Katznelson, Mann, Moore, Marshall and Runciman.

Strategies of explanation

Four strategies of explanation recur throughout the works that have been explored here. These strategies emphasize, respectively: competitive selection, system contradictions, infrastructural capacities, and dominant routes of societal change. Figure 5.4 locates a number of historical sociologists according to which of these strategies they rely upon most heavily in the particular works discussed in this book. Smelser, for example, assumes that social change always follow a particular seven-stage sequence (A in figure 5.4). That is the strictest form of the 'dominant route' type of explanation. More typical is the strategy of identifying the origins and distinctive characteristics of a social configuration which typically produces the outcome you are particularly interested in; and contrasting it with the origins and distinctive characteristics of other social configurations which fail to produce this outcome. Both Moore's *Social Origins* and Anderson's *Passages–Lineages* sequence have this character.

Both are built upon dichotomies – in one case, between democracy and dictatorship (Moore), in the other between two kinds of absolutism developed in, respectively, Eastern Europe and Western Europe (Anderson). These dichotomies dominate the works. The main text of *Lineages* is divided almost equally between East and West. In *Social Origins*, the three case studies of democracy (England, France, United States) take up the same amount of space (152 pages) as the two studies devoted to dictatorship in the forms of fascism (Japan) and communism

(China). The long chapter on India concerns a society that is difficult to locate in terms of the previous analysis of democracy's social origins.

Barrington Moore and Perry Anderson both use comparison in at least two ways: first to indicate the unique character of each national case; and second, to produce generalizations which refer to several

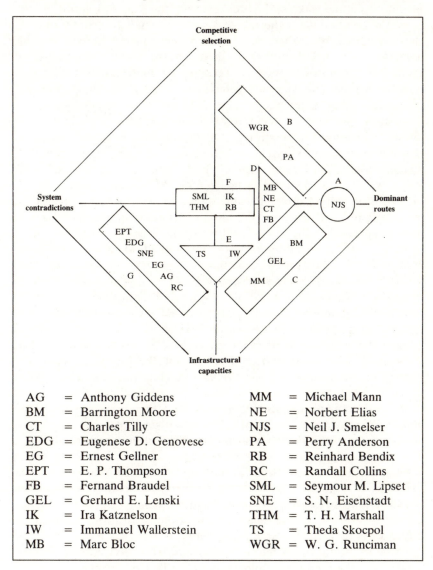

AG	= Anthony Giddens	MM	= Michael Mann
BM	= Barrington Moore	NE	= Norbert Elias
CT	= Charles Tilly	NJS	= Neil J. Smelser
EDG	= Eugenese D. Genovese	PA	= Perry Anderson
EG	= Ernest Gellner	RB	= Reinhard Bendix
EPT	= E. P. Thompson	RC	= Randall Collins
FB	= Fernand Braudel	SML	= Seymour M. Lipset
GEL	= Gerhard E. Lenski	SNE	= S. N. Eisenstadt
IK	= Ira Katznelson	THM	= T. H. Marshall
IW	= Immanuel Wallerstein	TS	= Theda Skocpol
MB	= Marc Bloc	WGR	= W. G. Runciman

Figure 5.4 Strategies of explanation

cases, e.g. the class/state configurations leading to democracy, fascism and communism (Moore), and the different varieties of absolutism prevailing in Eastern Europe and Western Europe (Anderson). *Social Origins* begins roughly where *Lineages of the Absolutist State* ends. Anderson focuses upon the conditions for the rise of a specific mode of production in the wake of the breakdown of the Roman Empire, Moore upon the conditions for the rise of a specific social class in the wake of the breakdown of the agrarian social order. In both cases, a specific configuration carried the vital 'seed', so to speak. The sequence feudalism–absolutism was the necessary precondition for capitalism (Anderson). Where the bourgeoisie achieved a dominant position within the polity, democracy ensued (Moore).

In each case, the argument about dominant routes is complemented by another explanatory strategy. Anderson incorporates evolutionist assumptions about the relative propensity of competing polities to become feudal (and, later, capitalist). He meets Runciman coming the other way, so to speak (B in figure 5.4). As has been seen, the 'old question' of why Europe became capitalist while other parts of the world did not – a version of the 'dominant route' approach – hovers in the background of the second volume of his *Treatise*.

Moore pays great attention to the infrastructural capacities of dominant and subordinate classes within agrarian polities, especially their ability to revolt and repress, respectively. Travelling in this direction, he encounters Mann coming the other way (C in figure 5.4). The latter's analysis of the sources of social power – crudely, the means available for getting things done – was open-ended. In order to 'close it down' and reduce the wide range of potential empirical analyses that could be conducted, Mann engaged in a search for the origins of European dynamism. As with Runciman, Weber's 'old question' continued to cast its spell.

A third occupant of this location between 'infrastructural capacities' and 'dominant routes' is Lenski. His *Power and Privilege* sketches an evolutionary pathway whose stages are distinguished with reference to the means of producing material surpluses. There is also a clutch of scholars – Elias, Bloch, Braudel, and Tilly (D in figure 5.4) – who each interweave three elements: a view of social life as a competition for survival, an emphasis on the power balances arising from infrastructural capacities, and a strong sense of direction in historical change (as expressed in, respectively, the civilizing process, the movement from the first to the second feudal ages, the shift from city-states to national states, and the increasing dominance of capitalized coercion).

By contrast, Wallerstein in *The Modern World-System*, and Skocpol in *States and Social Revolutions*, each combine the following: an emphasis on a single historical route, a concern for infrastructural capacities and a stress on system contradictions – focusing in one case upon agro-bureaucratic states (Skocpol), and, in the other, upon the modern world-system (Wallerstein). Furthermore, both are interested in the interplay between intra-societal and inter-societal relations, with special regard to the involvement of class actors and the state (E in figure 5.4). Skocpol stresses military conflicts between states, Wallerstein economic relations between national bourgeoisies. Skocpol interprets past social revolutions as being the outcome of contradictions within agro-bureaucratic societies exacerbated by pressure *from outside*, exerted by foreign states. Wallerstein forsees a future revolutioii as being the outcome of contradictions within the world-system exacerbated by pressure *from within*, exerted by antisystemic movements.

Although both minimize the part played by human volition in shaping the character of historical transformations, both nevertheless accept that groups can consciously alter their situation by mobilizing resources and responding positively to their situation – as in the case of revolutionary elites strengthening the state apparatus to defend their political position (Skocpol) or national bourgeoisies in the semiperiphery strengthening the state apparatus in order to move into the core.

Finally, there are two other clusters. One includes Marshall, Bendix, Lipset and Katznelson (F in figure 5.4). They all trace the 'unfolding' of the citizen-state relationship, identifying the main routes followed. Each focuses on contradictions within the process, such as the tension between citizenship and social class (Marshall), the authority crises brought about by modernization (Bendix), conflicts between the values dominant in the polity and economy (Lipset), and the divisions of a 'split consciousness' (Katznelson).[9] The other cluster includes Thompson, Genovese, Eisenstadt, Gellner, Collins and Giddens (G in figure 5.4). The explanatory strategies of these scholars all give a large place to the internal logic of empires, nation-states, class situations, global orders, and other kinds of 'system'. Their analyses indicate the resulting tensions and possibilities for transformation, including, on the one hand, the access of various groups to 'free-floating' resources or other means of facilitating human action and, on the other hand, the systemic limitations within which structuration occurs.

Historical sociology and capitalist democracy

So far, some important internal tensions within historical sociology have been identified with respect to established/outsider orientations, involvement and detachment, methodological approaches and strategies of

Phase I	Power and value conflicts marginalized.	Democracy expounded.
Phase II	Power and value conflicts rediscovered.	Democracy exposed.
Phase III	Power explored.	Capitalism explored and exposed.
Phase IV	Values explored.	Democracy re-examined.

Figure 5.5   Values, power and capitalist democracy

explanation. Now it is time to return to the content of the works examined, taking an overall view. Two arguments are to be developed. First, that the question of capitalist democracy's acceptability and viability links work in all three phases of post-war historical sociology. Second, that political and ideological changes within Western capitalist democracies and in their external relations have helped shape the problematic of historical sociology in successive phases. See figure 5.5.

The first phase: democracy expounded

After World War II, the American way dominated. It was heavily promoted through the mass media, with the willing cooperation of intellectuals. The ideal was a strong consensus based on emotional commitment and rational assent to a self-evidently just social order offering equality of opportunity. This ideal shaped a sociological perspective which assumed that within advanced industrial societies, especially as they became more like the United States, mutual adjustment was to be expected between, on the one hand, integrating national values and, on the other hand, the needs and demands arising within increasingly differentiated institutions and groups. Social systems usually solved the problems that were set for them. Capitalist democracy worked. These assumptions informed the work of Parsons, Smelser and Lipset.

What happened when processes of differentiation produced discordance between legitimizing values and the perceived interests of specific groups? Answers to this were: social systems readjusted as a matter of course (Smelser); stable conflict (e.g. the two-party system) would reinforce consensus (Lipset); it largely depended on the resources controlled by groups in strategic structural locations (Eisenstadt).

Eisenstadt's major work from this period was on pre-industrial empires, not capitalist democracy (although he had some relevant comments, as has been seen). In fact, structural-functionalist analyses of capitalist democracy paid little attention to the content of fundamental value-related disputes between groups, or the part played by power in settling them.

T. H. Marshall's essay 'Citizenship and social class' (1963d) originally appeared the year before Parsons's *The Social System* (1951). What links Marshall and Parsons is that both took seriously the official ideology of capitalist democracy as a description of the prevailing economic order and political order in Britain and the United States, respectively. In one recent critique, Parsons's vision of 'the evolutionary development of western society, towards freedom from the grip of tradition, the constraints of kinship and the dominance of hierarchies based upon ascribed, particularistic criteria has been described as 'an extension and application of Marshall's analysis of citizenship' (Holton and Turner, 1986, p. 22).

Like Lipset in *The First New Nation*, Marshall saw a conflict between equality through citizenship, and inequality through the market. Lipset treated this tension as being manageable with relative ease, as did Morris Janowitz a decade and a half later (Janowitz, 1980, pp. 21–2), but Marshall was more aware of its disruptive potential. Reinhard Bendix, who drew on Marshall's analysis, saw not only – like Marshall – that system contradictions reduced the efficiency of institutions (e.g. education), but also that conflicts of values frequently coincided with lines of group differentiation (e.g. between employers and workers, or between aristocrats and industrialists).

Societies undergoing industrialization or political modernization did not always 'handle' these conflicts in ways that led to stable capitalist democracy. In this first phase, Bendix was one of the few articulate mainstream critics within American historical sociology of the prevailing structural-functionalist approach. This approach paid little attention to group conflict, value differences, and the systematic use of power advantages to enforce domination. It was not possible to dismiss Bendix as a prejudiced left-winger, a tactic adopted by the establishment when dealing with C. Wright Mills.[10]

The second phase: democracy exposed

Work by four historical sociologists helped to reorientate the academic culture. None was decisive, but their cumulative impact eased the transition between the first and second phases. Two books appearing in

1966, by G. E. Lenski and W. G. Runciman respectively, dealt with
social stratification as the major source of inequality within societies. In
Power and Privilege, Lenski emphasized the part played by power as
opposed to need in regulating social stratification. His approach challenged Parsons, by asserting that societies were very imperfect systems
with a large measure of coercion and conflict. Meanwhile, in *Relative
Deprivation and Social Justice*, Runciman drew attention to the way
inequality was perceived by members of a society. In particular, he
made two points. First, these perceptions were frequently at odds with
reality. Second, existing patterns of inequality were, in many respects,
invalid according to criteria of social justice.[11] Through the work of
Lenski and Runciman, the assumption that social order – and particularly capitalist democracy – was built upon spontaneous acceptance of
transparently justifiable norms was undermined. Their books helped to
make 'power' and 'values' available as terms within critical analyses,
sensitive to coercion and injustice.

Meanwhile, knowledge of Marc Bloch and Norbert Elias began to
percolate into English-speaking academic culture during the 1960s. In
the case of Bloch, publication of his *Feudal Society* (1961) was important. Although *The Civilizing Process* (1978a; 1982a) had not yet been
published in Britain or the United States, Elias's approach was influential in the provincial university which became the major provider of
sociology teachers in British higher education. The pace and extent of
the spread of the Eliasian perspective should not be exaggerated.
However, along with Bloch's work, Elias's teaching drew attention to
the fears and vulnerabilities of human beings participating in complex
and dynamic networks of interdependence; and the way the shaping
of cultural meanings and psychic traits was bound up with changing
power balances within these configurations. Neither Bloch nor Elias
regarded 'integrating values' or political ideologies as a datum handed
down by the 'system'.

Books by Barrington Moore and E. P. Thompson demonstrated the
effectiveness of such a critical approach (Moore, 1969; Thompson,
1968). Each demonstrated, in different ways, the violent character of
capitalist democracy's past. In other work they extended the critique to
argue that modern capitalist democracies were 'predatory' (Moore,
1972, pp. 105ff) or 'parasitical' (Thompson, 1978b, pp. 48–9), treating
citizens as victims. The distance between work by Smelser and Thompson, and between Lipset and Moore, dramatically shows the change that
occurred in historical sociology in the early and mid-1960s.[12] Not
surprisingly, there were links with the previous phase. For example, the
issue of paternalism explored by Bendix recurred in Genovese's work

on plantation society.[13] However, Genovese was interested in its repressive aspects, rather than its capacity to foster social integration. Like Marshall, Ira Katznelson examined the impact of social differentiation on the development of civil and political rights. Katznelson, too, saw divergent trends at work in these separate spheres. However, his focus was not the implications for system integration, but the consequences for class consciousness.[14]

The third phase: capitalism explored and exposed

Marxian historians such as Thompson and Genovese had concentrated on digging out the experiences and perceptions of subordinate groups whose existence was ignored or neglected by established ideology. They used values embedded in democratic citizenship – especially the right to freedom and fulfilment – as a touchstone for a trenchant critique of actual practice. By the mid-1970s, some practitioners of Marxian historical sociology were becoming bolder. They wanted to fill the vacuum left after the crumbling of structural-functionalism, by developing an alternative world-encompassing system.

Immanuel Wallerstein began his enterprise of charting the course of the capitalist world-economy. Perry Anderson mapped the evolution of the feudal mode of production across several countries and epochs. The emphasis changed in the implicit debate within historical sociology on the nature of capitalist democracy. The centre of attention moved away from democracy and towards capitalism, away from the national and towards the international.

However, Marxian approaches had to come to terms with and, increasingly, give way before two tendencies: first, exploration of the active contribution made by relatively autonomous state apparatuses in their civic and military guises to the shaping of capitalist society; and second, a greater readiness to treat economic, political and other forms of coercion as alternative expressions of 'power' – without privileging any particular form of power within theoretical explanations. Contributions by Theda Skocpol, Charles Tilly, Fernand Braudel, Michael Mann and Anthony Giddens all moved the centre of gravity in this direction.[15]

In fact, these developments reacted on Wallerstein's project. As Michael Mann pointed out in a review of the third volume of *The Modern World System*, Wallerstein laid great stress upon the military progress of the geopolitical contest between the French and the British in the late eighteenth century. The British were successful: 'It was these politico-military victories that critically increased the economic gaps – in agriculture, in industry, in trade and in finance' (Wallerstein, 1989a, pp. 112–13). Mann's response to this passage conveys the flavour of the debate under way in the 1980s:

> If Wallerstein has an economic explanation for political-military victories, he keeps it very quiet . . . [His] general drift is against it, since he is particularly concerned to argue that the British were not more economically powerful than the French at the beginning of their rivalry, only at the end and as a *consequence* of military rivalry. He has conceded game-set-and-match to writers like Skocpol, Tilly and me, who argue against Marxists and for the critical importance of political-military power relations in social development. Actually, we don't argue it as strongly as he does, for we all (in different ways) give a greater explanatory role to domestic class relations and the level of development of the domestic economy. We have been outflanked by a more committed militarist!.
> (1990, p. 198; emphasis in original)

Mann welcomed Wallerstein's stress on international connectedness, but discounted his economic reductionism.[16] This aspect of Marxism, the insistence upon the priority of economics, has an element of mystification about it. In fact, a steady onslaught against mystifications of many kinds had been under way since the late 1970s. For example (to mention only authors considered here), Marxist theories of class and revolution, technocratic myths about education, American urban reform programmes in the 1960s and early 1970s, romantic myths of nationhood, Russian imperialism, and the market theory of value had all come under the whip.[17] This process has not been anxiety-free. Illusions are being destroyed in the name of rationality – but what are they to be replaced with?

The fourth phase: democracy re-examined

The protest movements in Eastern Europe and the USSR during the late 1980s certainly put the West European and American movements of two decades before into perspective. The earlier movements raised consciousness and stimulated some legislative change, especially for Blacks and women. But the latter toppled governments.

It is relevant to stress one similarity and one difference between the 1960s and 1980s. On the one hand, the later movement was in many respects a continuation of the earlier one. The main actors were in both cases drawn from the white- and blue-collar sections of the population.

These groups were represented, with varying effectiveness, by the 'intelligentsia' and union leaders. Between the 1960s and the 1980s the slogans changed – from student power, black power and female liberation to *perestroika*, *glasnost*, and 'Gorby' – but not the underlying issues. In both periods, the principal target was abuse of power, and the main demand fulfilment of the rights of citizenship.

On the other hand, the repertoire of political responses to these demands was quite different from two decades before. In the 1960s the big winner in the West, for a while at least, was the socialist dream of non-repressive communitarian togetherness in its many utopian guises. It did not last. Over the medium term, materialism and individualism triumphed. Thatcher and Reagan represented a return to populist capitalism, evoking Victorian values and the open frontier. Neither of these two responses – the communitarian and the individualistic – was so readily available in the late 1980s and early 1990s. The moral force of Marxism was shattered by the progressive liberalization of Soviet Russia, and successful uprisings against communism in Eastern Europe. This occurred at the very point when the free-market rhetoric of the Thatcher–Reagan *entente* during the 1980s was losing its self-confidence.

Conventional ideological explanations which used to handle the problems of power, morality and human experience have been undermined. However, people have certainly not abandoned their concern for human interests – what is 'good', 'just', 'fulfilling' and so on. They have discarded one set of answers but not forgotten the questions. On the contrary, they do not want to be sucked into an ethical vacuum. Widespread support for 'green' lifestyles shows how unattractive many find a world of amoral individualism and cynical geopolitics.

The disintegration of the Russian empire has raised the question: what kinds of economic and political entities are going to take shape in Europe over the next twenty years? This is the same question that was being asked in 1918 after the collapse of the Austro-Hungarian, Ottoman and German empires. The eventual outcome on that occasion was disadvantageous for European humanity. Historical sociology itself was one of the casualties. In the 1990s, the socialist utopia is an unwanted import in Europe. Meanwhile, the costs of exporting the American Dream are becoming prohibitive for the United States. That leaves the German Dream and the Japanese Dream. Germany and Japan have been very efficient capitalist societies, but their record as democracies is less promising. In these circumstances, it would not be surprising if sociologists, historians and others in the West began to explore the meaning and potential of democracy.

In fact, a critical re-examination of democracy as a political model is well under way. It still seems to be what most people want, especially if it can be shorn of any fanatical excesses. This may explain why, after years of neglect, Parsons and Marshall became fashionable again in the late 1980s. Since the 1950s, the reputations of Parsons and Marshall have undergone dramatic fluctuations. Both were pushed into the background during the second wave of historical sociology inaugurated by the great success of works by E. P. Thompson and Barrington Moore. By comparison, Parsons and Marshall seemed to be unreasonably bland and optimistic. Parsons, especially, was the object of attack, for example at the hands of Daniel Foss (1963) and Alvin Gouldner (1971).

However, during the 1980s, Parsons and Marshall have attracted new attention – much of it of a positive kind.[18] Without lapsing into free-market formulae, Parsons and Marshall took very seriously both the aspirations and the difficulties of capitalist democratic ideology. Their revival in the 1980s stems from the need to find a convincing replacement for existing versions of this ideology. These have become very threadbare, whether looking back to John Maynard Keynes or Adam Smith.[19]

To focus, for the moment, on Marshall, the revived interest in his ideas surfaced a few years after his death in 1981. As has already been noticed, both Mann and Giddens found it useful to debate with the ghost of Marshall. Both were critical. Others, such as Brian S. Turner and David Held have been more enthusiastic.[20] A. H. Halsey has argued that Marshall's analysis provides a way of developing the part played by the state, the professions and local community organizations in providing moral regulation of social stratification (Halsey, 1984, p. 14).[21] One interpretation of this suggestion is that means might be found through citizenship to move towards social justice, with proper regard for need.[22]

One academic who has taken very seriously his professional obligation with respect to citizenship is Morris Janowitz. He found Marshall's argument 'highly persuasive' (Janowitz, 1980, p. 4), especially his insistence that citizenship rights should be balanced by duties. Janowitz offered a number of refinements, especially in four areas – taxation, education, military service, and the promotion of community welfare – where the obligations of citizenship were particularly relevant. In each case, current practice was inadequate and some of Marshall's expectations pitched too low, in Janowitz's view. The taxpayer's obligations should include active efforts to influence patterns of governmental expenditure. Education should overcome, rather than reinforce, narrow ethnic loyalties. Its object should be to create '*effective national identification and an operative sense of citizenship*' (p. 13; emphasis in original). Military participation should be informed by the ideal of 'the citizen soldier' (p. 16), Britain being more advanced than the United States in this respect.

Finally, Marshall had underestimated the strength and significance of voluntary organizations. Unfortunately, such organizations tended to be more concerned with rights than obligations. They were 'highly localistic and narrow in territorial scope' (p. 17). Janowitz was in favour of more effective representation of voluntary bodies at the regional and national levels (Janowitz, 1978; Janowitz and Suttles, 1978; Smith, 1988a). This was at least as important as trade union organization – which should, in any case, be complemented by wide-ranging citizen representation in private industry and public corporations. A process of institution-building was needed to promote 'moral consciousness' (Janowitz, 1980, p. 22).[23]

The debate has drawn in analysts of 'Marshall's war between citizenship and social class' (Marshall *et al.*, 1985, p. 279).[24] It has also produced the suggestion that, properly understood, citizenship should mean 'taking the growth of job tenure rights not just as an unfortunate rigidity, but as an opportunity for developing a sense of community in business enterprises' (Dore, 1983, p. 480).[25] The list of contributors could be extended, but a more important point is that the renewed interest in models of capitalist democracy extends far beyond Marshall's work.[26] What contribution can historical sociologists make to this enterprise of rethinking capitalist democracy?

In fact, their 'infrastructural capacity' has grown considerably in recent years. During the 1970s and early 1980s historical sociologists made their way into established positions throughout higher education. As they settled into their tenured posts, a debate was under way about the condition of public culture and education.[27] History was a major battleground. Journalists and politicians told historians they had a responsibility to promote national values under threat. Official committees in both the United States and Britain reported on history teaching in schools.[28]

In this heightened atmosphere, a major breakthrough into the mass market occurred during the late 1980s: historical sociology found its way on to the airport bookstalls. Two prominent examples were Simon Schama's *The Embarrassment of Riches. An Interpretation of Dutch Culture in the Golden Age* (1987), and Paul Kennedy's *The Rise and Fall of the Great Powers* (1988) (subtitled 'Economic change and military conflict from 1500 to 2000'). Both books rapidly became international bestsellers. Apart from the professional skills of their authors, why should this be so?

A new audience for historical sociology

Simon Schama's book was about Dutch culture in the 'golden age' of Rembrandt and the Baroque. His theme – 'the anxieties of super abundance' (1987, p. xi) – had a very modern ring. North Americans in the late twentieth century were bound to warm to his description of the seventeenth-century Dutch temperament. It was reassuring to read about a stable human-sized society in which the 'embarrassment of riches' was successfully managed. Dutch culture was suffused with patriotism and morality. The Dutch approach to life reconciled world empire with small-town domestic happiness. Its virtues and obsessions were shaped by puritanism, trading habits and the struggle for national independence. The echoes of New England (and New Amsterdam) are clear. The Dutch remained true to themselves: 'in the acid test of allegiance and sacrifice in a murderous and terrifying war, in the burden of heavy taxes, and in the perennial alarms and anxieties that hung around Dutch diplomacy, their belief in themselves as a common tribe held firm' (Schama, 1987, p. 567).

Since then, Schama has enjoyed even greater success with his *Citizens. A Chronicle of the French Revolution* (1989). This is a dazzling work, with the pace of a thriller. It mixes erudition with wit, marrying enormous scope with sharp detail. The immediate point, however, is that having evoked the homely origins of modern capitalist culture in the Netherlands, Schama went on to explore the violent birth of political democracy in France. This choice of subjects illustrates a wider pattern, linking the resurgence of historical sociology to the troubles of transatlantic capitalist democracy.

To return to *The Embarrassment of Riches*, it provided an optimistic model for hegemonic powers under threat. When the Dutch empire declined, Dutch 'moral geography' stayed the same. Inhabitants of the Netherlands remained 'adrift between the fear of the deluge and the hope of moral salvage, in the tidal ebb and flow between worldliness and homeliness, between the gratification of appetite and its denial, between the conditional consecration of wealth and perdition in its surfeit' (p. 609). The moral struggle continued. It was intrinsic to being Dutch – as it is to being American. Schama's book put American and other English-speaking heirs of the puritan tradition back in touch with their cultural predecessors in early modern Europe.

The Dutch belonged to a 'first new nation' which had remained true to itself.[29] They were admirable and likeable. Schama did not draw any explicit parallel between Dutch experience and American ideals. He may even have been unconscious of it.[30] However, the comparison was implicit in the enterprise and had much to do with the book's appeal.

Paul Kennedy's book dealt with another aspect of imperial decline. He covered strategy and economics in the pre-industrial world, the industrial era and the post-war scene of today and tomorrow. Kennedy concluded:

> . . . it has been a common dilemma facing previous 'number-one' countries that even as their relative economic strength is ebbing, the growing foreign challenges to their position have compelled them to allocate more and more of their resources into the military sector, which in turn squeezes out productive investment and, over time, leads to the downward spiral of slower growth, heavier taxes, deepening domestic splits over spending priorities, and a weakening capacity to bear the burdens of defence. If this, indeed, is the pattern of history, one is tempted to paraphrase Shaw's deadly serious quip and say: 'Rome fell; Babylon fell; Scarsdale's turn will come'. (Kennedy, 1988, p. 689).

The Rise and Fall of the Great Powers argued that national decline was part of the natural way of things. Nothing much could be done about it. We could understand what was happening, but there was no way we could alter the intrinsic logic of the rise and fall of nations.

Critics had mixed feelings about the book, contrasting it unfavourably with his previous work.[31] Michael Mann and Anthony Giddens both pointed out that Kennedy ignored the part played by alliances in mediating the rise and fall of great powers. Samuel P. Huntingdon's rebuttal was one of many.[32] In Immanuel Wallerstein's opinion, Kennedy's book 'merely provides us with the homespun wisdom of a sage observer' (1989d, p. 340). However, it was wisdom with a huge popular following.

In fact Schama's and Kennedy's books both reached over the heads of specialist academic critics, to the public at large. They appealed strongly to American and British readers trying to come to terms with diminishing national power. It is fascinating that this larger audience should have been discovered in the later years of the Reagan–Thatcher decade, an era when the ethos of government was at best indifferent, and at worst hostile, to the models and theories developed in historical sociology. This neglect by government is ironic in view of the large amount of attention historical sociologists have paid to the development of capitalism, political culture, citizenship, social policy, nationalism and the modern state.

What should be the relationship between historical sociologists and their audience? Who should this audience be? One approach to these issues may be illustrated from the classic era of historical sociology. When the first volume of David Hume's *History of England* (Hume, 1983) appeared in 1754, it had a very rough ride. As Hume later recorded, he had stood above party politics and 'neglected present power, interest, and authority, and the cry of popular prejudices'. The result was 'one cry of reproach, disapprobation, and even detestation; English, Scotch, and Irish, Whig and Tory, churchman and sectary, freethinker and religionist, patriot and courtier, united in their rage' (Hume, 1987b, p. xxxvii). However, despite the opposition of so many vested interests the project was not abandoned. Later volumes were better received. When the completed version was published in 1762 it was an 'instant best seller' (Phillipson, 1989, p. 137). It went through five editions in its first fourteen years, then fifty more in the half-century after that. The completed version of the history was not only popular, as has been seen, but also scholarly, relevant and detached.

Hume's book was written for responsible members of the political nation. In his view, it was essential that people should be able to think critically about their own private interests and the public interest. Nicolas Phillipson has summarized this approach. Hume's history

> . . . is written for those who are curious about their past, and want to rethink the stories they have been told about the world they have lost. He sets agenda for those who want to discuss the past seriously; he provides the data and sets the contexts in which great events took place; he provides intellectual tools which are worthy of intelligent people; and invites his readers to exercise their own judgement about the significance of these events in their own ways and their own time. (Phillipson, 1989, pp. 140–1)

Hume treated his readers neither as a 'market', nor as a political 'constituency', but as fellow citizens. This provides a worthwhile model for modern historical sociology.

The future of the past

The best contribution historical sociology could make in the 1990s would be the discovery and dissemination of knowledge relevant to the development of capitalist democracy, even if this meant a diversion of attention from the discussion of philosophies of history. It is worth making this last point, since the mutual attraction between sociology and philosophy is so strong at present, not least in the most recent instances of historical sociology in the grand manner.[33] Giddens comments, 'There is a range of issues – to do with agency, intentionality, structure and meaning – about which it would be difficult to say whether they should properly be called "philosophical" or "sociological" '. He adds that such concepts are 'only of enduring value if they usefully help guide the practice of empirical research' (1987d, p. 72). This last comment must be regarded as more than a routine disclaimer. In fact, if historical sociology is to make a useful contribution to the debate about capitalist democracy, attention has to be paid to specific forms of human agency, specific intentions, particular structures, and particular meanings. John Hall has recently argued that there is a need for more 'philosophic history' whose 'concern is with distinguishing different types of society and explaining the transitions from one type to another in order thereby to reflect systematically on the nature of power and human life chances' (Hall, 1986, p. 3). He is right. However, the 'history' is as important as the 'philosophy'. In other words, detached reasoning must be closely related to empirical work, to historical exploration informed but not dominated by current debates in theory and the empirical generalizations being made by other scholars.[34] The ability of historical sociologists to make a contribution to the current debate on capitalist democracy will be increased if they are producing relevant knowledge. To cite an obvious example, the authority of Ronald Dore's contribution to this debate is greatly enhanced by his detailed research into the development of Japanese society.[35]

In fact, there are two related issues. On the one hand, more knowledge is needed. On the other hand, it should be communicated more widely within and between societies. Both matters are urgent, especially for the British and Americans. These two nations have, in turn, enjoyed the experience of global supremacy in the nineteenth and twentieth centuries. As a consequence they are known by the world far better than they, in turn, know that world. To use an analogy, the slave always has to know his or her master, in order to maximize the chances for survival. The master can enjoy the luxury of ignorance – at least until his throat is cut. It is ironic that the British, at least, currently know and understand the Germans as little, or perhaps even less, than they know and understand the Japanese.

During the 1990s historical sociology can make a major contribution to a more informed and open-minded civic culture. It has the potential to demonstrate by its achievements the practical value of investigating the past and carrying out systematic comparisons across time and space, drawing out similarities and differences, tracing long-term processes, seeking out causes and pursuing effects, indicating the way people shape and are shaped by the institutions which bind them together and keep them apart. Hopefully, it may offer a route to increased understanding and more effective action through rational, critical and imaginative inquiry.

Historical sociology can help citizens understand how opportunity structures and ways of life have been shaped and may, in some respects at least, be reshaped. To recall an image from the first chapter, the reality-testing function of historical sociology can help us distinguish between open doors and brick walls. It can also show us that some walls, at least, are temporary – as in Berlin.

Historical sociology may even help to introduce more rationality into popular understanding of relations between states, displacing the fantasy and fear which currently prevail. This leads to a more general point. For a long time capitalist democracies such as Britain and the United States have survived (some would say thrived upon) widespread ignorance and prejudice within their populations. This possibility is being progressively undermined as industrial competitiveness demands ever higher levels of education and training. The raising of education levels has implications for citizenship as well as productivity. The educated worker wants to know what he or she is working for, just as the educated soldier wants to know why he or she is fighting. Historical sociology should be ready to help fill the gap – not by providing pre-packaged answers but by indicating relevant questions, relevant evidence and rational ways of bringing them together. The case has been well made by Reinhard Bendix:

> Social scientists should have an abiding faith in human reason . . . . This is a more humane creed than a concern with improving the techniques of social manipulation. It is the only position worthy of the great intellectual traditions in which they stand. It is the baseline of the intellectual defense against the threat of totalitarianism. (Bendix, 1984, p. 127; emphasis in original)

Notes

NOTES TO CHAPTER 1

1　See Adorno *et al*, 1964.
2　See Adorno and Horkheimer, 1979; Smith, 1988a; Banks, 1989, pp. 521–3; Collini, 1979.
3　Knapp, 1984, p. 51; Hunt, 1989, p. 1; Calhoun, 1987, p. 615; Hall, 1989; Smith, 1982c, p. 299.
4　See also Smith, 1988b.
5　See, for example, Aymard, 1972; Kedourie, 1975; Andrews, 1978; Gurevitch, 1983; Baker, 1984; Clark, 1985.
6　Bloch, 1961; Braudel, 1972a; Braudel, 1972b; Braudel, 1981; Braudel, 1982; Braudel, 1984.
7　cf. Banks and Banks, 1964b.
8　e.g. Rosaldo and Lamphere, 1974; Humphries, 1977; Kuhn and Wolpe, 1978; Tilly and Scott, 1978; Hollis, 1979; Banks, 1981; Braybon, 1981; Sargent, 1981; Wemple, 1981; Ulrich, 1983; Chamberlain, 1983; Pahl, 1984; Alexander, 1984; Charles and Duffin, 1985; Banks, 1986; Hanawalt, 1986; Davidoff and Hall, 1987; Bradley, 1989.
9　Anderson, 1974a; Anderson, 1974b; Wallerstein, 1974; Wallerstein, 1980; Wallerstein, 1989a; Braudel, 1981; Braudel, 1982; Braudel, 1984; Mann, 1986; Skocpol, 1979.
10　e.g. Le Roy Ladurie, 1979; Braudel, 1980; Burke, 1980; Tilly, 1981; McLennan, 1981; Abrams, 1982; Runciman, 1983; Skocpol, 1984; Tilly, 1984; Neale, 1985; Hirst, 1985; Lloyd, 1986; Ragin, 1987; Callinicos, 1987.

NOTES TO CHAPTER 2

1　For Bloch's war memoirs, see Bloch, 1988.
2　Marshall, 1973, p. 89; Mennell, 1989, p. 19; Braudel, 1972b, p. 454.
3　Katz, 1987; Stouffer *et al*, 1949.

4   See, for example, Spengler, 1926–8; Hughes, 1959; Giddens, 1971.
5   Mommsen and Osterhammel 1987; Runciman, 1972; Giddens 1972; Beetham, 1985.
6   Buxton, 1985, p. 217; Lipset and Raab, 1971, p. xviii; Lipset, 1964; Lipset, 1969; Lipset, 1971, pp. xvi–xvii; Lipset and Smelser, 1961, p. 51.
7   See also Bendix, 1990.
8   e.g. Bendix and Lipset, 1957; Bendix and Lipset, 1967.
9   e.g. Parsons, 1937; Parsons, 1951; Parsons, Bales and Shils, 1953; Parsons and Smelser, 1956.
10   See also Parsons, 1971.
11   Charles Camic has suggested that Parsons's shift of emphasis from action to evolution might be one example of 'a necessary oscillation between these two species of social theory' (Camic, 1979, p. 544). It is worth noting that a similar 'oscillation', this time between utilitarian and Hegelian approaches, occurred in the work of one of Parson's early post-war critics, Barrington Moore (Smith, 1984a, pp. 160–2; Moore, 1953).
12   See Runciman, 1965, pp. 118–21; Sztompka, 1986, pp. 252–7.
13   See also Homans, 1984.
14   See also Eisenstadt, 1970; Eisenstadt and Rokkan, 1973.
15   See Smith, 1986.
16   Collini, 1979; Marshall, 1963b, p. 13; Marshall, 1973, p. 95.
17   See also Lehman, 1972, p. 291.
18   See Bendix, 1966; Bendix and Roth, 1970.

NOTES TO CHAPTER 3

1   Runciman, 1966; Lenski, 1966. The books by W. G. Runciman and Gerhard Lenski have a 'transitional' or 'in between' character. Lenski's theory of social stratification drew upon but also moved away from the 'conservative tradition' (1966, p. 14) to which Talcott Parsons belonged. Lenski accepted this tradition's broadly nominalist definition of 'class', its view that human beings were 'strongly self-seeking' and its assumption that inequality was 'inevitable' (pp. 441–2). However, he also accepted the radical tradition's assumption that societies were very imperfect systems, with a large measure of coercion and conflict. Runciman's work in the mid-1960s picked up themes which had intrigued Marshall: the historical interweaving of class, status and political power in British society, its tendency to generate discontent, and the implications for social justice. The sense of continuity with Marshall is strengthened by the fact that at different periods both men held fellowships at Trinity College, Cambridge. In fact, Runciman has an even more solid establishment background, as a titled old-Etonian, ex-guards officer and (since 1976) chairman of a shipping company. However, Runciman paid more attention than Marshall to,

firstly, how individuals and groups experienced and responded to relative deprivation, and secondly, what should be the proper criteria of social justice. To oversimplify, Runciman asked: what upset people about social stratification? why? and what did they have a right to expect? Runciman was tackling questions which were also central to the work of Thompson and Moore. Runciman dealt mainly with the subjective consequences of social stratification. By contrast, Lenski was principally interested in the causal aspect of social stratification, especially its objective manifestations or, as he put it '*Who gets what and why?*' (Lenski, 1966, p. 3; italics in original).

2　See, for example, Fink, 1989, ch 2.
3　e.g. Bloch, 1941; see also Bloch, 1963a; Bloch, 1967b.
4　See Giddens, 1987e.
5　Durkheim, 1964; Bloch, 1973; Rhodes, 1978.
6　cf. Bloch, 1954, pp. 90–110.
7　Fink, 1989, p. 106; see also Perrin, 1948; Stenger, 1953.
8　Bloch, 1967a; Sewell, 1967; Walker, 1963.
9　Hamilton, 1983, p. 35; Mennell, 1989, p. 10.
10　e.g. Elias, 1956; Elias, 1978b; Elias, 1987a; Elias, 1987c.
11　e.g. Elias, 1950; Elias, 1969; Elias, 1970; Elias, 1974; Elias, 1982–3; Elias, 1983; Elias, 1985; Elias, 1987b; Elias and Dunning, 1986.
12　e.g. Elias, 1971a; Elias, 1971b; Elias, 1982b; Elias, 1989a; Elias, 1989b; Elias, 1990.
13　For some recent critiques, see e.g. Sathaye, 1973; Bauman, 1979; Kuzmics, 1984; Sampson, 1984; Fulbrook, 1985; Lasch, 1985; Bogner, 1986; Robinson, 1987; Dunning, 1989; Mennell, 1990. See also the special double issue on Norbert Elias and figurational sociology in *Theory, Culture and Society*, 4, 2–3 (1987).
14　e.g. Elias, 1982a, pp. 146–7; Bloch, 1961, pp. 370–4.
15　cf. Smith, 1984b.
16　Elias, 1971a; Elias, 1971b; Elias, 1989a; Elias, 1989b; Elias, 1990; Smith, 1984b.
17　cf. Gay, 1967; Gay, 1969.
18　e.g. Anderson, 1964; Nairn, 1964; Anderson, 1966; Johnson, 1978; Johnson, 1981; cf. Thompson, 1978b; McClelland, 1979; Hall, 1981; Thompson, 1981; Kent, 1986; Magarey, 1987.
19　For a review of criticism, see Wiener, 1976 and Smith, 1983, pp. 25–9. See also Tilton, 1974; Castles, 1973; Downing, 1988; Stephens, 1989; Tumin, 1982.
20　cf. Smith, 1983, pp. 100–107; Smith, 1984a; Smith, 1984c.
21　On Methodism, see Laqueur, 1976; Thompson, 1976b; Smith, 1982a; McLeod, 1984; on the significance of time and work-discipline, see Thompson, 1967; Hopkins, 1982; Harrison, 1986; on the dynamics of class consciousness see Thompson, 1978b; Anderson, 1980; Calhoun, 1983a; Calhoun, 1983b; Jones, 1983a; Jones, 1983b; Kirk, 1987; Giddens, 1987c;

and, more generally, on the culture of capitalism see Thompson, 1972; Coats, 1972; Genovese, 1973; Macfarlane, 1978; Macfarlane, 1987; Corrigan and Sayer, 1985.

22   For a slightly different approach, see Runciman's *Relative Deprivation and Social Justice* (1966). Runciman's evidence did not provide much grounds for confidence in the accuracy or philosophical basis of popular judgements about inequalities of status and class. However, there are some interesting convergences between Runciman and Moore in other respects. For example, both argued that the discomfort of radical political change had to be taken into account and measured against the possible gains and losses of a more just society. Runciman believed it was certainly possible 'to envisage a just society with the social and economic lineaments of twentieth-century Britain which would be neither an inchoate and undisciplined rat-race nor an army of sullen and mediocre conformists' (p. 343). American society provided a model. Despite its obvious failings, in terms of status it came nearer than any other country to being 'a society at approximately the economic level of twentieth-century Britain that was already just' (p. 340). (For an alternative view, see the discussion in Randall Collins's *The Credential Society* (1979)). Runciman's warmth towards twentieth-century America was complemented by Moore's admiration for nineteenth-century Britain. It was as if patricians in each troubled capitalist democracy were turning for moral comfort towards its transatlantic sister.

23   Thompson, 1980; Thompson, 1982.

24   Katznelson, 1981b; Katznelson and Zolberg, 1986.

25   For a critique of Moore, see Skocpol, 1973.

26   On Gramsci, see Katznelson, 1981, p. 19; Genovese and Genovese, 1976, p. 206; cf. Thompson, 1978b; p. 73.

27   Skocpol, 1988a, p. 642. See also, for example, Skocpol and Finegold, 1982; Skocpol and Ikenberry, 1983; Orloff and Skocpol, 1984; Skocpol, 1988b.

28   cf. Himmelstein and Kimmel, 1981, pp. 1153–4; Smith, 1983, pp. 158–63; Smith, 1984a.

29   See also Skocpol, 1987.

30   For more recent contributions on these issues, see Skocpol, 1987; Skocpol, 1989; Goodwin and Skocpol, 1989. For other critiques and responses, see, for example, Shugart, 1989; Parsa, 1985; Meadwell, 1987; van den Braembussche, 1989.

31   e.g. Amenta and Skocpol, 1988; Skocpol, 1988b.

32   See also Tilly, 1963; Tilly, 1989.

33   For an alternative view, see Zagorin, 1982a, pp. 51–4.

NOTES TO CHAPTER 4

1   Anderson, 1974a; Anderson, 1974b; Wallerstein, 1974; Wallerstein, 1980; Wallerstein, 1989a; Braudel, 1981; Braudel, 1982; Braudel, 1984; Mann, 1986; Runciman, 1983; Runciman, 1989e; Giddens, 1981; Giddens, 1985.

2   For critiques, see, e.g. Johnson, 1976; Hechter, 1977; Runciman, 1989c.
3   cf. Anderson, 1966; Anderson, 1980.
4   For critiques of 'The figures of descent', see Nicholls, 1988; Callinicos, 1988; Barratt Brown, 1988; Ingham, 1988.
5   Wallerstein, 1969; Ragin and Chirot, 1984, p. 282.
6   For elaborations and critiques of world-system theory see, for example, Hechter, 1975; Brenner, 1977; Skocpol, 1977; Thirsk, 1977; Janowitz, 1977; Alapuro, 1977; Hunt, 1978–9; Chase-Dunn, 1980; Aronowitz, 1981; Garst, 1985; Hall, 1986; Smith, 1986; Hugill, 1988; Kearns, 1988; Boswell, 1989; Wallerstein, 1990a; Wallerstein, 1990b; Boyne, 1990; Bergsen, 1990; Mann, 1990.
7   See also Brenner, 1976; Goldstone, 1988.
8   See Bosserman, 1968; Balandier, 1975; Gurvitch, 1950; Gurvitch, 1955; Gurvitch, 1956; Gurvitch, 1962; Gurvitch, 1964; Gurvitch, 1971; Braudel, 1981; 479, 560; Braudel, 1982, 458–66, 50; Braudel, 1988, 26, 72.
9   cf. Braudel, 1958a.
10 cf. Braudel, 1958a, p. 746.
11 For critiques of *The Mediterranean* see, for example, Tevor-Roper, 1972; Hexter, 1972; Kellner, 1979; Kinser, 1986.
12 e.g. Mann, 1970; Mann, 1973; Mann, 1975.
13 Gellner's *Thought and Change* (1964) anticipates some aspects of Giddens's approach to evolutionism, as the latter acknowledges. Gellner's *Plough, Sword and Book* (1988) draws together themes from his own earlier work (e.g. Gellner, 1964; Gellner, 1969; Gellner, 1974; Gellner, 1979; Gellner, 1981; Gellner, 1983) in an impressive synthesis. Key works by Collins include *Conflict Sociology* (1975), *The Credential Society* (1979), *Sociology Since Mid-century* (1981), and the essays in *Weberian Sociological Theory* (1986b; see, for example, 1986c; 1986d). See also Collins, 1985; Collins, 1986a.
14 cf. Runciman, 1972.
15 cf. Collins, 1975, pp. 4–5 for a similar point.
16 This line of argument is reminiscent of Barrington Moore in his *Reflections on the Causes of Human Misery*, and *Injustice* (Moore, 1972, 1978).
17 For a longer discussion see Giddens, 1984, chapter five.
18 For a critique, see Smith, 1982b.
19 Turner, 1986; Held, 1989; see also Barbalet, 1988.
20 Runciman, 1989e, p. 297; Anderson, 1974b, pp. 420–1.
21 e.g. Bloch, 1961, pp. 35–8, 443; Gellner, 1988, pp. 154–70.
22 See also Febvre, 1982; Le Roy Ladurie, 1980.
23 e.g. Poster, 1984; Dodghson, 1987; Hallpike, 1986; Chartier, 1988; Veeser, 1989; Giddens, 1989b; Cohen, 1989; Coser, 1990; Bottomore, 1990; Gregory, 1990; Sayer, 1990; Giddens, 1990.

NOTES TO CHAPTER 5

1   Influences include, for example, the new interest of geographers in history, sociology and philosophy (e.g. Johnston, 1983; Jackson and Smith, 1984; Harvey, 1982; Dodgshon, 1987), the sociologists' rediscovery of spatiality and time (e.g. Gregory and Urry, 1985; Giddens, 1981), the awakening curiosity about anthropology (especially the work of Clifford Geertz) among historians (Walters, 1980), and the reciprocal concern of anthropologists such as Marshall Sahlins and Ernest Gellner with the historical dimension (Sahlins, 1985; Gellner, 1988; Cohn, 1980). Other influences stem from developments in historical political economy and archaeology (e.g. North and Thomas, 1973; North, 1981; Parker, 1986; Maier, 1987; Sahlins, 1974; Hodges, 1989; Tainter, 1988). Michel Foucault's challenges to established methodologies in history and the social sciences (e.g. Foucault, 1972; Foucault, 1974; Foucault, 1979; Sheridan, 1980; Smart, 1985; Kennedy, 1979; O'Neill, 1986; Weightman, 1989; Fraser, 1985; Dumm, 1985), work by Quentin Skinner on political thought and the methodology of history and social science (e.g. Skinner, 1978; Tully, 1988), the growing recognition of the role of language, texts and narrative structures in shaping historical interpretation (e.g. Stone, 1979; White, 1978; LaCapra, 1983), and continuing debates within moral and political philosophy (e.g. Rawls, 1972; Nozick, 1974; MacIntyre, 1981).

2   See, for example, Bourdieu, 1969; Bourdieu, 1985; Tully, 1988; White, 1978; Chartier, 1988; LaCapra, 1983; Ringer, 1990; Jay, 1990; Lemert, 1990.

3   Giddens, 1985, pp. 187–8; Mann, 1986, pp. 256–7; Runciman, 1983, p. 270; Collins, 1975, pp. 187–216.

4   Examples of the first include Tilly, 1964; Le Roy Ladurie, 1980 and Blok, 1974. Examples of the second include Bendix, 1964, Moore, 1969, and Skocpol, 1979. Examples of the third include Lenski, 1966; Giddens, 1985 and Gellner, 1988.

5   For example, the present writer's *Conflict and Compromise* (1982a), a comparative study of class formation in Birmingham and Sheffield between 1830 and 1914, lies on the dimension between historical exploration and empirical generalization. John Foster's *Class Struggle and Industrial Revolution* (1974) lies on the line between historical exploration and theory. Perez Zagorin's scholarly *Rebels and Rulers 1500–1660* (1982) is much closer to empirical generalization than theory construction. He produced a typology of revolutions in early modern Europe, but restricted himself to pointing out resemblances and parallels between national cases. He did not search for 'uniform or identical causal explanations' (1982a, p. 57).

6   e.g. Jones, 1974; Jones, 1976.

7   cf. Knapp, 1984.

8   Thompson, 1978a; Smith, 1982a, p. 302.
9   The reference is to Katznelson's *City Trenches* (1981). Katznelson shows how the interplay of state formation and class formation in the American case produced a split consciousness in the working class. They thought of themselves as 'workers' when at their place of work, but as 'ethnics' or residents of specific local communities when outside work.
10 e.g. Lipset and Smelser, 1961, p. 51.
11 It is worth comparing Runciman's book with the 'affluent worker' study which appeared shortly after (Goldthorpe, Lockwood, Bechhofer and Platt, 1968a; Goldthorpe, Lockwood, Bechhofer and Platt, 1968b; Goldthorpe, Lockwood, Bechhofer and Platt, 1969). Its authors were in favour of bold political strategies to bring about a more equal and just society. Runciman was more pessimistic about the prospects for planned improvement. In a rather Hayekian way, he pointed out the difficulties of securing agreement about how criteria of justice should be defined and implemented. Although their conclusions about political action differed from Runciman, the affluent worker team implicitly acknowledged the relevance of Runciman's analysis. In particular, they argued that the Labour Party should encourage a shift of instrumental collectivism from 'local and narrowly economic issues' to 'the level of national politics' (p. 190). It should strengthen its appeal as 'the party of the working man' (p. 191) and, in general, 'expand and diversify . . . wants and expectations in ways that would carry radical implications' (p. 194). In other words, political radicalism would attract more support if the reference groups of working-class voters were broadened, producing increased sensitivity to injustice and inequality. Runciman reached a similar conclusion, but in a more negative form. In his view, the very narrowness of working-class reference groups, especially regarding class, were a formidable obstacle to radical change. For an interesting review of Runciman, see Burns, 1966.
12 Smelser, 1959; Thompson, 1968; Lipset, 1963; Moore, 1969.
13 Bendix, 1974; Bendix, 1964; Genovese, 1974.
14 Katznelson, 1981b; see also Katznelson, 1988.
15 Skocpol, 1979; Tilly, 1990b; Braudel, 1981–4; Mann, 1986; Giddens, 1981; Giddens, 1985.
16 cf. Giddens, 1985, p. 167.
17 See Skocpol, 1979; Giddens, 1981; Collins, 1979; Katznelson, 1981b; Gellner, 1983; Collins, 1986b, chap 8; Gellner, 1988, chap 7; Gellner, 1975.
18 On Parsons see: Hamilton, 1983; Alexander, 1984; Holton and Turner, 1986; Turner, 1986; Munch, 1988; Robertson and Turner, 1990; Lidz, 1989; Parsons, 1989; Adriaansens, 1989; Barber, 1989; on Marshall, see later citations.
19 See Smith, 1990 for a discussion of historical and contemporary debates on capitalist democracy.
20 Turner, 1986; Held, 1989.

21   cf. Lockwood, 1974.
22   Runciman, 1966; Lenski, 1966.
23   On Janowitz, see Smith, 1988a; chap 10.
24   See also Marshall *et al.*, 1987; Goldthorpe, 1984a.
25   See also Dore, 1987a; Meade, 1984.
26   See, for example, Keane, 1984; Dahl, 1985; Bowles and Gintis, 1987; Held, 1987; Hoffman, 1988; Roper, 1989; Smith, 1990 – to list a very small sample from recent years.
27   e.g. Bloom, 1987; Bellah *et al.*, 1988; Wolin, 1989.
28   Bender, 1986; Monkonnen, 1986; Painter, 1987; Fox, 1987; Rosenzweig, 1987; Gagnon, 1988; Cannadine, 1987; Coss, 1988; Lamont, 1988; Evans, 1988; Bedarida, 1987; Hill, 1983.
29   cf. Lipset, 1963.
30   cf. Rogers, 1990, p. 270.
31   e.g. Kennedy, 1980; Kennedy, 1981.
32   Giddens, 1989a, pp. 330–1; Mann, 1989, p. 333; Huntington, 1988a; cf. Smith, 1978.
33   See, for example, Giddens, 1987d; Collins, 1988.
34   A few examples can be taken at random from a range of fields. Our understanding of the intersection between gender, class and the public and private spheres would be advanced by more studies like Leonore Davidoff and Catherine Hall's *Family Fortunes. Men and Women of the English Middle Class 1780–1850* (1987) and Ray Pahl's *Divisions of Labour* (1984), enquiring about other classes, other periods, other societies. John Brewer's *The Sinews of Power. War, Money and the English State 1688–1783* (1989) and Charles S. Maier's *Recasting Bourgeois Europe* (1975) provide models that could be applied elsewhere also. So, in their different spheres, do Joel Mokyr's *Why Ireland Starved. A Quantitative and Analytical History of the Irish Economy, 1800–1850* (1985), Barrington Moore's *Injustice* (especially part two) and Stuart M. Blumin's *The Emergence of the Middle Class. Social Experience in the American City, 1760–1900* (1989). Norbert Elias's magnificent *The Court Society* (1983), a study of the French absolutist court, is complemented, in some respects at least, by Pierre Bourdieu's *Distinction. A Social Critique of the Judgement of Taste* (1984). The inner workings of capitalism will be better understood as we acquire more empirical analyses such as Braudel's *Civilization and Capitalism* (1981–4), Alfred D. Chandler's *Scale and Scope* (1990), William M. Reddy's *The Rise of Market Culture* (1984), Charles A. Jones's *International Business in the Nineteenth Century* (1987) and R. P. T. Davenport-Hines's *Dudley Docker. The Life and Times of a Trade Warrior* (1984). Theda Skocpol's current research on the American state, and John Scott's work on the management of their wealth by the English propertied class, are two further examples of what is required.
35   Dore, 1959; Dore, 1965; Dore, 1967; Dore, 1973; Dore, 1983; Dore, 1986; Dore, 1987a; Dore, 1987b.

Bibliography

Abrams, P. 1982: *Historical Sociology*. London: Open Books.

Adorno, T., *et al*. 1964: *The Authoritarian Personality*. New York: John Wiley (originally published in 1950).

Adorno, T., and Horkheimer, M. 1979: *Dialectic of Enlightenment*. London: Verson (originally published in 1944).

Adriaansens, H. P. M. 1989: Talcott Parsons and beyond: recollections of an outsider. *Theory, Culture and Society*, 6, 4, pp. 613–21.

Alapuro, R. 1977: Peasants, states and the capitalist world system. *Acta Sociologica*, 20, 2, pp. 181–93.

Alexander, S. 1984: Women, class and sexual differences in the 1830s and 1840s. *History Workshop Journal*, 17, pp. 125–49.

Amenta, E., and Skocpol, T. 1988: Redefining the New Deal: World War II and the development of social provision in the Unites States. In Weir *et al*. 1988, pp. 81–122.

Anderson, M. 1971: *Family Structure in Nineteenth-Century Lancashire*. Cambridge: Cambridge University Press.

Anderson, P. 1964: Origins of the present crisis. *New Left Review*, 23, pp. 26–53.

Anderson, P. 1966: Socialism and pseudo–empiricism. *New Left Review*, 35, pp. 2–42.

Anderson, P. 1974a: *Passages from Antiquity to Feudalism*. London: Verso.

Anderson, P. 1974b: *Lineages of the Absolutist State*. London: Verso.

Anderson, P. 1976: *Considerations on Western Marxism*. London: New Left Books.

Anderson, P. 1980: *Arguments Within English Marxism*. London: New Left Books.

Anderson, P. 1987: The figures of descent, *New Left Review*. 161, pp. 20–77.

Anderson, P. 1990: A culture in contraflow – I. *New Left Review*, 180, pp. 41–78.

Andrews, R. M. 1978: Some implications of the *Annales* school and its methods for a revision of historical writing about the United States. *Review*, 1, pp. 165–80.

Aronowitz, S. 1981: A metatheoretical critique of Immanuel Wallerstein's *The Modern World System. Theory and Society*, 10, pp. 503–19.

Arrighi, G. *et al.* 1989: *Antisystemic Movements*. London: Verso.

Aymard, M. 1972: The *Annales* and French historiography (1929–1972). *Journal of European Economic History*, 1, pp. 491–511.

Baker, A. R. H. and Gregory, D. (eds) 1984: *Explorations in Historical Geography*. Cambridge: Cambridge University Press.

Balandier, G. 1975: *Gurvitch*. Translated by M. A. Thompson and K. A. Thompson, Oxford: Basil Blackwell (originally published in 1972).

Banks, J. A. 1954: *Prosperity and Parenthood. A Study of Family Planning in the Victorian Middle Classes*. London: Routledge.

Banks, J. A. 1989: From universal history to historical sociology. *British Journal of Sociology*, 40, 4, pp. 521–43.

Banks, J. A. and Banks, O. 1964a: Feminism and social change – a case study of a social movement. In Zollschan and Hirsch, 1964, pp. 547–69.

Banks, J. A. and Banks, O. 1964b: *Feminism and Family Planning in Victorian England*. Liverpool: Liverpool University Press.

Banks, O. 1981: *Faces and Feminism*. Oxford: Martin Robertson.

Banks, O. 1986: *Social Origins of First Wave Feminism*. Brighton: Wheatsheaf.

Barbalet, J. M. 1988: *Citizenship. Rights, Struggle and Class Inequality*. Milton Keynes: Open University Press.

Barber, B. 1989: Talcott Parsons and the sociology of science: an essay in appreciation and remembrance. *Theory, Culture and Society*, 6, 4, pp. 623–35.

Barker, A. R. H. 1984: Reflections on the relations of historical geography and the *Annales* school of history. In Baker and Gregory, 1984, pp. 1–27.

Barratt Brown, M. 1988: Away with all the great arches: Anderson's history of British capitalism. *New Left Review*, 88, pp. 22–51.

Bauman, Z. 1979: The phenomenon of Norbert Elias, *Sociology*. 13, 1, pp. 117–25.

Bedarida, F. 1987: The modern historian's dilemma: conflicting pressures from science and society. *Economic History Review*, 40, 3, pp. 335–48.

Beetham, D. 1985: *Max Weber and the Theory of Modern Politics*. Cambridge: Polity Press (originally published in 1974).

Bell, C. and Newby, H. (eds) 1974: *The Sociology of Community: A Selection of Readings*. London: Frank Cass.

Bell, D. 1962: *The End of Ideology*. Glencoe, Ill.: The Free Press.

Bellah, R., *et al.* 1988: *Habits of the Heart. Middle America Observed*. London: Hutchinson (originally published in 1985).

Bender, T. 1986: Wholes and parts: the need for synthesis in American history. *Journal of American History*, 73, 1, pp. 120–56.

Bender, T. 1987: Wholes and parts: continuing the conversation. *Journal of American History*, 74, 1, pp. 123–30.

Bendix, R. 1963: Concepts and generalizations in comparative sociological studies. *American Sociological Review*, (28), pp. 532–9.

Bendix, R. 1964: *Nation-Building and Citizenship. Studies of Our Changing Social Order*. New York: Wiley.

Bendix, R. 1966: *Max Weber. An Intellectual Portrait*. London: Methuen (originally published in 1959).

Bendix, R. 1970a: *Embattled Reason. Essays on Social Knowledge*. New York: Oxford University Press.

Bendix, R. 1970b: The age of ideology: persistent and changing. In Bendix, 1970a, pp. 18–61 (originally published in 1964).

Bendix, R. 1970c: Images of society and problems of concept formation in sociology. With Bennett Berger, in Bendix 1970a, pp. 116–38.

Bendix, R. 1970d: Sociology and the distrust of reason. In Bendix and Roth, 1970, pp. 84–105.

Bendix, R. 1970e: The comparative analysis of historical change. In Bendix and Roth, 1970, pp. 207–24.

Bendix, R. 1974: *Work and Authority in Industry*. Berkeley: University of California Press (originally published in 1956).

Bendix, R. 1978: *Kings or People. Power and the Mandate to Rule*. Berkeley: University of California Press.

Bendix, R. 1984: *Force, Fate and Freedom. On Historical Sociology*. Berkeley: University of California Press.

Bendix, R. 1990: How I became an American sociologist. In Berger, 1990, pp. 452–75.

Bendix R. and Lipset, S. M. (eds) 1957: *Class, Status and Power: a reader in social stratification*. Glencoe, IU: Free Press.

Bendix R. and Lipset, S. M. (eds) 1967: *Class, Status and Power: social stratification in comparative perspective*, second edition. London: Routledge and Kegan Paul.

Bendix, R. and Roth, G. 1970: *Scholarship and Partisanship Essays on Max Weber*. Berkeley: University of California Press.

Berger, B. M. (ed.) 1990: *Authors of Their Own Lives. Intellectual Autobiographies by Twenty American Sociologists*. Berkeley: University of California Press.

Bergsen, A. 1990: Turning world-system theory on its head. *Theory, Culture and Social*, 7, 2–3, pp. 67–81.

Bloch, M. 1941: The rise of dependent cultivation and seigneurial institutions. In Clapham and Power, 1941, pp. 224–77.

Bloch, M. 1949: *Strange Defeat. A Statement of Evidence Written in 1940*. Oxford: Oxford University Press (originally published in 1946).

Bloch, M. 1954: *The Historian's Craft*. Translated by Peter Putman, Manchester: Manchester University Press (originally published in 1949).

Bloch, M. 1961: *Feudal Society* , (2 vols). Translated by L. A. Manyon, London: Routledge.

Bloch, M. 1963a: *Mélanges Historiques*. Paris: SEVPEN.

Bloch, M. 1963b: Reflexions d'un historien sur less fausses nouvelles de la guerre. In Bloch, 1963a, pp. 41–57.

Bloch, M. 1966: *French Rural History. An Essay on its Basic Characteristics*. Translated by J. Sondheimer, Berkeley: University of California Press (originally published in 1931).

Bloch, M. 1967a: A contribution towards a comparative history of European societies. In Bloch, 1967b, pp. 44–81 (originally published in 1928).

Bloch, M. 1967b: *Land and Work in Medieval Europe. Selected Papers by Marc Bloch*. Translated by J. E. Anderson, London: Routledge.

Bloch, M. 1973: *The Royal Touch. Sacred Monarchy and Scrofula in England and France*. Translated by J. E. Anderson, London: Routledge (originally published in 1923).

Bloch, M. 1988: *Memoirs of War, 1914–15*. Translated and with an introduction by Carol Fink, Cambridge: Cambridge University Press (originally published in 1969).

Blok, A. 1974: *The Mafia of a Sicilian Village, 1860–1960*. Oxford: Basil Blackwell.

Bloom, A. 1987: *The Closing of the American Mind. How Higher Education Has Failed Democracy and Impoverished the Souls of Today's Students*. Harmondsworth: Penguin.

Blumin, S. 1989: *The Emergence of the Middle Class. Social Experience in the American City, 1760–1900*. Cambridge: Cambridge University Press.

Bogner, A. 1986: The structure of social processes: a commentary on the sociology of Norbert Elias. *Sociology*, 20, 3, pp. 387–411.

Bosserman, P. 1968: *Dialectical Sociology. An Analysis of the Sociology of Georges Gurvitch*. Boston, Mass.: Porter Sargent.

Boswell, T. 1989: Colonial empires and the capitalist world-economy: a time series analysis of colonization, 1640–1960. *American Sociological Review*, 54, 2, pp. 180–96.

Bottomore, T. 1990: Giddens's view of historical materialism. In Clark *et al.*, 1990, pp. 205–10.

Bourdieu, P. 1969: Intellectual field and creative project. *Social Science Information*, 8, pp. 89–119.

Bourdieu, P. 1984: *Distinction. A Social Critique of the Judgement of Taste*. London: Routledge and Kegan Paul.

Bourdieu, P. 1985: The genesis of the concepts of *habitus* and of *field*. *Sociocriticism*, 2, pp. 11–24.

Bourdieu, P. 1988: *Homo Academicus*. Translated by Peter Collier, Cambridge: Polity Press (originally published in 1984).

Bowersock, G. W. 1988: Gibbon's historical imagination. *American Scholar*, 57, 1, pp. 33–47.

Bowles, S. and Gintis, S. 1987: *Democracy and Capitalism. Property, Community and the Contradictions of Modern Social Thought*. London: Routledge and Kegan Paul.

Boyne, R. 1990: Culture and the world-system. *Theory, Culture and Society*, 7, 2–3, pp. 57–62.

Bradley, H. 1989: *Men's Work, Women's Work. A Sociological History of the Sexual Division of Labour in Employment*. Cambridge: Polity Press.

Braudel, F. 1953: Georges Gurvitch ou la discontinuité du social. *Annales: Economies, Sociétés, Civilisations*, 8, 3, pp. 347–61.

Braudel, F. 1958a: La longue durée. *Annales: Economies, Sociétés, Civilisations*, 13, 4, pp. 725–53.

Bruadel, F. 1958b: Histoire et sociologie. In Gurvitch, 1958, pp. 83–98.

Braudel, F. 1972a: *The Mediterranean and the Mediterranean World in the Age of Philip II* (2 vols). Translated by Siân Reynolds. London: Fontana.

Braudel, F. 1972b: Personal testimony. *Journal of Modern History*, 44, 4, pp. 447–67.

Braudel, F. 1973: *Capitalism and Material life 1400–1800*. London: Weidenfeld and Nicolson.

Braudel, F. 1980: *On History*. London: Weidenfeld and Nicolson.

Braudel, F. 1981: *Civilization and Capitalism 15th–18th Centuries. Vol 1: The Structures of Everyday Life*. Translated by Siân Reynolds, London: Collins (originally published 1979).

Braudel, F. 1982: *Civilization and Capitalism 15th–18th Centuries. Vol II: The Wheels of Commerce*. Translated by Siân Reynolds, London: Collins (originally published 1979).

Braudel, F. 1984: *Civilization and Capitalism 15th–18th Centuries. Vol III: The Perspective of the World*. Translated by Siân Reynolds, London: Collins (originally published 1979).

Braudel, F. 1988: *The identity of France. Vol I: History and Environment*. Translated by Siân Reynolds, London: Fontana (originally published in 1986).

Braybon, G. 1981: *Women Workers in the First World War*. London: Croom Helm.

Brenner, R. 1976: Agrarian class structure and economic development in pre-industrial Europe. *Past and Present*, 70, pp. 30–75.

Brenner, R. 1977: The origins of capitalist development: a critique of neo-Smithian Marxism. *New Left Review*, 105, pp. 25–92.

Brewer, J. 1989: *The Sinews of Power. War, Money and the English State, 1688–1783*. London: Unwin Hyman.

Burawoy, M. 1989: Two methods in search of science. Skocpol versus Trotsky. *Theory and Society*, 18, 6, pp. 759–805.

Burke, P. 1980: *Sociology and History*. London: Allen and Unwin.

Burns, T. 1966: Review of Runciman 1966. *British Journal of Sociology*, 17, 4, pp. 430–4.

Buxton, W. 1985: *Talcott Parsons and the Capitalist Nation-State. Political Sociology as a Strategic Vocation*. Toronto: University of Toronto Press.

Calhoun, C. 1983a: *The Question of Class Struggle*. Oxford: Basil Blackwell.

Calhoun, C. 1983b: Industrialization and social radicalism. British and French workers' movements and the mid-nineteenth century crises. *Theory and Society*, 12, 4, pp. 485–504.

Calhoun, C. 1987: History and sociology in Britain. *Comparative Studies in Society and History*, 29, 3, pp. 615–25.

Callinicos, A. 1987: *Making History. Agency, Structure and Change in Social Theory*. Cambridge: Polity Press.

Callinicos, A. 1988: Exception or symptom? The British crisis and the world system. *New Left Review*, 169, pp. 97–106.

Camic, C. 1979: The utilitarians revisited. *American Journal of Sociology*, 85, 3, pp. 516–50.

Cannadine, D. 1987: British history: past, present – and future? *Past and Present*, 116, pp. 169–91.

Castles, F. G. 1973: Barrington Moore's thesis and Swedish political development. *Government and Opposition*, 8, 3, pp. 313–331.

Chamberlain, M. 1983: *Fenwomen*. London: Routledge, Kegan and Paul.

Chandler, A. D. 1990: *Scale and Scope. The Dynamics of Industrial Capitalism*. Cambridge, Mass.: Harvard University Press.

Charles, L. and Duffin, L. 1985: *Women and Work in Pre-Industrial England*. London: Croom Helm.

Chartier, R. 1988: *Cultural History: Between Practices and Representations*. Translated by L. G. Cochrane, Cambridge: Polity Press.

Chase-Dunn, C. K. 1980: Socialist states in the capitalist world-economy. *Social Problems*, 27, 3, pp. 505–32.

Chirot, D. 1984: The social and historical landscape of Marc Bloch. In Skocpol (ed.), 1984, pp. 22–46.

Chirot, D. 1985: The rise of the West. *American Journal of Sociology*, 50, 2, pp. 181–95.

Clapham, J. H. and Power, E. (eds) 1941: *The Cambridge History of Europe from the Decline of the Roman Empire. Vol 1: The Agrarian Life of the Middle Ages*. Cambridge: Cambridge University Press.

Clark, J. *et al.*, 1990: *Anthony Giddens. Consensus and Controversy*. London: Falmer Press.

Clark, S. 1985: The *Annales* historians. In Skinner, 1985, pp. 177–203.

Coats, A. W. 1972: Contrary moralities: plebs, paternalists and political economists. *Past and Present*, 54, pp. 130–3.

Cohen, G. A. 1978: *Karl Marx's Theory of History: A Defence*. Oxford: Clarendon Press.

Cohen, I. 1989: *Structuration Theory. Anthony Giddens and the Constitution of Social Life*. London: Macmillan.

Cohn, B. S. 1980: History and anthropology: the state of play. *Comparative Studies in Society and History*, 22, 2, pp. 199–21.

Collini, S. 1979: *Liberalism and Sociology. L. T. Hobhouse and Political Argument in England 1880–1914*. Cambridge: Cambridge University Press.

Collins, R. 1975: *Conflict Sociology. Towards an Explanatory Science*. New York: Academic Press.

Collins, R. 1977: Some comparative principles of educational stratification. *Harvard Educational Review*, 47, pp. 1–27.

Collins, R. 1979: *The Credential Society. An Historical Sociology of Education and Stratification*. New York: Academic Press.

Collins, R. 1981: *Sociology Since Midcentury. Essays in Theory Cumulation*. New York: Academic Press.

Collins, R. 1985: *Three Sociological Traditions*. Oxford: Oxford University Press.

Collins, R. 1986a: *Max Weber. A Skeleton Key*. Beverley Hills: Sage.

Collins, R. 1986b: *Weberian Sociological Theory*. Cambridge: Cambridge University Press.

Collins, R. 1986c: Weber's last theory of capitalism, In Collins, 1986a, pp. 19–44.

Collins, R. 1986d: The Weberian revolution of the High Middle Ages. In Collins, 1986a, pp. 45–76.

Collins, R. 1988: For a sociological philosophy. *Theory and Society*, 17, pp. 669–702.

Corrigan, P. and Sayer, D. 1985: *The Great Arch. English State Formation as Cultural Revolution*. Oxford: Basil Blackwell.

Coser, L. A. 1990: Giddens on historical materialism. In Clark, *et al.*, 1990, pp. 195–204.

Coss, P. R. 1988: Debate: British history: past, present – and future. (Reply to Cannadine 1987). *Past and Present*, 119, pp. 171–83.

Coulbourn, R. 1956: *Feudalism*. Princeton, NJ: Princton University Press.

Dahl, R. A. 1985: *A Preface to Economic Democracy*. Cambridge: Polity Press.

Davenport-Hines, R. P. T. 1984: *Dudley Docker. The Life and Times of a Trade Warrior*. Cambridge: Cambridge University Press.

Davidoff, L. and Hall, C. 1987: *Family Fortunes. Men and Women of the English Middle Class 1780–1850*. London: Hutchinson.

Dodd, P. and Colls, R. 1986: *Englishness. Politics and Culture 1880–1920*. London: Croom Helm.

Dodgshon, R. A. 1987: *The European Past*. London: Macmillan.

Dore, R. P. 1959: *Land Reform in Japan*. Oxford: Oxford University Press

Dore, R. P. 1965: *Education in Tokugawa Japan*. London: Routledge and Kegan Paul.

Dore, R. P. (ed.) 1967: *Aspects of Social Change in Modern Japan*. Princeton: Princeton University Press.

Dore, R. P. 1973: *British Factory – Japanese Factory. The Origins of National Diversity in Industrial Relations*. Berkeley: University of California Press.

Dore, R. P. 1983: Goodwill and the spirit of capitalism. *British Journal of Sociology*, 34, 4, pp. 459–82.

Dore, R. P. 1986: *Flexible Rigidities. Industrial Policy and Structural Adjustment in the Japanese Economy 1970–80*. London: The Athlone Press.

Dore, R. P. 1987a: Citizenship and employment in an age of high technology. *British Journal of Industrial Relations*, 25, 2, pp. 201–25.

Dore, R. P. 1987b: *Taking Japan Seriously. A Confucian Perspective on Leading Economic Issues*. London: The Athlone Press.

Downing, B. M. 1988: Constitutionalism, warfare, and political change in early modern Europe. *Theory and Society*, 17, 7, pp. 7–56.

Downing, B. M. 1989: Medieval origins of constitutional government in the West. *Theory and Society*, 18, 2, pp. 213–47.

Dumm, T. L. 1985: Friendly persuasion. Quakers, liberal toleration, and the birth of the prison. *Political Theory*, 13, 3, pp. 387–407.

Dunning, E. 1989: A response to R. J. Robinson's 'The civilizing process': some remarks on Elias's social history. *Sociology*, 23, 2, pp. 299–307.

Durkheim, E. 1964: *The Division of Labour in Society*. New York: Free Press.

Eisenstadt, S. N. 1963: *The Political Systems of Empires*. New York: Free Press.

Eisenstadt, S. N. (ed.) 1970: *Readings in Social Evolution and Development*. Elmsford, NY: Pergamon Press.

Eisenstadt, S. N. and Rokkan, S. (eds) 1974: *Building States and Nations*. Beverley Hills, Cal: Sage.

Elias, N. 1950: Studies in the genesis of the naval profession. *British Journal of Sociology*, 1, 4, pp. 291–309.

Elias, N. 1956: Problems of involvement and detachment. *British Journal of Sociology*, 7, 3, pp. 226–52.

Elias, N. 1969: Sociology and psychiatry. In Foulkes and Prince, 1969, pp. 117–44.

Elias, N. 1970: Processes of state formation and nation building. *Transactions of the Seventh World Congress of Sociology*, 3, pp. 274–84.

Elias, N. 1971a: Sociology of knowledge: new perspectives (part one). *Sociology*, 5 (2), pp. 149–68.

Elias, N. 1971b: Sociology of knowledge: new perspectives (part two). *Sociology*, 5, (3), pp. 355–70.

Elias, N. 1974: Towards a theory of communities. In Bell and Newby, 1974, pp. ix–xi.

Elias, N. 1978a: *The Civilizing Process. Vol I: The History of Manners*. Oxford: Basil Blackwell (originally published in 1939).

Elias, N. 1978b: *What Is Sociology?*. London: Hutchinson (originally published in 1970).

Elias, N. 1982a: *The Civilizing Process. Vol 2: State Formation and Civilization*. Oxford: Basil Blackwell (originally published in 1939).

Elias, N. 1982b: Scientific establishments. In Elias *et al.*, 1982, pp. 3–29.

Elias, N. 1982–83: Civilization and violence. *Telos*, 54, winter, pp. 134–54.

Elias, N. 1983: *The Court Society*. Translated by Edmund Jephcott, Oxford: Basil Blackwell (originally published in 1969).

Elias, N. 1985: *The Loneliness of the Dying*. Oxford: Basil Blackwell (originally published in 1982).

Elias, N. 1987a: *Involvement and Detachment*. Translated by Edmund Jephcott, Oxford: Basil Blackwell (originally published in 1983).

Elias, N. 1987b: On human beings and their emotions: a process–sociological essay. *Theory, Culture and Society*, 4, 2–3, pp. 339–61.

Elias, N. 1987c: The retreat of sociologists into the present. *Theory, Culture and Society*, 4, 2–3, pp. 223–47.

Elias, N. 1989a: The symbol theory: an Introduction, part one. *Theory, Culture and Society*, 6, 2, pp. 169–217.

Elias, N. 1989b: The symbol theory: an Introduction, part two. *Theory, Culture and Society*, 6, 3, pp. 339–83.

Elias, N. 1990: The symbol theory: an Introduction, part three. *Theory, Culture and Society*, 6, 4, pp. 499–537.

Elias, N. and Dunning, E. 1986: *The Quest for Excitement: Sport and Leisure in the Civilizing Process*. Oxford: Basil Blackwell.

Elias, N. *et al.*, (eds) 1982: *Scientific Establishments and Hierarchies*. Dordrecht: D. Reidel.

Elias, N. and Scotson, J. 1965: *The Established and the Outsider: A Sociological Enquiry into Community Problems*. London: Frank Cass.

Evans, N. 1988: Debate: British history: past, present – and future (reply to Cannadine 1987). *Past and Present*, 119, pp. 194–203.

Febvre, L. 1982: *The Problem of Unbelief in the Sixteenth Century*. Cambridge: Mass.: Harvard University Press (originally published in 1942).

Ferguson, A. 1980: *An Essay on the History of Civil Society*. London: Transaction Books (originally published in 1767).

Fink, C. 1989: *Marc Bloch: A Life in History*. Cambridge: Cambridge University Press.

Fogel, W., and Engerman, S. L. 1974: *Time on the Cross* (2 vols). Boston, Mass.: Little, Brown.

Foss, D. 1963: The World of Talcott Parsons. In Stein and Vidich, 1963, pp. 96–126.

Foster, J. 1974: *Class Struggle and Industrial Revolution*. London: Weidenfeld and Nicolson.

Foucault, M. 1965: *Madness and Civilisation. A History of Insanity in the Age of Reason*. Translated by Richard Howard, New York: Random House (originally published in 1961).

Foucault, M. 1972: *The Archaeology of Knowledge*. London: Routledge.

Foucault, M. 1974: *The Order of Things. An Archaeology of the Human Sciences*. London: Tavistock/Routledge.

Foucault, M. 1979: *Discipline and Punish. The Birth of the Prison*. Harmondsworth: Penguin.

Foucault, M. 1981: *The History of Sexuality. Vol I: An Introduction*. Translated by Robert Hurley, Harmondsworth: Penguin (originally published in 1976).

Foulkes, S. H., and Prince, G. S. (eds) 1969: *Psychiatry in a Changing Society*. London: Tavistock Publications.

Fox, R. W. 1987: Public culture and the problem of synthesis. *Journal of American History*, 74, 1, pp. 113–6.

Fox–Genovese, E., and Genovese, E. D. 1983a: *Fruits of Merchant Capital: Slavery and Bourgeois Property in the Rise and Expansion of Capitalism*. Oxford: Oxford University Press.

Fox–Genovese, E. and Genovese, E. D. 1983b: The debate over *Time on the Cross*: a critique of bourgeois criticism. In Fox–Genovese, E. and Genovese, E. D. 1983a, pp. 136–71.

Fraser, F. 1985: Michel Foucault: a 'young conservative'. *Ethics*, 96, 1, pp. 165–84.

Fulbrook, M. 1985: The emergence of modernity: patterns and people in sociocultural history. A review article. *Comparative Studies in Society and History*, 27, 1, pp. 130–7.

Gagnon, P. 1988: Why study history?. *Atlantic Monthly*, Nov, pp. 43–66.

Garst, D. 1985: Wallerstein and his critics. *Theory and Society*, 14, 4, pp. 469–95.

Gay, P. 1967: *The Enlightenment: An Interpretation. Vol I: The Rise of Modern Paganism*. New York: Alfred Knopf.

Gay, P. 1969: *The Enlightenment: An Interpretation. Vol 2: The Science of Freedom*. New York: Alfred Knopf.

Geertz, C. 1973: *The Interpretation of Cultures*. New York: Basic Books.

Geertz, C. 1980: *Negara. The Theatre State in Nineteenth-Century Bali*. Princeton: Princeton University Press.

Geertz, C. 1983: *Local Knowledge. Further Essays in Interpretive Anthropology*. New York: Basic Books.

Gellner, E. 1959: *Words and Things. A Critical Account of Linguistic Philosophy and a Study of Ideology*. London: Victor Gollancz.

Gellner, E. 1965: *Thought and Change*. London: Weidenfeld and Nicolson.

Gellner, E. 1969: *Saints of the Atlas*. London: Weidenfeld and Nicolson.

Gellner, E. 1973: *Cause and Meaning in the Social Sciences*. London: Routledge and Kegan Paul.

Gellner, E. 1974: *Legitimations of Belief*. Cambridge: Cambridge University Press.

Gellner, E. 1975: A social contract in search of an idiom. The demise of the Danegold state?. *Political Quarterly*, 46, 2, pp. 127–52.

Gellner, E. 1979: *Spectacle and Predicaments. Essays in Social Theory*. Cambridge: Cambridge University Press.

Gellner, E. 1981: *Muslim Society*. Cambridge: Cambridge University Press.

Gellner, E. 1983: *Nations and Nationalism*. Oxford: Basil Blackwell.

Gellner, E. 1985: *Relativism and the Social Sciences*. Cambridge: Cambridge University Press.

Gellner, E. 1988: *Plough, Sword and Book. The Structure of Human History*. London: Collins Harvill.

Genovese, E. D. 1971a: *In Red and Black. Marxian Explorations in Southern and Afro–American History*. New York: Random House.

Genovese, E. D. 1971b: On being a socialist and a historian. In Genovese, 1971a, pp. 3–22.

Genovese, E. D. 1974: *Roll, Jordan, Roll. The World The Slaves Made*. New York: Random House.

Genovese, E. D., and Genovese, E. 1976: The political crisis of social history. *Journal of Social History*, 10, 2, pp. 205–20.

Genovese, E. F. 1973: The many faces of moral economy: a contribution to a debate (a reply to Coats 1972). *Past and Present*, 58, pp. 161–68.

Giddens, A. 1971: *Capitalism and Modern Social Theory. An Analysis of the Writings of Marx, Durkheim and Max Weber*. Cambridge: Cambridge University Press.

Giddens, A. 1972: *Politics and Sociology in the Thought of Max Weber*. London: Macmillan.

Giddens, A. 1973: *The Class Structure of the Advanced Societies*. London: Hutchinson.

Giddens, A. 1976: *New Rules of Sociological Method: A Positive Critique of Interpretative Sociologies*. London: Hutchinson.

Giddens, A. 1979: *Central Problems in Social Theory*. London: Macmillan.

Giddens, A. 1981: *A Contemporary Critique of Historical Materialism. Vol. 1: Power, Property and the State*. London: Macmillan.

Giddens, A. 1982: *Profiles and Critiques in Social Theory*. London: Macmillan.

Giddens, A. 1984: *The Constitution of Society. Outline of the Theory of Structuration*. Cambridge: Polity Press.

Giddens, A. 1985: *The Nation-State and Violence. Volume Two of A Contemporary Critique of Historical Materialism*. Cambridge: Polity Press.

Giddens, A. 1987a: *Social Theory and Modern Sociology*. Cambridge: Polity Press.

Giddens, A. 1978b: Out of the Orrery: E. P. Thompson on consciousness and history. In Giddens, 1987a, pp. 203–24.

Giddens, A. 1987c: What do sociologists do? In Giddens, 1987a, pp. 1–21.

Giddens, A. 1987d: The social sciences and philosophy – trends in recent social theory. In Giddens, 1987a, pp. 52–72.

Giddens, A. 1987e: Weber and Durkheim: coincidence and convergence. In Mommsen and Osterhammel, 1987, pp. 182–9.

Giddens, A. 1989a: Comments on Paul Kennedy's *The Rise and Fall of the Great Powers*. *British Journal of Sociology*, 40, 2, pp. 328–31.

Giddens, A. 1989b: A reply to my critics. In Held and Thompson, 1989, pp. 249–301.

Giddens, A. 1990: Structuration theory and sociological analysis. In Clark *et al.*, 1990, pp. 297–315.

Giddens, A., and Stanworth, P. H. (eds) 1974: *Elites and Power in British Society*. Cambridge: Cambridge University Press.

Gleichman, P. *et al.* (eds) 1977: *Human Figurations. Essays for Norbert Elias*. Amsterdam: Amsterdam Sociologisch Tijdschrift.

Goldstone, J. 1988: East and west in the seventeenth century: political crises in Stuart England, Ottoman Turkey and Ming China. *Comparative Studies in Society and History*, 30, 1, pp. 103–42.

Goldthorpe, J. H. 1984a: The end of convergence: Corporatist and dualist tendencies. In Goldthorpe, 1984b, pp. 315–43.

Goldthorpe, J. H. (ed.) 1984b: *Order and Conflict in Contemporary Capitalism*. Oxford: Clarendon Press.

Goldthorpe, J. H., *et al.* 1968a: *The Affluent Worker: Industrial Attitudes and Behaviour*. Cambridge: Cambridge University Press.

Goldthorpe, J. H., *et al.* 1968b: *The Affluent Worker: Political Attitudes and Behaviour*. Cambridge: Cambridge University Press.

Goldthorpe, J. H., *et al.* 1969: *The Affluent Worker and the Class Structure*. Cambridge: Cambridge University Press.

Goodwin, J., and Skocpol, T. 1989: Explaining revolutions in the contemporary Third World. *Politics and Society*, 17, 4, pp. 489–509.

Goudsblom, J. 1977: Responses to Norbert Elias's work in England, Germany, the Netherlands and France. In Gleichman *et al.* (eds), 1977, pp. 37–97.

Goudsblom, J. 1988: The sociology of Norbert Elias: its resonance and significance. *Theory, Culture and Society*, 4, 2–3, pp. 323–37.

Gouldner, A. 1971: *The Coming Crisis of Western Sociology*. London: Heinemann.

Gregory, D. 1990: 'Grand maps of history': structuration theory and social change. In Clark *et al.* 1990, pp. 217–33.

Gregory, D., and Urry, J. (eds) 1985: *Social Relations and Spatial Structures*. London: Macmillan.

Gurevich, A. J. 1983: Medieval culture and mentality according to the new French historiography. *European Journal of Sociology*, 14, 1, pp. 167–95.

Gurr, T. R. 1970: *Why Men Rebel*. Princeton, NJ: Princeton University Press.

Gurvitch, G. 1950: *La Vocation Actuelle de la Sociologie*. Paris: Presses Universitaires de France.

Gurvitch, G. 1955: *Déterminismes Sociaux et Liberté Humaine*. Paris: Presses Universitaires de France.

Gurvitch, G. 1956: La crise de l'explication en sociologie. *Cahiers Internationaux de Sociologie*, 21, pp. 3–18.

Gurvitch, G. 1957: Continuité et discontinuité en histoire et en sociologie. *Annales: Economies, Sociétés, Civilisations*, 12, 1, pp. 73–85.

Gurvitch, G. (ed.) 1958: *Traite de Sociologie, Vol I*. Paris: Presses Universitaires de France.

Gurvitch, G. 1962: *Dialectique et Sociologie*. Paris: Flammarion.

Gurvitch, G. 1964: *The Spectrum of Social Time*. Dordrecht: D. Reidel.

Gurvitch, G. 1971: *The Social Frameworks of Knowledge*. Translated by M. A. Thompson and K. A. Thompson. Oxford: Basil Blackwell (originally published in 1966).

Gutman, H. G. 1975: *Slavery and the Numbers Game: A Critique of 'Time on the Cross'*. Urbana.

Gutman, H. G. 1977a: *Work, Culture and Society in Industrializing America*. New York: Vintage Books.

Gutman, H. G. 1977b: Work, culture and society in industrializing America, 1815–1919. In Gutman, 1977a, pp. 3–78.

Hall, J. A. 1985: *Powers and Liberties*. Harmondsworth: Penguin.

Hall, J. A. 1989: They do things differently there, or, the contribution of British historical sociology. *British Journal of Sociology*, 40, 4, pp. 544–64.

Hall, S. 1981: In defence of theory. In Samuel, 1981, pp. 378–85.

Hall, T. D. 1986: Incorporation and the world-system. *American Sociological Review*, 51, 3, pp. 390–402.

Hallpike, C. R. 1988: *The Principles of Social Evolution*. Oxford: Clarendon Press.

Halsey, A. H. 1984: T. H. Marshall: past and present 1893–1981. *Sociology*, 18, 1, pp. 1–18.

Hamilton, P. 1983: *Talcott Parsons*. London: Tavistock.

Hamilton, R. 1978: *The Liberation of Women. A Study of Patriarchy and Capitalism*. London: Allen and Unwin.

Hammond, P. E. (ed.) 1964: *Sociologists at Work*. New York: Basic Books.

Hanawalt, B. 1986: *Women and Work in Pre-Industrial Europe*. Bloomington: Indiana University Press.

Harrison, M. 1986: The ordering of the urban environment: time, work and the occurrence of crowds 1790–1835. *Past and Present*, 110, pp. 134–68.

Harvey, D. 1982: *The Limits to Capital*. Oxford: Basil Blackwell.

Hatt, P. K., and Reiss, A. J. (eds) 1957: *Cities and Societies. The Revised Reader in Urban Sociology*. Glencoe, Ill: Free Press.

Hawthorn, G. 1976: *Enlightenment and Despair. A History of Sociology*. Cambridge: Cambridge University Press.

Hayek, F. 1976: *The Road to Serfdom*. London: Routledge (originally published in 1944).

Hechter, M. 1975: Review of Wallerstein, 1974. *Contemporary Sociology*, 4, pp. 217–22.

Hechter, M. 1977: Lineages of the capitalist state (review of Anderson, 1974b). *American Journal of Sociology*, 82, 5, pp. 1057–74.

Held, D. 1987: *Models of Democracy*. Cambridge: Polity Press.

Held, D. 1989: Citizenship and autonomy. In Held and Thompson, 1989, pp. 162–84.

Held, D. and Thompson, J. B. 1989: *Social Theory of Modern Societies. Anthony Giddens and his Critics*. Cambridge: Cambridge University Press.

Hexter, J. H. 1972: Fernand Braudel and the *Monde Braudelien . . . . Journal of Modern History*, 44, 4, pp. 480–539.

Hill, C. 1983: History is a matter of taking liberties. *Guardian*, 30 July.

Himmelstein, J., and Kimmel, M. S. 1981: Skocpol's structural model of revolution. *American Journal of Sociology*, pp. 1145–54.

Hirst, P. Q. 1985: *Marxism and Historical Writing*. London: Routledge.

Hobhouse, L. T. 1911: *Liberalism*, London: Williams and Northgate.

Hodges, R. 1989: *Dark Age Economics. The Origins of Towns and Trade AD 600–1000*. London: Duckworth.

Hoffman, J. 1988: *State, Power and Democracy. Contentious Concepts in Practical Political Theory*. New York: St Martin's Press.

Hollis, P. 1979: *Women in Public*. London: Allen and Unwin.

Holton, R. J. and Turner, B. S. 1986: *Talcott Parsons on Economy and Society*. London: Routledge.

Homans, G. C. 1942: *English Villagers of the Thirteenth Century*. Cambridge: Mass.: Harvard University Press.

Homans, G. C. 1984: *Coming to my Senses. The Autobiography of a Sociologist*. New Brunswick: Transaction.

Hopkins, E. 1982: Working hours and working conditions during the industrial revolution: a re-appraisal. *Economic History Review*, 35, 1, pp. 52–66.

Hopper, E. I. 1971: *Readings in the Theory of Education Systems*. London: Hutchinson.

Horowitz, I. L. (ed.) 1969: *Sociological Self-Images*. Beverly Hills: Sage.

Howell, M. C. 1986: *Women, Production and Patriarchy in Late Medieval Cities*, Chicago: University of Chicago Press.

Hughes, S. H. 1959: *Consciousness and Society. The Reorientation of European Social Thought 1890–1930*. London: Paladin.

Hugill, P. J. 1988: Structural changes in the core regions of the world-economy, 1830–1945. *Journal of Historical Geography*, 14, 2, pp. 111–27.

Hume, D. 1983: *The History of England from the Invasion of Julius Caesar to the Revolution in 1688*, 6 vols, ed. W. B. Todd. New York: Liberty Classics.

Hume, D. 1987a: *Essays Moral, Political and Literary*. Indianapolis: Liberty Classics (originally published in 1777).

Hume, 1987b: My own life. In Hume 1987a, pp. xxxii–x1i.

Humpries, J. 1977: The working class family, women's liberation and class struggle: the case of nineteenth-century British history. *Review of Radical Political Economy*, 9, 3, pp. 25–41.

Hunt, L. (ed.) 1989: *The New Cultural History*. Berkeley: University of California Press.

Hunt, V. F. 1978–9: The rise of feudalism in Eastern Europe: a critical appraisal of the Wallerstein 'world-system' thesis. *Science and Society*, 42, 1, pp. 43–61.

Huntington, S. P. 1988–9: The United States – decline or renewal? *Foreign Affairs*, 67, 2, pp. 76–96.

Ingham, G. 1970: Social stratification: individual attributes and social relationships. *Sociology*, 4, 1, pp. 105–13.

Ingham, G. 1984: *Capitalism Divided? The City and Industry in British Social Development*. London: Macmillan.

Ingham, G. 1988: Commercial capital and British development: a reply to Michel Barratt Brown. *New Left Review*, 88, pp. 45–65.

Jackson, P. and Smith, S. J. 1984: *Exploring Social Geography*. London: Allen and Unwin.

Janowitz, M. 1977: A sociological perspective on Wallerstein. *American Journal of Sociology*, 82, 5, pp. 1090–96.

Janowitz, M. 1978: *The Last Half-Century. Social Change and Politics in America*. Chicago: University of Chicago Press.

Janowitz, M. 1980: Observations on the sociology of citizenship: obligations and rights. *Social Forces*, 59, 1, pp. 1–24.

Janowitz, M., and Suttles, G. D. 1978: The social ecology of citizenship. In Sarri and Hasenfeld, 1978, pp. 80–104.

Jarvie, I. C., and Agassi, J. 1973: Preface. In Gellner, 1973, pp. vii–ix.

Jarvie, I. C., and Agassi, J. 1985: Editorial preface. In Gellner, 1985, pp. v–viii.

Jay, M. 1990: Fieldwork and theorizing in intellectual history. A reply to Fritz Ringer. *Theory and Society*, 19, 3, pp. 311–21.

Johnson, R. 1976: Barrington Moore, Perry Anderson and English social development. *Working Papers in Cultural Studies*, 9, Centre for Contemporary Cultural Studies. Birmingham University, UK.

Johnson, R. 1978: Edward Thompson, Eugene Genovese, and socialist–humanist history. *History Workshop Journal*, 6, pp. 79–100.

Johnson, R. 1981: Against absolutism. In Samuel, 1981, pp. 386–96.

Johnston, R. J. 1983: *Philosophy and Human Geography*. London: Edward Arnold.

Jones, C. A. 1987: *International Business in the Nineteenth Century. The Rise and Fall of a Cosmopolitan Bourgeoisie*. Brighton: Wheatsheaf.

Jones, G. S. 1971: *Outcast London. A Study of the Relationship between Classes in Victorian Society*. Oxford: Clarendon Press.

Jones, G. S. 1975: Review of Foster 1974. *New Left Review*, 90, pp. 35–69.

Jones, G. S. 1976: From historical sociology to theoretical history. *British Journal of Sociology*, 27, 3, pp. 295–305.

Jones, G. S. 1983a: *The Language of Labour. Studies in English Working Class History 1832–1982*. Cambridge: Cambridge University Press.

Jones, G. S. 1983b: The mid-century crisis and the 1848 revolutions. *Theory and Society*, 12, 4, pp. 505–19.

Joyce, P. 1982: *Work, Society and Politics*. London: Methuen.

Katz, B. M. 1987: The criticism of arms: the Frankfurt school goes to war. *Journal of Modern History*, 59, pp. 439–478.

Katznelson, I. 1973: *Black Men, White Cities. Race, Politics and Migration in the United States, 1900–30, and Britain, 1948–68*. London: Oxford University Press.

Katznelson, I. 1981a: Lenin or Weber? Choices in Marxist theories of politics. *Political Studies*, 29, 4, pp. 632–40.

Katznelson, I. 1981b: *City Trenches. Urban Politics and the Patterning of Class in the United States*. Chicago: Chicago University Press.

Katznelson, I. 1988: The welfare state as a contested institutional idea. *Politics and Society*, 16, 4, pp. 517–31.

Katznelson, I., and Zolberg, A. (eds) 1986: *Working-Class Formation. Nineteenth-Century Patterns in Western Europe and the United States*. Princeton, NJ: Princeton University Press.

Kaye, B. 1960: *The Development of the Architectural Profession in Britain. A Sociological Study*. London: Allen and Unwin.

Kaye, H. 1984: *The British Marxist Historians. An Introductory Analysis*. Cambridge: Polity Press.

Keane, J. 1984: *Public Life and Late Capitalism*. Cambridge: Cambridge University Press.

Kearns, G. 1988: History, geography and world-systems theory. *Journal of Historical Geography*, 14, 3, pp. 281–92.

Kedourie, 1975: New histories for old. *Times Literary Supplement*, 7 March, p. 238.

Kellner, H. 1979: Disorderly conduct: Braudel's Mediterranean satire. *History and Theory*, 18, 1, pp. 197–222.

Kennedy, D. 1979: The archaeology and sociology of knowledge. *Theory and Society*, 8, 2, pp. 269–90.

Kennedy, P. 1980: *The Rise of Anglo–German Antagonism 1860–1914*. London: Allen and Unwin.

Kennedy, P. 1981: *The Realities Behind Diplomacy. Background Influences on British External Policy, 1865–1980*. London: Fontana.

Kennedy, P. 1988: *The Rise and Fall of the Great Powers. Economic Change and Military Conflict from 1500 to 2000*. London: Fontana.

Kent, C. 1986: Presence and absence: history, theory and the working class. *Victorian Studies*, 29, 3, pp. 437–62.

Kinser, S. 1986: *Annaliste* paradigm? The geohistorical structuralism of Fernand Braudel. *American Historical Review*, 86, 1, pp. 63–105.

Kirk, N. 1987: In defence of class. A critique of recent revisionist writing upon the nineteenth-century English working class. *International Review of Social History*, 32, pp. 2–47.

Knapp, P. 1984: Can social theory escape from history? Views of history in social science. *History and Theory*, 23, 1, pp. 34–52.

Kuhn, A., and Wolpe, A. (eds) 1978: *Feminism and Materialism. Women and Modes of Production*. London: Routledge and Kegan Paul.

Kumar, K. 1983: Class and political action in nineteenth-century England. *European Journal of Sociology*, 24, 1, pp. 3–43.

Kuzmics, H. 1984: Elias's theory of civilization. *Telos*, 61, Fall, pp. 83–100.

LaCapra, D. 1983: *Rethinking Intellectual History: Texts, Contexts, Language*. Ithica, NY: Cornell University Press.

Lachmann, R. 1989: Elite conflict and state formation in 16th- and 17th-century England and France. *American Sociological Review*, 54, 2, pp. 141–62.

Lamont, W. 1988: Debate: British history: past, present – and future (reply to Cannadine, 1987). *Past and Present*, 119, pp. 183–93.

Laqueur, W. 1976: *Religion and Respectability. Sunday Schools and Working-Class Culture 1780–1850*. Princeton: Yale University Press.

Lasch, C. 1985: Historical sociology and the myth of maturity. Norbert Elias's 'very simple formula'. *Theory and Society*, 14, 5, pp. 705–21.

Laslett, P. 1965: *The World We Have Lost*. London: Methuen.

Lattimore, O. 1962: *Studies in Frontier History*. London: Oxford University Press.

Le Goff, J. 1980: *Time, Work and Culture in the Middle Ages*. Chicago: University of Chicago Press (originally published in 1977).

Le Goff, J. 1988: *Medieval Civilization 400–1500*. Translated by Julia Barrow. Oxford: Basil Blackwell (originally published in 1964).

Lehman, E. W. 1972: Review of Lipset and Raab, 1970. *Contemporary Sociology*, 1 (4), pp. 291–5.

Lemert, C. 1990: The habits of intellectuals. Response to Ringer. *Theory and Society*, 19, 2, pp. 295–310.

Lenski, G. 1966: *Power and Privilege. A Theory of Social Stratification*. New York: McGraw-Hill.

Le Roy Ladurie, E. 1977: *Peasants of the Languedoc*. Urbana, Ill.: Illinois University Press (originally published in 1966).

Le Roy Ladurie, E. 1979: *The Territory of the Historian*. Hassocks: Harvester Press.

Le Roy Ladurie, E. 1980: *Montaillou. Cathars and Catholics in a French Village 1294–1324*. Translated by Barbara Bray. Harmondsworth: Penguin (originally published in 1978).

Le Roy Ladurie, E. 1981: *Carnival in Romans. A People's Uprising at Romans 1579–80*. Translated by Mary Feeney, Harmondsworth: Penguin (originally published in 1979).

Le Roy Ladurie, E. 1982: *Love, Death and Money in the Pays d'Oc*. Translated by Alan Sheridan, London: Scolar Press (originally published in 1980).

Le Roy Ladurie, E. 1987: *The French Peasantry 1450–1660*. Translated by Alan Sheridan, Aldershot: Scolar Press (originally published in 1977).

Levi–Strauss, C. 1963–77: *Structural Anthropology*. Translated by Arthur Goldhammer, New York: Basic Books.

Lidz, V. 1989: The American value system: a commentary on Talcott Parson's pespective and understanding. *Theory, Culture and Society*, 6, 4, pp. 559–76.

Lindberg, L. N., *et al.* (eds) 1975: *Stress and Contradiction in Modern Capitalism*. Toronto: Lexington Books.

Lipset, S. M. 1963: *The First New Nation. The United States in Comparative and Historical Perspective*. London: Heinemann.

Lipset, S. M. 1964: The biography of a research project: *Union Democracy*. In Hammond, 1964, pp. 96–120.

Lipset, S. M. 1968a: History and sociology: some methodological considerations. In Lipset, 1968, pp. 3–28.

Lipset, S. M. 1968b: *Revolution and Counterrevolution. Change and Persistence in Social Structures*. New York: Basic Books.

Lipset, S. M. 1969: Socialism and sociology. In Horowitz, 1969, pp. 143–75.

Lipset, S. M. 1971: *Rebellion in the University*. Boston: Little, Brown and Company.

Lipset, S. M. 1981: *Political Man. The Social Bases of Politics*. Baltimore: Johns Hopkins Press (originally published in 1960).

Lipset, S. M., *et al* 1956: *Union Democracy. The Internal Politics of the International Typographical Union*. New York: Free Press.

Lipset, S. M., and Raab, E. 1971: *The Politics of Unreason. Right-Wing Extremism in America 1790–1970*. London: Heinemann.

Lipset, S. M., and Rokkan, S. 1967a: Cleavage structures, party systems, and voter alignments. In Lipset and Rokkan, 1967b, pp. 1–64.

Lipset, S. M., and Rokkan, S. (eds) 1967b: *Party Systems and Voter Alignments*. New York: Free Press.

Lipset, S. M., and Smelser, N. 1961: Change and controversy in recent American sociology. *British Journal of Sociology*, 12, 6, pp. 41–51.

Lloyd, C. 1986: *Explanation in Social History*. Oxford: Basil Blackwell.

Lockwood, D. 1974: For T. H. Marshall. *Sociology*, 8, pp. 363–7.

Lowenthal, D. 1968: Review of Moore, 1966. *History and Theory*, 7 (2), pp. 257–78.

Lukes, S. 1973: *Emile Durkheim. His Life and Work. A Historical and Critical Study*. London: Allen Lane.

McClelland, K. 1979: Reply to Johnson, 1978. *History Workshop*, 7, Spring, pp. 101–15.

MacFarlane, A. 1978: *The Origins of English Individualism*. Oxford: Basil Blackwell.

MacFarlane, A. 1987: *The Culture of Capitalism*. Oxford: Basil Blackwell.

MacIntyre, A. 1981: *After Virtue: A Study in Moral Theory*. London: Duckworth.

McLellan, G. 1981: *Marxism and the Methodologies of History*. London: Verso.

McLellan, G. 1984: History and theory: contemporary debates and directions. *Literature and History*, 10, 2, pp. 139–64.

McLeod, H. 1984: *Religion and the Working Class in Nineteenth-Century Britain*. London: Macmillan.

Magarey, S. 1987: That hoary old chestnut, free will and determinism: culture vs structure, or history vs theory in Britain. *Comparative Studies in Society and History*, 29, 3, pp. 626–39.

Maier, C. S. 1987: *In Search of Stability. Explorations in Historical Political Economy*. Cambridge: Cambridge University Press.

Mann, M. 1970: The social cohesion of liberal democracy. *American Sociological Review*, 35, 3, pp. 423–39.

Mann, M. 1973: *Consciousness and Action among the Western Working Class*. London: Macmillan.

Mann, M. 1975: The ideology of intellectuals and other people in the development of capitalism. In Lindberg *et al.*, 1975, pp. 275–307.

Mann, M. 1986: *The Sources of Social Power. Vol I: A History of Power from the Beginning to AD 1760*. Cambridge: Cambridge University Press.

Mann, M. 1988: *States, War and Capitalism. Studies in Political Sociology*. Oxford: Basil Blackwell.

Mann, M. 1989: Comments on Paul Kennedy's *The Rise and Fall of the Great Powers*. *British Journal of Sociology*, 40, 2, pp. 331–5.

Mann, M. 1990: Review of Wallerstein, 1989. *Contemporary Sociology*, 19, 2, pp. 196–8.

Maravall, J. A. 1986: *Culture of the Baroque. Analysis of a Historical Structure*. Manchester: Manchester University Press.

Marshall, G. *et al.* 1985: Class, citizenship, and distributional conflict in modern Britain. *British Journal of Sociology*, 36, 2, pp. 259–84.

Marshall, G. *et al.* 1987: Distributional struggle and moral order in a market society. *Sociology*, 21, 1, pp. 55–73.

Marshall, G. *et al.* 1988: *Social Class in Modern Britain*. London: Hutchinson.

Marshall, T. H. 1963a: *Sociology at the Crossroads and Other Essays*. London: Heinemann.

Marshall, T. H. 1963b: Sociology at the crossroads. In Marshall, 1963a, pp. 3–4 (originally published in 1946).

Marshall, T. H. 1963c: Sociology – the way ahead. In Marshall, 1963a, pp. 25–43.

Marshall, T. H. 1963d: Citizenship and social class. In Marshall, 1963a, pp. 67–127 (originally published in 1950).

Marshall, T. H. 1965: *Social Policy in the Twentieth Century*. 5th edition. London: Hutchinson.

Marshall, T. H. 1971: Social selection in the welfare state. In Hopper, 1971, pp. 38–55.

Marshall, T. H. 1973: A British sociological career. *International Social Science Journal*, 25 (1–2), pp. 89–100.

Marshall, T. H. 1981a: *The Right to Welfare and Other Essays*. London: Heinemann.

Marshall, T. H. 1981b: Value problems of welfare–capitalism. In Marshall, 1981a, pp. 104–22 (originally published in 1972).

Marshall, T. H. 1981c: *Afterthought* – The 'Hyphenated Society'. In Marshall, 1981a, pp. 123–36.

Marshall, T. H. 1981d: Reflections on power. In Marshall, 1981a, pp. 137–53 (originally published in 1969).

Marx, K. 1970: *Capital*. London: Lawrence and Wishart (originally published in 1867–94).

Marx, K., and Engels, F. 1962: *Selected Works* (2 vols). Moscow: Foreign Languages Publishing House.

Meade, J. E. 1984: Full employment, new technologies and the distribution of income. *Journal of Social Policy*, 13, 2,

Meadwell, H. 1987: Exchange relations between lords and peasants. *European Journal of Sociology*, 28, 1, pp. 3–49.

Mehta, V. 1983: *Fly and the Fly-Bottle. Encounters with British Intellectuals*. New York: Columbia University Press (originally published in 1962).

Mennell, S. 1989: *Norbert Elias. Civilization and the Human Self-Image*. Oxford: Basil Blackwell.

Mennell, S. 1990: The globalization of human society as a very long-term social process: Elias's theory. *Theory, Culture and Society*, 7, 2–3, pp. 359–71.

Merton, R. K. 1970: *Science, Technology and Society in Seventeenth Century England*. New York: Howard Fertig (originally published in 1938).

Mills, C. W. 1956: *The Power Elite*. New York: Oxford University Press.

Mills, C. W. 1970: *The Sociological Imagination*. Harmondsworth: Penguin (originally published in 1959).

Mokyr, J. 1985: *Why Ireland Starved. A Quantitative and Analytical History of the Irish Economy, 1800–1850*. London: Allen and Unwin.

Mommsen, W. J., and Osterhammel, J. (eds) 1987: *Max Weber and his Contemporaries*. London: Unwin Hyman.

Monkonnen, E. H. 1986: The dangers of synthesis. *American Historical Review*, 91, pp. 1146–57.

Montesquieu, C. de 1989: *The Spirit of the Laws* (L'Esprit des Lois). Translated by A. M. Cohler, *et al.* Cambridge: Cambridge University Press (originally published in 1748).

Moore, B. 1950: *Soviet Politics – The Dilemma of Power: The Role of Ideas in Social Change*. Cambridge, Mass.: Harvard University Press.

Moore, B. 1953: The new scholasticism and the study of politics. *World Politics*, 1, 6, pp. 122–38.

Moore, B. 1954: *Terror and Progress USSR: Some Sources of Change and Stability in the Soviet Dictatorship.* Cambridge, Mass.: Harvard University Press.

Moore, B. 1958: *Political Power and Social Theory.* Cambridge, Mass.: Harvard University Press.

Moore, B. 1969: *Social Origins of Dictatorship and Democracy. Lord and Peasant in the Making of the Modern World.* Harmondsworth: Penguin (originally published in 1966).

Moore, B. 1972: *Reflections on the Causes of Human Misery and on Certain Proposals to Eliminate Them.* Harmondsworth: Penguin.

Moore, B. 1978: *Injustice. The Social Bases of Obedience and Revolt.* London: Macmillan Press.

Moore, B. 1984: *Privacy. Studies in Social and Cultural History.* Armonk, NY: M. E. Sharpe.

Moore, B. 1987: Austerity and unintended riches. *Comparative Studies in Society and History*, 29, 4, pp. 787–810.

Moore, B. 1988: *Authority and Equality under Capitalism and Socialism.* Oxford: Oxford University Press.

Mumford, L. 1961: *The City in History.* New York: Harcourt, Brace and World.

Munch, R. 1988: *Theory of Action. Towards a New Synthesis Going Beyond Parsons.* London: Routledge and Kegan Paul.

Nairn, T. 1964: The English working class. *New Left Review*, 64, pp. 43–57.

Neale, R. S. 1985: *Writing Marxist History. British Society, Economy and Culture.* Oxford: Basil Blackwell.

Newby, H. 1977: *The Deferential Worker.* Harmondsworth: Penguin.

Newby, H. *et al.* 1985: *Restructuring Capital.* London: Macmillan.

Nicholls, D. 1988: Fractions of capital: the aristocracy, the city and industry in the development of modern British capitalism. *Social History*, 13, 1, pp. 71–83.

North, D. C. 1981: *Structure and Change in Economic History.* New York: W. W. Norton.

North, D. C., and Thomas, R. P. 1973: *The Rise of the Western World. A New Economic History.* Cambridge: Cambridge University Press.

Nozick, R. J. 1974: *Anarchy, State, and Utopia.* Oxford: Basil Blackwell.

Nye, J. S. 1988: Understanding US strength. *Foreign Policy*, 72, Fall, pp. 105–29.

O'Neill, J. 1986: The disciplinary society: from Weber to Foucault. *British Journal of Sociology*, 37, 1, pp. 42–60.

Orloff, A. S., and Skocpol, T. 1984: Why not equal protection? Explaining the politics of public societal spending in Britain, 1900–1911, and the United States, 1880–1920. *American Sociological Review*, 49, 6, pp. 726–50.

Pahl, R. E. 1984: *Divisions of Labour.* Oxford: Basil Blackwell.

Painter, N. I. 1987: Bias and synthesis in history. *Journal of American History*, 74, 1, pp. 107–12.

Parker, W. N. (ed.) 1986: *Economic History and the Modern Economist.* Oxford: Oxford University Press.

Parsa, M. 1985: Economic development and political transformation. A comparative analysis of the United States, Russia, Nicaragua and Iran. *Theory and Society*, 14, 3, pp. 623–75.

Parsons, T. 1937: *The Structure of Social Action. A Study in Social Theory with Special Reference to a Group of Recent European Writers*. New York: Free Press.

Parsons, T. 1942: Some sociological aspects of the fascist movements. *Social Forces*, 21 (2), pp. 138–47.

Parsons, T. 1951: *The Social System*. New York: Free Press.

Parsons, T. 1966: *Societies: Evolutionary and Comparative Perspectives*. Englewood Cliffs, NJ: Prentice-Hall.

Parsons, T. 1970: On building social systems theory: a personal history. *Daedalus*, 99, pp. 826–81.

Parsons, T. 1971: *The System of Modern Societies*. Englewood Cliffs, NJ: Prentice-Hall.

Parsons, T. 1989: 'A tentative outline of American values'. *Theory, Culture and Society*, 6, 4, pp. 577–612.

Parsons, T., *et al*. 1953: *Working Papers in the Theory of Action*. New York: Free Press.

Parsons, T., and Smelser, N. J. 1956: *Economy and Society. A Study in the Integration of Economic and Social Theory*. London: Routledge.

Perrin, C.-E. 1948: L'oeuvre historique de Marc Bloch. *Revue Historique*, 199, 2, pp. 161–88.

Phillipson, N. 1989: *Hume*. London: Weidenfeld and Nicolson.

Poggi, G. 1968: Review of Moore, 1966. *British Journal of Sociology*, 19 (2), pp. 215–17.

Popper, K. R. 1945: *The Open Society and its Enemies* (2 vols). London: Routledge and Kegan Paul.

Popper, K. R. 1957: *The Poverty of Historicism*. London: Routledge and Kegan Paul.

Poster, M. 1984: *Foucault, Marxism and History. Mode of Production versus Mode of Information*. Cambridge: Polity Press.

Ragin, C. 1987: *The Comparative Method. Moving Beyond Qualitative and Quantitative Strategies*. Berkeley, Cal: University of California Press.

Ragin, C. and Chirot, D. 1984: The world system of Immanuel Wallerstein: sociology and politics as history. In Skocpol (ed.), 1984, pp. 276–312.

Rawls, J. 1972: *A Theory of Justice*. Oxford: Oxford University Press.

Reddy, W. H. 1984: *The Rise of Market Culture. The Textile Trade and French Society, 1750–1900*. Cambridge: Cambridge University Press.

Rhodes, R. C. 1978: Emile Durkheim and the historical thought of Marc Bloch. *Theory and Society*, 5 (1), pp. 45–73.

Ringer, F. 1990: The intellectual field, intellectual history, and the sociology of knowledge. *Theory and Society*, 19, 3, pp. 269–94.

Robertson, R., and Turner, B. S. 1990: Talcott Parsons and modern social theory – an appreciation. *Theory, Culture and Society*, 6, 4, pp. 539–58.

Robinson, R. J. 1987: The 'civilizing process': some remarks on Elias's social history. *Sociology*, 21, 1, pp. 1–17.

Rogers, B. 1990: Philosophy for historians: the methodological writings of Quentin Skinner. *History*, 75, 244, pp. 262–71.

Roper, J. 1989: *Democracy and its Critics. Anglo–American Democratic Thought in the Nineteenth Century*. London: Unwin Hyman.

Rosaldo, M. and Lamphere, L. (eds) 1974: *Women, Culture and Society*. Stanford: Stanford University Press.

Rosenzweig, R. 1987: What *is* the matter with history?. *Journal of American History*, 74, 1, pp. 117–22.

Rothman, S. 1970: Barrington Moore and the dialectics of revolution. *American Political Science Review*, 64 (1), pp. 61–83.

Rubinstein, W. D. 1977: Wealth, elites and the class structure of modern Britain. *Past and Present*, 76, pp. 99–124.

Runciman, W. G. 1965: *Social Science and Political Theory*. Cambridge: Cambridge University Press.

Runciman, W. G. 1966: *Relative Deprivation and Social Justice*. London: Routledge.

Runciman, W. G. 1970a: *Sociology in its Place and Other Essays*. Cambridge: Cambridge University Press.

Runciman, W. G. 1970b: Charismatic legitimacy and one-party rule in Nkrumah's Ghana. In Runciman, 1970a, pp. 157–75.

Runciman, W. G. 1972: *A Critique of Max Weber's Philosophy of Social Science*. Cambridge: Cambridge University Press.

Runciman, W. G. 1978: *Max Weber. Selections in Translation*. Cambridge: Cambridge University Press.

Runciman, W. G. 1983: *A Treatise on Social Theory. Volume One: The Methodology of Social Theory*. Cambridge: Cambridge University Press.

Runciman, W. G. 1989a: *Confessions of a Reluctant Theorist*. London: Harvester Wheatsheaf.

Runciman, W. G. 1989b: Confessions of a reluctant theorist. In Runciman, 1989a, pp. 1–19.

Runciman, W. G. 1989c: Comparative sociology or narrative history? In Runciman, 1989a, pp. 193–209.

Runciman, W. G. 1989d: Origins of states: the case of archaic Greece. In Runciman, 1989a, pp. 53–80.

Runciman, W. G. 1989e: *A Treatise on Social Theory. Volume Two: Substantive Social Theory*. Cambridge: Cambridge University Press.

Runciman, W. G. 1990: How many classes are there in contemporary British society? *Sociology*, 24, 3, pp. 1–96.

Sahlins, M. 1974: *Stone Age Economics*. London: Tavistock.

Sahlins, M. 1985: *Islands of History*. Chicago: University of Chicago Press.

Sampson, S. F. 1984: The formation of European national states, the elaboration of functional interdependence networks, and the genesis of modern self-control. (Review of Elias, 1982a). *Contemporary Sociology*, 13, 1, pp. 22–7.

Samuel, R. 1981: *People's History and Socialist Theory*. London: Routledge and Kegan Paul.

Sanderson, S. K. 1990: *Social Evolutionism: A Critical History*. Cambridge, Mass.: Basil Blackwell.

Sargent, L. 1981: *Women in Revolution: The Unhappy Marriage of Marxism and Feminism*. London: Pluto.

Sarri, R. C. and Hasenfeld (eds) 1978: *The Management of Human Services*. New York: Columbia University Press.

Sathaye, S. G. 1973: On Elias's developmental paradigm. *Sociology*, 7, 1, pp. 117–23.

Sayer, D. 1990: Reinventing the wheel: Anthony Giddens, Karl Marx and social change. In Clark *et al.*, 1990, pp. 235–50.

Schama, S. 1987: *The Embarrassment of Riches. An Interpretation of Dutch Culture in the Golden Age*. London: Collins.

Schama, S. 1989: *Citizens. A Chronicle of the French Revolution*. London: Viking.

Sennett, R. 1977: *The Fall of Public Man*. Cambridge: Cambridge University Press.

Sewell, W. H. 1967: Marc Bloch and the logic of comparative history, 6 (2), pp. 208–18.

Sheridan, A. 1980: *Michel Foucault. The Will to Truth*. London: Tavistock Publications.

Shils, E. 1980: *The Calling of Sociology and Other Essays on the Pursuit of Learning*. Chicago: Chicago University Press.

Shugart, M. S. 1989: Patterns of revolution. *Theory and Society*, 18, 2, pp. 249–71.

Simmel, G. 1950: *The Sociology of Georg Simmel*. Translated by Kurt H. Wolff, New York: Free Press.

Sjoberg, G. 1960: *The Preindustrial City*. New York: Free Press.

Skinner, Q. 1978: *The Foundations of Modern Political Thought* (2 vols). Cambridge: Cambridge University Press.

Skinner, Q. (ed) 1985: *The Return of Grand Theory in the Human Sciences*. Cambridge: Cambridge University Press.

Skocpol, T. 1973: A critical review of Barrington Moore's *Social Origins of Democracy and Dictatorship*. *Politics and Society*, 4, 1, pp. 1–34.

Skocpol, T. 1977: Wallerstein's world capitalist system: a theoretical and historical critique. *American Journal of Sociology*, 82, 5, pp. 1075–90.

Skocpol, T. 1979: *States and Social Revolutions*. Cambridge: Cambridge University Press.

Skocpol, T. 1982: Rentier state and Shi'a Islam in the Iranian revolution. *Theory and Society*, 11, 3, pp. 265–83.

Skocpol, T. (ed.) 1984: *Vision and Method in Historical Sociology*. Cambridge: Cambridge University Press.

Skocpol, T. 1987: Social revolutions and mass military mobilization. *World Politics*, 40, 2, pp. 147–68.

Skocpol, T. 1988a: An 'uppity generation' and the revitalization of macroscopic sociology: reflections at mid-career by a woman from the sixties. *Theory and Society*, 17 (5), pp. 627–43.

Skocpol, T. 1988b: The limits of the New Deal system and the roots of contemporary welfare dilemmas. In Weir *et al.*, 1988, pp. 293–311.

Skocpol, T. 1989: Reconsidering the French Revolution in world-historical perspective. *Social Research*, 56, 1, pp. 53–70.

Skocpol, T., and Finegold, K. 1982: State capacity and economic intervention in the early New Deal. *Political Science Quarterly*, 97, 2, pp. 255–78.

Skocpol, T., and Ikenberry, G. J. 1983: The political formation of the American welfare state in comparative and historical perspective. *Comparative Social Research*, 6, 1, pp. 92–119.

Skocpol, T., and Somers, M. 1980: The uses of comparative history in macrosocial inquiry. *Comparative Studies in Society and History*, 22, 2, pp. 174–97.

Smart, B. 1985: *Michel Foucault*. London: Routledge.

Smelser, N. J. 1959: *Social Change and the Industrial Revolution*. London: Routledge.

Smith, D. 1971: Selection and knowledge management in education systems. In Hopper, 1971, pp. 139–58.

Smith, D. 1978: Domination and containment: an approach to modernization. *Comparative Studies in Society and History*, 20, 2, pp. 177–213.

Smith, D. 1982a: *Conflict and Compromise. Class Formation in English Society 1830–1914. A Comparative Study of Birmingham and Sheffield*. London: Routledge.

Smith, D. 1982b: 'Put not your trust in princes': a commentary on Anthony Giddens and the absolutist state. *Theory, Culture and Society*. 1, 2, pp. 93–9.

Smith, D. 1982c: Social history and sociology – more than just good friends. *Sociological Review*, 30, 2, pp. 286–308.

Smith, D. 1983: *Barrington Moore. Violence, Morality and Political Change*. London: Macmillan.

Smith, D. 1984a: Morality and method in the work of Barrington Moore. *Theory and Society*, 13, pp. 151–76.

Smith, D. 1984b: Norbert Elias – established or outsider? *Sociological Review*, 32, 2, pp. 367–89.

Smith, D. 1984c: Discovering facts and values: the historical sociology of Barrington Moore. In Skocpol, 1984, pp. 313–55.

Smith, D. 1986: Englishness and the Liberal inheritance. In Dodd and Colls, 1986, pp. 254–82.

Smith, D. 1988a: *The Chicago School. A Liberal Critique of Capitalism*. London: Macmillan.

Smith, D. 1988b: History, geography and sociology: lessons from the *Annales* school. *Theory, Culture and Society*, 5, pp. 137–48.

Smith, D. 1990: *Capitalist Democracy on Trial: The Transatlantic Debate from Tocqueville to the Present*. London: Routledge.

Smith, P. 1986: Anglo–American religion and hegemonic change in the world-system, *c.*1870–1980. *British Journal of Sociology*, 37, 1, pp. 88–105.

Sombart, W. 1913: *The Jews and Modern Capitalism.* Translated by M. Epstein. London: T. Fisher Unwin.

Sombart, W. 1915: *The Quintessence of Capitalism: A Study of the History and Psychology of the Modern Businessman.* Translated by M. Epstein, London: T. Fisher Unwin.

Spengler, O. 1926–8: *The Decline of the West.* London: Allen and Unwin.

Stampp, K. 1956: *The Peculiar Institution. Slavery in the Ante-Bellum South.* New York: Alfred A. Knopf.

Stein, M., and Vidich, A. (eds) 1963: *Sociology on Trial.* Englewood Cliffs, NJ: Prentice-Hall.

Stengers, J. 1953: Marc Bloch et l'histoire. *Annales, Economies, Sociétés, Civilisations*, 8, 2, pp. 329–37.

Stephens, J. D. 1989: Democratic transition and breakdown in Western Europe, 1870–1939: A test of the Moore thesis. *American Journal of Sociology*, 94, 5, pp. 1019–77.

Stern, F. (ed.) 1956: *The Varieties of History. From Voltaire to the Present.* Cleveland: Meridian Books.

Stinchcombe, A. 1978: *Theoretical Methods in Social History.* New York: Academic Press.

Stoianovich, T. 1976: *French Historical Method. The Annales Paradigm.* Cornell, N.Y.: Cornell University Press.

Stone, L. 1977: *The Family, Sex and Marriage in England, 1500–1800.* London: Weidenfeld and Nicolson.

Stone, N. 1979: The revival of narrative: reflections on a new old history. *Past and Present*, 85, pp. 3–24.

Stouffer, S. A. *et al.* 1949: *The American Soldier, I: Adjustment during Army Life.* Princeton: Princeton University Press.

Sztompka, P. 1986: *Robert K. Merton. An Intellectual Profile.* London: Macmillan.

Tainter, J. A. 1988: *The Collapse of Complex Societies.* Cambridge: Cambridge University Press.

Thirsk, J. 1977: European and social development on a European-world scale. *American Journal of Sociology*, 82, 5, pp. 1097–1102.

Thompson, E. P. 1967: Time, work-discipline, and industrial capitalism. *Past and Present*, 38, pp. 56–97.

Thompson, E. P. 1968: *The Making of the English Working Class.* Harmondsworth: Penguin (originally published in 1963).

Thompson, E. P. 1971: The moral economy of the English crowd in the eighteenth century. *Past and Present*, 55, pp. 76–136.

Thompson, E. P. 1972: Anthropology and the discipline of historical context. *Midland History*, 1, 3, pp. 41–55.

Thompson, E. P. 1975: *Whigs and Hunters. The Origins of the Black Act.* London: Allen Lane.

Thompson, E. P. 1976a: *William Morris. Romantic to Revolutionary.* New York: Pantheon Books (originally published in 1955).

Thompson, E. P. 1976b: On history, sociology and historical relevance. *British Journal of Sociology*, 27, 3, pp. 387–402.

Thompson, E. P. 1978a: *The Poverty of Theory*. London: Merlin Press.

Thompson, E. P. 1978b: The peculiarities of the English. In Thompson, 1978a, pp. 35–91 (originally published in 1965).

Thompson, E. P. 1978c: An open letter to Leslek Kolakowski. In Thompson, 1978a, pp. 92–192.

Thompson, E. P. 1978d: The poverty of theory: or an orrery of errors. In Thompson, 1978a, pp. 193–397.

Thompson, E. P. 1978e: Eighteenth-century English society: class struggle without class? *Social History*, 3 (2), pp. 136–65.

Thompson, E. P. 1980: *Writing By Candlelight*. London: Merlin Press.

Thompson, E. P. 1981: The politics of theory. In Samuel, 1981, pp. 386–408.

Thompson, E. P. 1982: *Beyond the Cold War*. London: Merlin Press.

Tilly, C. 1963: The Analysis of a Counter-Revolution. *History and Theory*, 3, 1, pp. 30–58.

Tilly, C. 1964: *The Vendée*. London: Edward Arnold.

Tilly, C. 1978: *From Mobilization to Revolution*. Reading, Mass.: Addison-Wesley.

Tilly, C. 1981: *As Sociology Meets History*. New York: Academic Press.

Tilly, C. 1984: *Big Structures, Large Processes, Huge Comparisons*. New York: Russell Sage Foundation.

Tilly, C. 1988: Future history. *Theory and Society*, 17, 5, pp. 703–12.

Tilly, C. 1989: States and counterrevolution in France. *Social Research*, 56, 1, pp. 71–97.

Tilly, C. 1990a: George Caspar Homans and the rest of us. *Theory and Society*, 19, 3, pp. 261–68.

Tilly, C. 1990b: *Coercion, Capital and European States AD 990–1990*. Oxford: Basil Blackwell.

Tilly, C. *et al.*, 1975: *The Rebellious Century 1830–1930*. London: Dent.

Tilly, L., and Scott, J. N. 1978: *Women, Work and Family*. New York: Methuen.

Tilly, L., and Tilly, C. 1980: Problems in social history: a symposium. *Theory and Society*, 9, pp. 667–81.

Tilton, T. A. 1974: The social origins of liberal democracy: the Swedish case. *American Political Science Review*, 68, 2, pp. 561–71.

Trevor-Roper, H. 1972: Fernand Braudel, the *Annales*, and the Mediterranean. *Journal of Modern History*, 44, 4, pp. 468–79.

Tully, C. (ed.) 1975: *The Formation of Nation-States in Western Europe*. Princeton: Princeton University Press.

Tully, J. (ed.) 1988: *Meaning and Context. Quentin Skinner and his Critics*. Cambridge: Polity Press.

Tumin, J. 1982: The theory of democratic development: a critical revision. *Theory and Society*, 11, 2, pp. 143–78.

Turner, B. S. 1986: *Citizenship and Capitalism. The Debate over Reformism*. London: Allen and Unwin.

Ulrich, L. T. 1983: *Goodwives. Image and Reality in the Lives of Women in Northern New England, 1650–1750*. New York: A. A. Knopf.

van den Braembussche, A. A. 1989: Historical explanation and comparative method: towards a theory of the history of society. *History and Theory*, 1, pp. 1–24.

Veeser, H. A. (ed.) 1989: *The New Historicism*. London: Routledge.

von Thunen, 1966: *Isolated State*. Translated by C. M. Wartenberg. Oxford: Pergamon (originally published in 1826).

Walker, L. 1963: Review of Bloch 1961. *History and Theory*, 3, 2, pp. 247–55.

Wallerstein, I. 1969: *Universities in Turmoil: the politics of change*. New York: Atheneum.

Wallerstein, I. 1974: *The Modern World-System. Capitalist Agriculture and the Origins of the World-Economy in the Sixteenth Century*. New York: Academic Press.

Wallerstein, I. 1979: *The Capitalist World-Economy*. Cambridge: Cambridge University Press.

Wallerstein, I. 1980: *The Modern World-System II. Mercantilism and the Consolidation of the European World-Economy 1600–1750*. New York: Academic Press.

Wallerstein, I. 1983: *Historical Capitalism*. London: Verso.

Wallerstein, I. 1989a: *The Modern World-System III. The Second Era of Great Expansion of the Capitalist World-Economy 1730–1840s*. New York: Academic Press.

Wallerstein, I. 1989b: 1968, Revolution in the world-system. *Theory and Society*, 18, 4, pp. 431–49.

Wallerstein, I. 1989c: The bourgeois(ie) as concept and reality. *New Left Review*, 167, pp. 91–106.

Wallerstein, I. 1989d: Comments on Paul Kennedy's *The Rise and Fall of the Great Powers*. *British Journal of Sociology*, 40, 2, pp. 328–31.

Wallerstein, I. 1990a: Culture as the ideological battleground of the modern world-system. *Theory, Culture and Society*, 7, 2–3, pp. 31–55.

Wallerstein, I. 1990b: Culture is the world-system: a reply to Boyne. *Theory, Culture and Society*, 2–3, pp. 63–5.

Walters, R. G. 1980: Signs of the times: Clifford Geertz and the historians. *Social Research*, 47, pp. 537–56.

Weber, M. 1961: *General Economic History*. Translated by F. Knight. New York: Collier–Macmillan (originally published 1923).

Weber, M. 1976: *The Protestant Ethic and the Spirit of Capitalism* (second edition). Translated by Talcott Parsons. London: Unwin (originally published in 1905).

Weber, M. 1978: *Economy and Society* (2 vols). New York: Bedminster Press.

Weightman, J. 1989: On not understanding Michel Foucault. *American Scholar*, pp. 383–406.

Weir, M. *et al.* (eds) 1988: *The Politics of Social Policy in the United States.* Princeton: Princeton University Press.

Wemple, S. 1981: *Women in Frankish Society. Marriage and the Cloister, 500–900.* Philadelphia: University of Philadelphia Press.

White, H. 1978: *Tropics of Discourse: Essays in Cultural Criticism.* Baltimore: Johns Hopkins University Press.

Wiener, J. M. 1975: Planter–merchant conflict in Reconstruction Alabama. *Past and Present,* 68, pp. 73–94.

Wiener, J. M. 1976: Review of reviews (of Moore, 1969), *History and Theory.* 15, 2, pp. 146–75.

Wirth, L. 1939: Review of Parsons, 1937. *American Sociological Review,* 4 (3), pp. 399–404.

Wirth, L. 1948: Consensus and mass communication. *American Sociological Review,* 13, 1, pp. 1–15.

Wirth, L. 1957: Urbanism as a way of life. In Hatt and Reiss, 1957, pp. 46–63.

Wolin, R. 1989: Review of Bloom, 1987. *Theory and Society,* 18, pp. 273–87.

Zagorin, P. 1982a: *Rebels and Rulers 1500–1660. Vol I: Society, States and Early Modern Revolution. Agrarian and Urban Rebellions.* Cambridge: Cambridge University Press.

Zagorin, P. 1982b: *Rebels and Rulers 1500–1660, Vol II: Provincial Rebellions. Revolutionary Civil Wars 1560–1660,* Cambridge: Cambridge University Press.

Zeldin, T. 1976: Social history and total history. *Journal of Social History,* 10, 2, pp. 237–45.

Zollschan, G. K., and Hirsch, W. (eds) 1964: *Explorations in Social Change.* London: Routledge and Kegan Paul.

Index